D1549837

# BOUNDARY CROSSERS

MEG FOSTER is an award-winning historian of banditry, settler colonial and public history, and a Research Fellow at Newnham College, University of Cambridge. She was awarded the 2018 Aboriginal History Award from the History Council of New South Wales, has published academically as well as in popular publications like *Overland* and *Australian Book Review* and has a passion for connecting history with the contemporary world. Meg received her PhD in history from the University of New South Wales in March 2020.

'Full of intriguing detail, colourful stories and challenging ideas, *Boundary Crossers* offers new context for some of Australia's great central legends.'
ALAN ATKINSON

'Bushranging has furnished white Australia with a rich collection of lore, legends and heroes treated as representative of common and even admired national traits. In *Boundary Crossers*, Meg Foster provocatively unsettles this settler culture by telling the story of those 'other' bushrangers – men and women of colour – either ignored, forgotten or turned into monsters in Australian collective memory. Her deep research, brilliant detective work and creative storytelling invite us to reconsider what we think we know about this country's colonial history.'
FRANK BONGIORNO

'*Boundary Crossers* is excellent Australian history, thought-provoking and illuminating.'
BOOKS + PUBLISHING

'Meg Foster has at long last flipped a dominant white, male, egalitarian colonial trope to uncover a complex, challenging and fascinating Australian bushranging history that critically incorporates the experiences of women, Aboriginal people and other people of colour.'
PAUL DALEY

'This is a wonderful, questioning book that draws on the histories of four lesser-known bushrangers to confront enduring colonial legacies. As Meg Foster pieces together the traces of their lives, she offers a rich, complex view of the colonial world, and how it has been remembered and forgotten. *Boundary Crossers* is a lively and engaging work of scholarship, and a refreshing riposte to familiar bushranging folklore.'
BILLY GRIFFITHS

'A spellbinding journey into Australia's iconic bushranging history as you have never imagined it: the stories of bushrangers who were not white men. Like the "other" bushrangers themselves, Meg Foster defies the silence of the archives and the vast weight of traditional bushranger lore to unearth these remarkable stories of lives lived against the odds. Rich, absorbing and beautifully written, *Boundary Crossers* throws brilliant new light on our strange fascination with bushrangers and their legends, and why some are idolised and others forgotten.'
**GRACE KARSKENS**

'This is thrilling detective work. Bushrangers are Meg Foster's subject but her investigations lead deeper – to a true history of Australia's troubles with race, sex and gender, troubles that haven't gone away.'
**DAVID MARR**

'Meg Foster has uncovered an unknown and riveting side of bushranging that also manages to be relevant to current race politics. Stories are the glue that bind our national identity, and with meticulous research and a writer's prose, Foster manages to uncover the stories of people who should never have been forgotten and will now be forever remembered.'
**JASON PHU**

'With exemplary research and animated writing, Meg Foster introduces us to an extraordinary cast of characters. They were the boundary crossers – little known or half-forgotten bushrangers who did not fit the time-worn stereotypes.'
**HENRY REYNOLDS**

# BOUNDARY CROSSERS

## MEG FOSTER

THE HIDDEN
HISTORY OF
AUSTRALIA'S
OTHER
BUSHRANGERS

NEWSOUTH

**A NewSouth book**

*Published by*
NewSouth Publishing
University of New South Wales Press Ltd
University of New South Wales
Sydney NSW 2052
AUSTRALIA
https://unsw.press/

© Meg Foster 2022
First published 2022

10 9 8 7 6 5 4 3 2 1

This book is copyright. Apart from any fair dealing for the purpose of private study, research, criticism or review, as permitted under the Copyright Act, no part of this book may be reproduced by any process without written permission. Inquiries should be addressed to the publisher.

A catalogue record for this book is available from the National Library of Australia

ISBN       9781742237527 (paperback)
           9781742238494 (ebook)
           9781742239392 (ePDF)

*Internal design* Josephine Pajor-Markus
*Cover design* Regine Abos, Studio Regina
*Cover image* William Insull Burman, photographer, *Kelly on the Defensive,*
    1880, print. State Library Victoria.

All reasonable efforts were taken to obtain permission to use copyright material reproduced in this book, but in some cases copyright could not be traced. The author welcomes information in this regard.

Descendants of any of the individuals mentioned in this book are encouraged to contact the author or publisher.

*For Tracy*

# CONTENTS

*The greatest threat to recognition, in this case the recognition of both Indigenous histories of Australia and the at times difficult terrain of colonial history, is silence, absence.*

Tony Birch, 'The Trouble with History'

# INTRODUCTION

Imagine a piece of thick unpolished metal, rectangular in shape. Dents and grooves cover its crudely curved surface and a narrow rectangular slit punctures its otherwise sturdy façade. Two rectangles; two simple shapes are now an almost universally recognised symbol in this country. They represent the armour of Irish-Australian bushranger Ned Kelly. And Kelly, in turn, represents a national legend – the white, male, bushranging hero. Many Australians also know the names of the bushrangers who came before. Bold Jack Donohoe, Brave Ben Hall, Frank Gardiner, Captains William Geary, Thunderbolt and Moonlite – men of crime, men of the bush, and men of local and national fame. Australians are fascinated by bushrangers. Although these criminals are meant to have died out with Ned Kelly – on the scaffold in 1880 – they live on as some of the most potent symbols of our nation.

At its most basic, a bushranger was a criminal who survived by robbery with, or with at least the threat of, violence. These figures were able to evade capture by living and concealing themselves in the Australian bush. Today, Australians celebrate bushrangers for their bravery: their ability to challenge authority and fight back against an unjust system. Bushrangers epitomise the underdog, the Aussie battler, the pioneer spirit and the noble bushman traditions that Australians hold dear. Plus, bushranging tales make for ripping yarns.[1]

Few in this country are unaware of white, male bushrangers and their place in the nation's figurative heart. They saturate popular culture, from podcasts to films and folklore. They punctuate Australia's tourist trails. Their paraphernalia fills the shelves of big-city souvenir shops and local country stores. Travelling along the east coast of New South Wales you might pass Bushrangers Hill, Bushrangers Reserve, Bushrangers Cave, Bushrangers Bay, Bushranger Transport Pty Ltd, Kellyville Bushrangers Junior Rugby League Football Club, Bushrangers 4x4 Gear or Bushranger Mowing. Moving further inland you could find yourself travelling down roads, skirting alongside creeks or sipping a cold one at pubs featuring these bushrangers' names. Ned Kellys are dotted throughout the landscape. They travel on car bumper stickers, wait patiently out the front of properties collecting mail, stand erect in yards or small-town museums miles from where Ned and his men ever trod in their dusty boots. Bushrangers mark the bodies of ordinary Australians who tattoo themselves with bushrangers' faces, names and words. Dozens of bushrangers with blazing guns swarmed the opening ceremony of the Sydney 2000 Olympic Games, representing our nation to the world. Millions of Australians love these brave white men, and we think we know them. But our popular mythology is imperfect and critically incomplete.

Bushrangers were not all white men.

This book tells the hidden history of the 'other' bushrangers – the bandits who were not white men, and whose stories have been marginalised, obscured, erased or forgotten as a result. Aboriginal, African American, Chinese and female bushrangers have never been a part of the national mythos. We do not remember them in our merchandise or memorials, or in our films or songs or ceremonies. And this absence is no accident.

Black Douglas was a black bushranger renowned as the terror of the goldfields in 1850s Victoria. He was said to have murdered a white woman at Avoca and robbed enterprising miners the length and breadth of the diggings. Sam Poo was a Chinese man executed for murder and accused of bushranging in 1860s New South Wales. His alleged activities shaped critical debates about the 1860s bushranging crisis and the steps the authorities should take to restore colonial order. Worimi Aboriginal woman Mary Ann Bugg lived for several years on the run from the law with her white bushranging partner, Captain Thunderbolt. She taunted, evaded and outsmarted the police, and manipulated colonial expectations to further her own ends. In some settings, she described herself as 'the Captain's Lady'. In others, this educated 19th-century woman dressed in men's pants. Jimmy Governor (later fictionalised as 'Jimmie Blacksmith') is renowned for murdering white women, children and the elderly in 1900.[2] Few Australians realise that before these crimes he was known as a charismatic hard worker and family man. When he believed himself wronged by colonial society, Governor drew inspiration from white bushranging tales.

While there were certainly more white bushranging men than women or people of colour, this is not the reason for other bushrangers' historical exclusion. Their small numbers did not make them insignificant. Black Douglas, Sam Poo, Mary Ann Bugg and Jimmy Governor each led remarkable lives. They threatened colonial society. They had the authorities' attention, and the population's fascination and fear. Other bushrangers posed not only physical threats to colonists' lives and property, but ideological ones too. Their actions challenged colonial Australians' ideas about racial and gendered hierarchies, law and order, not to mention settlers' own sense of their place in the world. Other bushrangers often committed the same crimes at the same time as famous white bushranging men and yet they have not entered the pantheon of Australian bushranging legends. When they are remembered at all, their stories are largely peripheral; recalled in local lore or featured in family stories. In histories, they are often a colonial quirk or an odd footnote to the larger, white settler story.

But in their own times, these bushrangers were not simply curiosities, or blips on an otherwise white male history, and their stories deserve to be told on their own terms – their voices salvaged, as far as possible, from the imperfect sources that remain. Douglas, Poo, Bugg and Governor's lives were important in their own times, and they remain so today. They shine a stark and critical light on Australia's colonial past.

## WHY HIDE?

The celebration of white bushranging men to the exclusion of others is no accident. For centuries bushranging has been seen as the preserve of white men and associated with a unique brand of settler masculinity. Some of the first histories of the Australian colonies recorded white, male bushrangers' actions and crimes as part of the colonial experience, while settlers' reminiscences are laden with these controversial figures.[3] Bushranging stories featured in some of the first instances of settler folklore, bush ballads and plays.[4] Despite this early interest, the national bushranging mythos is a 20th-century phenomenon. And it is no coincidence that the first Australian bushranging histories were written at the time of national Federation.

In 1899, George E Boxall published *The Story of the Australian Bushrangers* while in 1900, Charles White's *History of Australian Bushranging* hit bookstore shelves.[5] These works concentrated on white bushranging men. Although they did not go as far as to openly celebrate these figures, they privileged white male characters and colonial tropes. Charles White in particular relied heavily on interviews with local residents to gather details for his stories and in this way, white colonists' ideas about bushranging were reinscribed in some of the first professional bushranging histories.[6] This colonial influence did not always take the form of complete exclusion, as at least one non-white character, the Chinese bushranger Sam Poo, appeared briefly in White's writing. But when other bushrangers were discussed, their stories were heavily distorted by colonial ideas about race and gender.

By 1901, bushrangers' display of physical prowess and manly strength increasingly became a symbol for the new nation's future. The real bushranging crisis had ended decades earlier in 1880 and by Federation the danger these figures posed to colonial society was increasingly forgotten. In the vacuum left by this selective memory, these criminal men came to represent Australians' egalitarianism, anti-authoritarianism and pioneering spirit. Ironically, bushrangers who in their own times were considered threats to the colonial project became romantic exemplars of it. Their success in the bush apparently epitomised colonists' capacity to be at home in the natural environment and use the bush for their own ends. Although they were originally treated as bandits who lived beyond the bounds of civilised society, white bushranging men progressively became heroic ancestors who contemporary Australians could be proud of.

White male bushrangers created a usable past for the new Australian nation that sought both national distinction and to be a part of a broader, masculine, Anglo world.[7] Settler Australians knew that their national tradition had been created transnationally, but they imagined points of connection with white British highwaymen and American cowboys, rather than Aboriginal resistance fighters, Fujianese bandits or emancipated African Americans.

Factual errors continued to plague bushranging histories well beyond Boxall and White's days because bushranging was seen as the natural domain of white men. Well into the 20th century, Irish convict 'Bold Jack Donohoe' was typically cited as one of the first men who escaped to live in the bush and engaged in 'robbery under arms' when in fact, the first bushranger in settler-Australian history was a six-foot-tall convict of African descent named John Caesar (more commonly known as 'Black Caesar'). In England, Caesar was tried at the Kent Assizes in 1786 for theft and sentenced to seven years' transportation to New South Wales. He arrived in the colony in the First Fleet.[8] Despite popular accounts to the contrary, our first bushranger was a black man who operated decades before Donohoe first ordered unsuspecting colonists to 'bail up'.[9]

The first big step towards addressing the absence of women and people of colour from Australian history came in the 1960s and 1970s, and this is when other bushrangers made a reappearance too. Spurred on by social justice movements at home and around the world, historians looked to history to understand contemporary injustice and remedy the male-dominated whitewashing of the nation's past. Caesar was first written about by historian Mollie Gillen in the 1980s, although it was not until the early 2000s that he was explicitly recognised by Cassandra Pybus as Australia's first bushranger.[10] Historian Henry Reynolds wrote about Aboriginal bushranging in his work on the frontier in the 1970s and 1980s, and since then there have been several invaluable yet isolated studies on individual figures.[11] A handful of scholars have pieced together the careers of select non-white bushrangers, while others have used these figures to illustrate broader themes such as colonial race relations and Aboriginal resistance to colonisation.

Although these studies are significant, they are far from exhaustive.[12] And they remain on the periphery of national consciousness. Not only were many studies published in academic journals and away from the public eye, the figures who did appear in popular publications did not match the idea of bushranging so pervasive in our culture. It was challenging for some Australians to recognise that a tradition epitomised by Ned Kelly began with a black convict, and that the settler-colonial icon of the bushranger had not always been white. Apart from clashing with cultural assumptions, studies of other bushrangers remained marginal because they emerged when public attention was consumed by the History Wars. In the 1990s and early 2000s, political attempts to undermine, detract from or actively refute the violence of colonial invasion dominated talk about the nation's past. Historians' public appearances were then largely concerned with defending the basic facts of colonial history and Indigenous dispossession. Debates between 'Black Armband' and 'Three Cheers' views of history largely eclipsed the remarkable lives of other bushrangers that were slowly being unearthed.[13]

## PAST IMPERFECT

Most bushranging books that are published today appear to seamlessly entwine action with biography. We are used to reading about daring hold-ups and high-stakes robberies, narrow escapes from the clutches of the police and adrenaline-inducing pursuits through rough and unforgiving country. These are the moments that draw us in, both to the book and the bushrangers whose lives we are witnessing play out on the page. Contemporary authors then situate these moments in bushrangers' life stories, just as our colonial ancestors did at the time these bushrangers were at large. In the 19th century, sympathetic newspaper articles, petitions for clemency, parliamentary debates and court defences often drew on white bushrangers' backgrounds. Through this information, colonists tried to make connections between these men's experiences and their turn to crime. Whether to advocate for social change to prevent more offenders, or to defend a bushranger's character or actions, white bushrangers were regarded as individuals. It was not only their actions that were significant, but their personal histories.[14]

The same cannot be said for other bushrangers. Absence not only characterises these bushrangers' place in our national consciousness, but their place in the archive – in the sources that remain for us to reconstruct their lives. This book is not a comprehensive account of all other bushrangers who existed in Australian history. It uncovers the lives of four individuals not only because they were exceptional but because they left exceptional traces; fragments of sources that together were large enough for me to chart something of their lives. But their archives are still grossly incomplete. While I would love to begin this book with Douglas, Poo, Bugg and Governor's escapades and then present perfectly rendered accounts of their lives from birth to death, that is impossible. The evidence is just not there. Although this book does contain other bushrangers' impressive feats, perilous adventures and derring-dos, it will never be as seamless, or complete, as the bushranging stories we are used to encountering. The violence of colonisation was not just wrought on the bodies of people of colour, and its inequities were not just faced by women or minorities at the time. It manifests in the material colonists kept about them. And it hampers our ability to access other bushrangers' lives, or see the world through their eyes.

This is not to say that Douglas, Poo, Bugg or Governor have left no trace. It is a lot easier to see marginalised people from the past if they were mixed up with crime. Locals gossiped, word spread, the press reported regularly on these cases and the colonial state had a fetish for recording, documenting and categorising these 'criminals' – as it still does. But there is something deeply problematic about drawing the contours of someone's life from material that was meant to control, punish and demean them. It is even worse when the people making these records were colonisers, intent on creating a 'white man's country' on stolen Indigenous land.

This is the structural story, but how these biases manifested in each bushranger's life, and in each source kept about them, is different. Black Douglas and Sam Poo's archives appear full but are riddled with silences. Douglas was renowned as one of the most dastardly figures of the Victorian Gold Rush. He was talked about the length and breadth of the colony, and was accused of assault and violent robbery and murder. Stories of his horrid misdeeds became cautionary tales to keep miners alert and watchful of their lives and property. But there was often only a sliver of truth to these dark and wide-reaching stories. In the records, we encounter Black Douglas most often as a nightmare of settlers' own creation. There was a man behind the myth. But he is largely hidden from view.

Sam Poo was said to have robbed unsuspecting settlers and murdered a white police constable in 1860s New South Wales. Although reporters noted that Poo was 'unfriended', his crimes caused a colonial sensation. That a Chinese man had entered the bushranging game shocked and astounded many, inflamed racial tensions in the colony, and was used by colonists to debate the nature and extent of the bushranging threat. But the evidence connecting Poo to these alleged crimes cannot be taken at face value. And little can be divined from colonial accounts about the man later labelled 'Australia's only Chinese bushranger'. The archive is not teeming with details about Douglas or Poo's lives. It is spewing forth colonial stories about them.

Even when we have more material of other bushrangers' actions and words, there is colonial distortion. The Aboriginal bushrangers of this book, Mary Ann Bugg and Jimmy Governor, were aware of the opinions, fears and hang-ups of the colonisers and actively sought to shape the stories told about them. Mary Ann Bugg lived the life of a fugitive for several years as the partner of prolific white bushranger Captain Thunderbolt, and this meant defying colonial norms. Mary Ann raised three children on the run, dressed and rode like a man, slaughtered cattle and physically assaulted the police. In the press and in the courtroom, she would find no understanding or sympathy for this life and so she crafted another. Mary Ann's lived experience differed dramatically both from colonial accounts and from the narrative she herself constructed. And she remained keenly aware of the importance of public reputation beyond her time as the 'Captain's Lady'. It is only by pushing beyond the caricatures that colonists created and the fictions that Mary Ann invented that we can see the messy brilliance of her life, and the full impact of her legacy.

Jimmy Governor caused a sensation in 1900. After killing the white family of his employer, Governor went on the run and with his brother, Joe, embarked on a crime spree around New South Wales. Books and a film capture fragments of his story, but they often fail to look beyond the horror of his crimes. Governor left a mark on his archive. He left notes for the police, spoke to the court and eagerly addressed the press. Jimmy Governor declared himself to be a bushranger. This book takes his claim seriously, not to defend his crimes, but to understand them and the world in which he lived. It also recognises that Governor was not the only one hunted and punished for his crimes. By recovering the experiences of Governor's white wife, Ethel, and his Aboriginal family in the rural town of Wollar, we can see that Governor's story was always larger than one man. It was a story of nation-building, the endurance of First Nations people and settlers reckoning with colonial violence.

Of necessity then, this book is as much about the ideas, prejudices and beliefs of colonists and the blind spots of their records as it is about other bushrangers. The only way to access these bushrangers' lives is to disentangle what they did and said from what colonists said about them. This process is not straightforward. It requires us to question what we know, and how we think we know it, at almost every turn. It is complex and messy, but it is also an inseparable part of the story. To access other bushrangers' lives we must first peel back, and understand, the layers of colonial distortion that are obscuring them from view.

There are some parts of this book that readers might find distressing. It deals with topics such as colonial violence, Stolen Generations, racism, sexism and sexual assault. First Nations readers are advised that this book contains names, words and images of people who have died. It also contains offensive language, such as slurs, and colonial views that are unacceptable today. This book does not treat this material lightly. It is not included to shock and offend but to paint an unvarnished picture of other bushrangers' lives. By showing the extent of colonial vitriol we can see the full scale of what these bushrangers were up against. And what they fought to overcome.

# CHAPTER 1

# THE LEGENDARY
# BLACK DOUGLAS

In May 1855, a storekeeper from the Maryborough goldfields penned a letter to the *Age* newspaper in Melbourne. This was one of many pieces of mail sent to the capital, as the booming tent city of Melbourne relied on such correspondence to get news of the interior and keep up to date with the ever-expanding web of diggings dotted across the colony's landscape. However, this letter was unique. Instead of relaying the usual news of gold discoveries, the weather or the cost of grog or grain, this storekeeper used the newspaper to mount an attack on the justice system of the diggings. The disgruntled author wrote that:

> Crime is fearfully on the increase, and the persons and properties of Her Majesty's subjects are quite unprotected in this quarter. Several storekeepers join with me in asking you to give Sir Charles [Hotham, the Governor of Victoria] a hint on the subject. For our part, we would suggest Lynch Law at once, and rid the colony of such blackguards.[1]

Storekeepers were rarely depicted at the vanguard of calls for rough justice nor as so insubordinate as to hint at how their Governor should do his job. However, this group apparently could not help but raise their voices in protest when the threat to their lives and livelihoods was so great. And while this correspondent wrote of the generally degraded and criminal state of the diggings, he felt compelled to write because of an event that had just occurred at the Alma diggings, a goldfield not far from his own: the capture of a notorious black bushranger known as 'Black Douglas'.

At about 1 pm on Sunday 6 May, word reached miners that Black Douglas and his gang were attempting to rob their tents while they were toiling in the afternoon sun. In response, between 100 and 400 miners captured the gang and its infamous leader.[2] The men were not taken peacefully. The *Geelong Advertiser* reported that '[t]he injuries sustained by the gang in their conflict with the diggers, who fought with picks, shovels &c, are said to be very severe ... one was so badly wounded that his life was in danger'.[3] At one point lynching was proposed, and it was only after considerable persuasion that the posse of diggers consented to cart the bound and gagged bushrangers 6 kilometres to the police in Maryborough instead.[4] We can imagine our storekeeper correspondent watching the procession of miners and their captives enter the town, for along with his comments about crime, he reported these diggers' actions to the press. Instead of condemning the outbreak of mob violence, this storekeeper suggested that the best way forward was 'Lynch Law'. In his view, the miners need not have bothered to make their journey, as they should have the right to kill the culprits; they should have the right to exact justice themselves.

When the diggers fell upon Douglas and his men that May afternoon they were not only responding to the immediate threat to their property, but to tales depicting Black Douglas as the worst of criminals. Although gold was only publicly discovered in the colony of Victoria in 1851, the following year, reports began to emerge of Black Douglas's criminal exploits. At a public meeting in Melbourne in April 1852, a military officer reported that:

> the notorious ruffian 'Black Douglas' ... was seen carrying on his shoulders the dead body of a man who doubtless was one of his victims, and which body he was endeavouring to conceal or bury: but such was the terror of his name that no one dared to attempt to ascertain the fact![5]

The passing of time did nothing to diminish Black Douglas's ill repute. Referring to Douglas and his criminal brethren in 1855, the *Geelong Advertiser* reported that:

> The whole neighbourhood of Simpson's, from Carisbrook to the Avoca and New Bendigo, has for several weeks past been kept in a continual state of terror and apprehension, by the depredations of gangs of scoundrels, whose maraudings [sic] gradually increased in violence and brutality ...[6]

In later years, it would become a mark of distinction to say that you had encountered Black Douglas on the Victorian goldfields, while tales of his horrid misdeeds were passed around campfires and greeted 'new chums' as they advanced into the bush and left their sea legs behind.[7] Although crimes all over the colony were attributed to him, it was the dreaded precincts of the Black Forest that stood between Melbourne and the diggings at Bendigo and Mount Alexander that were considered Black Douglas's favourite haunt (see Plate 3).[8] Even today, Douglas's infamy has not completely faded. The Australian Government included Douglas on its bushranging webpage in 2015, while *Australian Geographic* ran a piece on the bushranger the previous year. Although the government website was brief and has since been erased, the magazine took the time to regale its readers with tales of Douglas's transgressions. According to *Australian Geographic*, Douglas's modus operandi was to strip his victims naked, tie them to trees and fill their 'boots full of bull ants' leaving them 'to die a slow and excruciating death'.[9]

Despite Douglas's ignominy and the hysteria surrounding his escapades at the time and since, we hardly know anything about him. This is because colonists were only concerned with Douglas as a black man and a criminal. Douglas has no origin, no age, no religion, no occupation, no name beyond his bushranging title, no appearance beyond the colour of his skin and certainly no opinions or desires in the stories told about him from the Gold Rush. A colonial obsession with crime and colour clings to Douglas's history and clouds our view of his life and so, I want to start here – with the colonial perspective, and with the obsession. We need to see Black Douglas first through colonial eyes if we are to have any hope of separating fact from fiction, and extricating Douglas the man from Douglas of legend.

*

Although Black Douglas was renowned as a bushranger, murder was the crime that made him a colonial sensation. This was not as unusual as it may sound. Bushranging involved robbery, but it could also include anything from drunk and disorderly conduct to receiving stolen goods, and from burglary to assault and murder. The crime that ensured Douglas's downfall at the hands of the miners in 1855 and that left the most enduring legacy was the murder of a white woman at Avoca, in the central highlands of Victoria. Newspaper articles from Mount Alexander to Geelong, Maitland to Hobart connected this crime with the diggers' uprising in no uncertain terms.[10] According to the *Mount Alexander Mail*:

> The crowning act of the barbarities committed by these ruffians, was the murder of a woman at Avoca, as reported elsewhere, and the diggers became sensible that they must themselves take measures for securing their own lives and property.[11]

It appears that the murder of a defenceless woman was the impetus for so many men to bear arms and toy with the idea of murdering Douglas and his brothers in crime. Honour, revenge and the restoration of justice seem to have been the driving forces behind the diggers' uprising. This murder enhanced Black Douglas's notoriety and influenced his public persona for years to come. Decades later in 1887, the *Independent* still described the murder of this woman as a critical moment in Douglas's career, while in 1982 writer Allan Nixon repeated this story in his book *100 Australian Bushrangers*.[12]

But as soon as we cast a critical eye over these stories they unravel. Black Douglas was never convicted for any of these heinous crimes. He was never convicted for theft. Or highway robbery. And certainly not for murder. The spectacular scene of hundreds of miners joining forces to end Douglas's reign of terror is undercut by the fact he faced court accused only of unlawfully entering the tent of two Māori and was sentenced under the Vagrant Act to two years' hard labour.[13] The *Mount Alexander Mail* and *Geelong Advertiser* reporters struggled to contain their disbelief that:

> [n]otwithstanding the reputation which this chief of the robbers has obtained, it seems difficult to establish any serious charge against him, and ... he will have to be proceeded against ... as a consorter with thieves and vagabonds.[14]

Douglas was released early in February 1857 for good conduct, but within two months he was spotted among the rowdy crowds in grog tents on the Goulburn Diggings, and in another two he was in Beechworth Gaol for drunk and disorderly conduct. Only days after his release, he was before the bench again, fined 5 shillings for a similar offence, and ordered to leave the district.[15] According to his criminal record, the 'redoubtable' Douglas was a vagrant and a drunkard as opposed to a murderous, violent thief.[16]

Outside of goldfields gossip, there is no evidence that Black Douglas murdered a woman at Avoca. There were only two murders of white women on the diggings between March and early May 1855. The first was committed over 30 kilometres away from the Avoca district where Douglas was supposed to have committed this crime.[17] The second murder occurred on 29 April on the road between Avoca and New Bendigo. Five mounted men committed a series of crimes in that vicinity:

and among the outrages attacked, and robbed a party of four
men and one woman, near Hawkin's Hotel, shooting at and
wounding the woman, of which wound the woman died on
the following day.

This murder appears to match the one ascribed to Douglas but for
one crucial flaw. All five men were meticulously described in the
*Government Gazette*'s notice on the murder and none of the offenders
was black. When the *Gazette* took the time to describe one criminal as
a 'short, stout, full-faced man, with light hair, aged about 22, wearing
a light black coat and a Jim Crow hat, riding on a brown pony with a
tan muzzle', it appears a glaring absence that it did not describe a black
offender's race – unless a black man was not among the perpetrators of
this crime.[18]

How could the story of Black Douglas's murder of a white woman
have gained so much traction, when it had such little basis in fact?
How could a fabrication have such influence? One answer lies in
the turbulent nature of the Gold Rush. Thousands of people flowed
in and out of the ever-shifting goldfields. There was always word of
a 'New Eldorado' and miners hurried around the colony following
the latest reports of riches. As the decade progressed, people flooded
in from outside of the colony too. In 1852, the first ships from the
United Kingdom arrived bringing Brits eager to make their fortune
and others quickly followed. Although white men remained the
largest group on the fields throughout the Gold Rush, the diggings
were incredibly diverse.[19] The Chinese were the largest and the most
resented new immigrant population on the goldfields, but there were
also Māori, Poles, Germans and Americans – the list goes on.[20] In such
a tumultuous environment, witnesses to crimes could be hard to track
down. In gold camps, new identities could be assumed, and characters
remade. Although many found this anonymity liberating, it also made
it difficult to know who to trust.[21] If ostracised from one goldfield, an
offender could usually move on to the next without difficulty.

This reveals how criminals could escape justice on the diggings, but it does not solve our mystery. It does not explain how the murder of a woman by five white assailants could be attributed to a black man. Descriptions of the culprits were circulated in both metropolitan and regional papers, and the *Geelong Advertiser* reported both the description of the five guilty men and later, a report implicating Douglas in the same crime.[22] This glaring contradiction only makes sense if we look beyond our sources to the men who created them. The Black Douglas myth grew because it resonated with the white miners who spread and embellished it. This is not to say that these men were liars, or that there was some grand conspiracy to make Black Douglas a figure of crime and terror. The truth is never so simple. Many miners undoubtedly believed that the Black Douglas legend was real, or at the very least, that it represented something true. It aligned with their vision of the world – their ideas about men and women, and the meaning of black skin as well as their own white.

In some ways, we already know this story. Fictitious tales of black men murdering white women have been used to explain white men's violence towards people of colour before the 1850s and since. This is one part of a longer history of racialised violence, but it needs to be understood on its own terms. White miners' beliefs and the way these beliefs shaped their actions were uniquely their own. We need to see how men and women lived on the diggings to understand how the Black Douglas myth was so influential among *these* people, at *this* place, at *this* time.

## MEN AND WOMEN OF THE DIGGINGS

Although there were more men than women on the Victorian goldfields, the diggings were never simply a man's world. Women were an active and integral part of goldfields society. Forty-five per cent of the Ballarat population were women and children in 1854.[23]

Some women, like Elizabeth Ramsay-Laye, saw their main role on the goldfields as looking after their husbands, and bringing as much refinement and feminine delicacy as was possible to remote places. Caroline Chisholm's famous campaign to civilise the goldfields by bringing women to domesticate the 'wilderness' seems to have reflected how many women saw their own position.[24] Women courted, married, and made love on the diggings. They gave birth, maintained their tents, prepared meals, darned socks, washed clothes and performed myriad other tasks that were expected of them because of their gender.[25] In the 19th century, respectable women were not only meant to maintain hearth and home, they were supposed to be confined to them. Men protected and provided for their families, men engaged in trade and scoured the diggings for gold, men caroused and fought and engaged in politics. In polite circles, few believed the world outside of the home was something the 'weaker sex' should trouble their pretty heads about.[26]

Despite the weight of these ideas, women did not always follow them. Some women sought individual prosperity among the mine shafts instead of merely domestic bliss. Some became entrepreneurs. Martha Clendinning and her sister ran a small but prosperous shop on the goldfields, female entertainers found local fame and eager audiences on the diggings, while other women dug for gold alongside their male counterparts. These mining women were visible enough for the Governor to contemplate extending the miner's licence to include them (see Plate 4). Some women also had success in the more nefarious trades such as sex work and sly grog selling. In the Avoca district late in 1855, five women were arrested for sly grog selling while one managed to escape custody and go on the run.[27] Women were even involved in the Eureka Stockade Uprising of 1854. As historian Clare Wright has shown, the female rebels of Eureka fought alongside their male counterparts to end abuses of power by police and government officials.[28] Women were part of the social fabric of the goldfields. While some engaged solely in domestic labour, others worked independently or engaged in supposedly masculine pursuits like politics, rioting and manual labour. Women in both lawful and illicit business formed an essential part of the diggings' social landscape.

Against this backdrop the Black Douglas myth begins to make sense. The legend provided miners with a more palatable narrative about women's place on the diggings than the reality that surrounded them. In stories of the murder of the white woman at Avoca, there were no independent, strong women vying with men for a share in the riches of the Gold Rush. Women were not active participants, assertive partners or potential rivals to men in this tale. All the press reported was that an anonymous woman was shot by one of a gang of male bushrangers and later died of the wound.[29] Such scant information was helpful to miners as the bare bones of the murder could be used to confirm what white diggers already believed – that women were weak, vulnerable and far too delicate for the harsh reality of life on the diggings. For male miners, this story restored the natural order of things. The murdered woman at Avoca was incapable of gaining a foothold in, let alone threatening, male diggers' domain.

Newspapers on the goldfields were largely run by men, for men. Bearing this in mind, it comes as no surprise that newspaper accounts of the murder were censored. In a report sent from the authorities at Avoca to the Chief Commissioner of Police, as well as in the original proclamation sent by the police to be published in the *Government Gazette*, the murder victim was not just referred to as 'a woman', but as Margaret Wade. When this name reached the printing press, it was replaced by Margaret's sex alone. Newspapers and the *Government Gazette* could have used Margaret Wade's name to alert her family and acquaintances to her death but instead, they chose to refer to her merely as a woman. Despite women's presence and activity on the goldfields, their identities were commonly obscured in colonial reportage. When male reporters deigned to mention them at all, they were usually identified as the wives or daughters of certain men. Although the Gold Rush offered new opportunities to women, men still controlled essential public services like the press. Men could erase women's names from public view.

*

This is not to say that all white men were beyond reproach from their peers. Miners were constantly under attack from both the government and the press for violence on the goldfields. In April and June 1855, the months either side of Douglas's capture, there were two further instances of mass unrest and near-lynching in Alma and Maryborough in central Victoria. On 4 April, Assistant Commissioner Drummond reported that 5000 men assembled at Alma 'in a state of great excitement caused by a murderous assault alleged to have been committed by a party of foreigners ... [and that] preparations had already been made ... to try and lynch the accused'. It was only after speaking to the men and assuring them that the law was equipped to deal with the offenders that the party of miners dispersed. Not long afterwards, in June 1855 at Maryborough, over 1000 armed diggers dragged a group of 'disorderly' men to camp and there were fears that a riot would take place between the supporters of each party. All available reinforcements were called in to deal with the anticipated bloodshed, but luckily, the situation had de-escalated by the time the extra police reached the diggings.[30] Although in both instances lynching and rioting never occurred, they exposed a tendency towards mob violence that shocked the authorities and the conservative press alike.

Vigilante diggers were active in defending their character and demonstrating that their actions were necessary to *restore* order on the goldfields. In Alma and the surrounding areas, there was only one police officer to protect a population of over 25 000.[31] Miners used numbers such as these to argue that the police were incapable of protecting the population and that this forced diggers to mobilise for their own defence. Many also complained that the police only cared about retrieving licence fees. Diggers alleged that the police resorted to degrading and brutal tactics to arrest men whose only crime was to fail to show a piece of paper, rather than pursuing the real criminals who endangered life and livelihood.[32] Echoing the insurgents at Eureka, miners went dangerously close to asserting that their methods of governing the goldfields were superior to those of colonial officials.

To combat claims of sedition and to further promote the legitimacy of their actions, miners created protection societies. Soon after Douglas's dramatic capture at Alma, the Maryborough Mutual Protection Society was formed 'to apprehend, and vigorously to prosecute, all offenders, and specially to suppress crime'.[33] These organisations had a set of rules that controlled their members' conduct and participants sought to differentiate themselves from the criminal population by agreeing to assist the police and abide by the law. Governor Hotham even gave his support to mutual protection societies in recognition of their necessity.[34] Members hoped that this would dispel allegations that they were deaf to all but the authority of 'Judge Lynch'.

Unfortunately for miners, these strategies were not enough to legitimise protection societies in the eyes of the broader population. Similar arguments had been made about the need for rough justice on the American goldfields in California from the late 1840s. In that locale, lynching was not just threatened, but enacted as diggers claimed they were the only thing standing between the goldfields and complete lawlessness.[35] Colonial Australians knew of the violence of the Californian Gold Rush and were well aware that beneath the veneer of respectability, protection societies were more than capable of instigating violence, and their members capable of murder.[36]

The fiction that Black Douglas murdered a white woman was useful to miners here too, as it went some way to redeeming vigilante diggers in the eyes of polite society. Although violence had erupted when hundreds of miners rose up to capture Black Douglas and his gang in May 1855, the diggers had not delivered justice themselves. Despite the fact that Douglas and his gang were far outnumbered and well within the miners' grasp, the diggers decided to hand their quarry over to the authorities. This set them apart from lawless crusaders and illustrated their respect for the law. Even more significant was the fact that the Black Douglas myth added a moral dimension to the diggers' violence. The story that Douglas had killed a woman at Avoca allowed miners to cast themselves as righteous avengers seeking retribution for Douglas's female victim and striving to prevent further outrages. In respectable circles it was a white man's duty to defend and avenge the 'weaker sex' – so long as they too were white. By capturing Douglas and his men, the diggers were apparently righting the wrongs committed against one of 'their' women. This shifted their actions from senseless violence to fighting for a righteous cause.

These attempts to establish diggers' morality were made all the more pressing by the fact that white men committed violence against white women in the Gold Rush. Violence was usually condoned if it was inflicted by a woman's father or husband as she was under their supervision and control. Beyond this intimate group of male relatives, it was socially unacceptable, but this did not stop violence against women from being a major issue on the goldfields. As historian Margaret Anderson describes, '[a]lmost every chronicler of the diggings commented on the drunkenness and violence they saw around them, with women frequent victims'.[37] In the Avoca area only a few months after Douglas's capture:

> a man named Morris Beresford attempted to take liberties with
> a Mrs McDonald wife of a shepherd residing about three miles
> from Avoca Camp, and upon her resisting his advances, he struck
> her a violent blow upon the head from the effects of which she
> nearly lost her life.[38]

In the murder of Margaret Wade, the 'white woman at Avoca', the killers were also white men.

Violence was by no means the only threat that white men posed to women in the Gold Rush. Abandonment was also pervasive, as many men struck out alone to pursue the wealth of the diggings. Hundreds of husbands left their wives and fathers left their families, either in Melbourne or on older goldfields that no longer yielded easy riches.[39] In 1855, the *Geelong Advertiser* reported that charities were stretched to their limits trying to assist these broken families and described 'the abrupt manner in which ... [men] leave their wives and offspring for the ... gold fields' as 'a source of great distress'.[40] Welfare agencies were not the only ones who were concerned. Social reformers were terrified that without male supervision and support, women would be enticed into illicit trade and sex work, and their children would be corrupted by such blatant immorality.[41] Considering that upstanding men were supposed to provide for their dependants, abandonment reduced husbands' moral standing too.[42] Some commentators attempted to explain away these men's neglect of their families. Many blamed factors beyond men's control such as the absence of viable alternatives to the goldfields for men to earn a living.[43] Yet all of this talk did little to address the fact that many women lived in complete destitution due to being abandoned by their 'natural protectors'.

Conveniently for miners, the Black Douglas legend shifted the moral balance sheet so that white men were back on the ethical high ground. The fictitious story that Black Douglas murdered a white woman papered over white diggers' own failings and erased the ambiguities of real life. It provided a clear victim and villain, while allowing white men to be valiant champions and saviours. It showed miners the world as they wished it, and not as it was.

## PEOPLE OF COLOUR

Fraught relationships between men and women were not the only problems on the diggings. White colonists were also deeply anxious about race. At the same time that white men's morality was brought into disrepute, black men held positions of status and authority on

FIGURE 1. William Strutt, *Cohunguiam and Munight*, 1851.

State Library of Victoria Pictures Collection, H88.21/112.

the goldfields. The most obvious examples of this were the Aboriginal police officers who first patrolled the diggings. The Native Police was originally created in the 1830s to control the colony's Aboriginal population, but when gold was discovered they were an obvious choice to establish law and order on the diggings. These officers were already tried and tested, their aptitude in the bush was widely recognised, and they were a lot less expensive than white police who might occupy the same role. To white miners, however, there was a difference between 'Native' troopers policing Aboriginal people, and policing whites (see Plate 5). Many of the white population resented being sanctioned by men whom they believed to be their racial inferiors.[44]

The Black Douglas myth distracted white miners from this uncomfortable state of affairs. For them, Douglas embodied the crime and disorder of the Gold Rush. With little to no evidence, he could be blamed for almost any crime. A nervous digger requesting government protection assumed it was Douglas who took a dish of his tailings. A man on trial for selling sly grog declared that he committed the crime because 'he lived in a state of excitement, fearing his life to be in danger from Black Douglas'.[45] When miners heard of murder, or tales of unfortunate travellers robbed of their possessions, stripped of their clothes, tied to trees and attacked by ferocious ants, they were warned to be watchful, aware and ready to defend their person and property.[46] Through repeated telling, these stories ensured that Black Douglas was as familiar in miners' 'ears as household words'.[47] While this terrorised many, it was easier for colonists to obsess over one black man than confront the fact that most criminals on the goldfields were white.

Racial prejudice notwithstanding, it is peculiar that Douglas was known by his skin colour alone. Goldmining communities made racial distinctions.[48] In 1852 newspapers reported that 'Black Douglas and an African black' had been arrested, giving a specific racial identity to one man but not the other.[49] This difference makes sense if Black Douglas was viewed as a symbol of racial disorder, rather than a man. British beliefs about black inferiority had a long history. For centuries, the colour black had been associated with evil and villainy, and in the 19th century these ideas were legitimised by supposedly 'objective' science. Both stereotypes and scientific ideas placed black people at the bottom of the racial hierarchy, and so Black Douglas's depredations aligned nicely with white prejudices.[50] Black Douglas came to represent the supposed 'fiendishness' of all black men rather than a specific racial group, and this too protected white colonists from confronting uncomfortable truths. If we explore a counterfactual – if we engage in a little speculation, and ask what might have happened if history unfolded differently – we can see this most clearly. Imagine, for a moment, what might have happened if Douglas was an Aboriginal man.

*

Alongside policing and goldmining, some Aboriginal people declared their sovereignty over the land and made claims to rights and recognition, much to the discomfort of the white community. When white mounted police asked a group of Aboriginal people to show their miner's licences at Forest Creek in 1852, they apparently replied that 'the land was theirs by right so why should they pay money to the Queen?' In other instances, Aboriginal people requested goods, food or equipment as recompense for the miners' use of their land and tried to teach goldfields migrants the laws of reciprocity that governed Aboriginal communities. A Djadjawurrung man complained to one settler that, 'when a native discovers a [bee] hive, he invites the neighbours to partake of the honey, but when a white Christian discovers it, he keeps the produce for himself'. In Aboriginal groups, members had a responsibility to share their possessions and wealth among their kin, and some clearly believed that migrants had the same obligations.[51]

Aboriginal people's assertions of their customs and rights were increasingly made out of necessity. As diggers pushed deeper into Aboriginal Country, it became harder for Aboriginal people to live off the land alone. Their foodstuffs were either destroyed by the creation of goldfields or else appropriated by miners, while their waterholes were muddied or dredged by diggers.[52] In extreme cases, Aboriginal people used violence to ensure that their customary and material needs were met. Goldminer George Robins described how an Aboriginal man threatened to shoot him if he did not give his group supplies, while digger Abraham Abrahamsohn barely escaped with his life after evading payback for assaulting an Aboriginal man.[53]

This was not a veiled issue. The 1859 Select Committee into Victoria's Aboriginal population recognised that when the government took from Aboriginal people 'their hunting grounds and their means of living, proper provision should have been made for them'. To not have done so was 'a great injustice'.[54] Britons were meant to be a benevolent and civilising force upon foreign lands – this was a big part of how they justified their colonisation of Aboriginal Country.[55] But in Victoria there was official recognition that colonists' actions had resulted in 'a great injustice'. The colonisers knew they had not improved the lives of Aboriginal people. Yet colonisation continued apace.

Had Black Douglas been depicted as an Aboriginal man, tales about him might have reminded miners of these issues. Few wanted to entertain the idea that they might owe something to the country's First Peoples, and no one wanted to be confronted with the fact that they had taken someone else's land. In contrast to Aboriginal people, diggers depicted Black Douglas as an external threat. He had no pre-existing connection or entitlement to the land. In miners' minds, Black Douglas was an outsider who came to wreak havoc on the diggings. And although he was dangerous, the idea that he was an interloper brought with it a sense of relief.

## THE MAN BEHIND THE LEGEND

We now know why the Black Douglas legend was created and where the myth starts and stops but who was the *real* Black Douglas? If we remove the clinging film of colonial misrepresentation, it becomes clear that Douglas was never an isolated figure. In many ways, his life was representative of Victoria's goldfields population. Ex-convicts from Van Diemen's Land (Tasmania) were some of the first to descend upon the diggings, and they were frequently depicted as the goldfields' criminal class.[56] It is fitting then, that Black Douglas was actually William Douglas, an ex-convict from Van Diemen's land.[57] He came to Victoria in 1851 as a steerage passenger on board the *City of Melbourne* steamer and was one of 2437 men to enter the colony from Van Diemen's Land that year.[58] It is very likely that Douglas's 'gang' was composed of former convicts. Almost 60 per cent of the men and women who sailed with Douglas on the *City of Melbourne* had been convicts themselves.[59] Black Douglas was part of a larger group of ex-convicts and might have been condemned as such, had diggers ever concerned themselves with his origins.

Although Douglas only arrived in Victoria in 1851, by the end of the following year he had been arrested for a slew of offences on various goldfields. In the most extreme of these cases, Douglas came before the Supreme Court for assaulting a police officer. According to the *Argus*:

> Mr John Tucker, the Chief Constable at Kyneton, stated that on the 23rd of January a man named Fahey was given into his custody on a charge of stealing gold. He was on his way to the Watch House with Fahey when the prisoner Douglas came up to him, and seizing Fahey by the arm, said that witness should not take him to the Watch House. Douglas carried a short bludgeon, which he brandished in the face of the witness, and threatened to use it if Fahey was not released. Fahey then began to struggle and with the assistance of the prisoner contrived to effect his escape.[60]

In this instance, Douglas risked his life and freedom to liberate one of his associates and was later found guilty of assault for his efforts. While he could have saved Fahey to protect his own interests, this seems unlikely. Assaulting a police officer was the most serious crime that Douglas was convicted of in Victoria and stands in stark contrast to the majority of minor offences that he committed. The risk that Douglas might be implicated if Fahey passed information to the authorities was small compared to his risk of arrest for assaulting a police officer.

It appears that Douglas was looking out for his mate, and so upholding the most 'sacred' of Australian values. The loyalty and support of a mate is something Australians prize today, but this distinctive national trait has a long history. Historian Russel Ward has shown that mateship was a feature of early colonial life – that this tradition was forged among convicts and in the pastoral industry, as well as on the goldfields. The diggings provided a unique space for this collective ethos to grow and mature, as mining often demanded parties of two or more for success, while solidarity was encouraged by diggers' resentment of miner's licences and the police's heavy-handed approach to law and order.[61] Mateship meant watching each other's backs and standing tall, together, no matter the risks or odds. Despite the fact that Douglas was never connected to this tradition in his own time or by historians since, 'mateship' seems to have propelled him to act. There appears to have been honour among thieves.

William Douglas also showed a keen awareness of manly conduct and the law in the case of Fahey's liberation. The *Argus* reported that Douglas 'cross-examined Mr Tucker [the police constable] with great tact' and addressed the jury with his own closing remarks. His defence rested on turning attention from his criminal actions and back onto the arresting officer, as Douglas contended that 'he could not have rescued the prisoner from an armed constable except the latter was an arrant coward'. Through cross-examination, Douglas gained evidence that when the incident took place, the constable had a loaded revolver but had never used it. Although Douglas ultimately lost the case, it was not for want of trying.[62]

At another trial for assault in April 1852, Douglas similarly proved his legal acumen. When asked if he knew of any reason why the court should not sentence him according to the law, Douglas:

> ... pleaded the long period he had been already in confinement, and the hardships he had undergone since his arrest. He had been kept without food, and chained to trees without sufficient shelter from the weather, and all this before he had been brought to trial, and ... when, according to the law, he was to be considered innocent.[63]

One of the central tenets of British law, upon which the Victorian legal system was founded, is that the accused is seen as innocent until they are proven guilty. Eighteenth-century jurist William Blackstone famously declared that 'the law holds that it is better that ten guilty persons escape than that one innocent suffer' and by the 19th century this was clearly articulated in treatises on criminal law.[64] Douglas was not the only convict to possess this legal knowledge. From the very beginning of colonisation, convict men and women mobilised the law to achieve their own ends, and as Douglas illustrates, not all of these convicts were white.[65]

Abuses of police power similarly crossed the racial divide, as Douglas suffered the same brutal treatment by police of which white miners so often complained. George Chislehurst wrote in 1855 of a strikingly similar incident to the one Douglas described in court. After being captured by the police for failing to produce his mining licence, Chislehurst was chained with a group of like offenders. There, he met a man who remarked that their situation was not as bad as it could be, for the last time that he had been taken by the authorities 'twenty of us was chained to a gum-tree and the rain come down till we was almost drowned'.[66]

William Douglas was most often convicted for alcohol-related offences on the Victorian goldfields and in this, he was perhaps most typical of the goldfields population. Douglas was imprisoned for selling sly grog, and repeatedly apprehended for drunk and disorderly conduct.[67] Drunkenness was pervasive on the goldfields even though it was illegal to sell alcohol on diggings themselves. The goldfields contained a mobile, predominately male population, freed from the grounding influences of established society. In such circumstances, the Victorian government feared that alcohol would prove a major threat to order on the diggings, and they were right.[68] Charles Latrobe, the Lieutenant-Governor of Victoria before Hotham took the office in 1854, believed that 'the illicit trade of spirits [was] the root of nine tenths of the crime and disorder on the diggings', and involvement in this trade was not confined to men or the criminal classes.[69]

Women not only ran sly grog stores on the diggings – some were also customers and drunkards themselves. A Victorian colonist named Samuel Lazarus remarked in his diary that drunkenness on the diggings was so ubiquitous that 'even women, feeling themselves relieved from the salutatory checks which society in civilized life lays on them, fall ...'[70] Upstanding folk were equally susceptible to the lure of alcohol. In evidence put before the 1853 Select Committee on the Goldfields, for instance, EN Emmet declared that sly grog tents were also frequented by 'respectable persons ... for men will have liquor and they are unable to get it except at these tents' (see Plate 6).[71]

People continued to visit sly grog tents despite their illegality, their extortionate prices, and the harm that the government and temperance advocates believed these beverages caused to civilised society.[72] Spirits were the drink of the diggings. They could be transported more easily than beer and this meant that enterprising sly grog sellers could be as mobile as the miners themselves.[73] It was easier to get drunk on liquors such as these, with their high alcohol content, and many batches were adulterated to keep up with demand. This lethal combination of spirits and spiked concoctions 'killed many, and made many more insane'.[74] In humanitarian and temperance circles, it was blamed for breaking up families and friendships, increasing crime and impoverishing mining men.[75] And so the question remains as to why drinking was so prevalent. When people on the diggings apparently witnessed their neighbours drinking themselves to death and destroying 'in a few weeks the chance of placing himself [sic] in easy and happy circumstances for life ...' why did they seek out alcohol?[76]

Historian AE Dingle offers us part of the picture. In his article, 'A Truly Magnificent Thirst', Dingle proposes that as 'incomes were high and alternatives few', miners sought alcohol on the goldfields.[77] This idea was not confined to Victoria alone, as the 1854 Select Committee into Intemperance in New South Wales contained a similar opinion, that gold had 'increased the wage so much' that people were more likely to indulge in liquor.[78] However, Dingle's suggestion that 'alternatives [were] few' deserves our critical attention. There were other ways that diggers spent their newfound wealth. Gambling was a particularly popular pastime, with prize fights, card games and

Chinese 'gambling dens' rife on the diggings.[79] Miners did not have to spend their money on liquor.

A more convincing reason for diggers' consumption of alcohol can be found when we look at the environmental impact of the Gold Rush. Rivers and waterways were muddied and polluted by the miners, in many instances making the water contaminated and unsafe to drink.[80] Water was a precious commodity on the goldfields but it was predominately used, hoarded and traded to assist miners to find gold through practices such as sluicing, and not to satiate their thirst.[81] And so, despite temperance advocates' push for the goldfields' population to drink water, this was not a feasible suggestion or a top priority on many diggings.[82]

Attempts to limit or prohibit drinking and drunkenness were also hampered by the cultural significance of alcohol. There was a sense among some of the colonial elite that the growing criminal problem of drunkenness was part of 'a wider British culture, in which intoxication was a subject of levity and drinking was regarded as healthy and normal'.[83] For many, drinking alcohol was essential for hard work, and a part of sociability. Few men drank alcohol alone. In the 18th century in particular, heavy drinking was associated with manliness across all classes, while the consumption of liquor was intertwined with almost all aspects of life. It was a way to seal a bargain, to solidify friendships, to celebrate success and drown out misfortune. Babies had alcohol mixed in with some of their first meals, doctors prescribed it as medicine and families farewelled their loved ones by drinking to their memory.[84] Historian Roy Porter summed up the situation neatly when he remarked that 'from cradle to grave, drink gratified and compensated'.[85] It was woven into the fabric of community life.

The customs and rituals surrounding alcohol took on an even greater meaning in the context of the Gold Rush. In such a tumultuous time, some miners clung to the familiar as a way to anchor their lives.[86] Archaeologist Susan Lawrence's research has shown this in material terms, as remains from the Moorabool goldfields included cups and plates in a 'multitude of patterns and colours': the trappings of domesticity brought to maintain the outward signs of civilised life.[87] Drinking culture appears to have served a similar role, as it was a known mode of interaction, expression and performance in a rapidly changing landscape. Despite its illegality, storekeepers would often provide their customers with a glass of alcohol at the end of their transaction, and it was rude to refuse.[88] Emmet was right when he declared that no matter the regulation 'men will have liquor'.[89] Indeed, many believed it to be their right to access the intoxicating beverage.

The language of freedom and liberty was increasingly used to speak about alcohol, as mining communities believed that the government was unfairly intervening in their lives when they curtailed their access to liquor.[90] This was not just the preserve of radicals. The 'majority of moderate men … objected to [liquor laws'] interference with their liberty'.[91] The position of the police exacerbated resistance. As one man testified to the Select Committee in 1853, 'the present spirit law places a great number of persons outside the pale of the law' while another declared that '[t]he police have been engaged in looking after … grog shops, instead of protecting the people, so that at last they have come to be viewed as the oppressors of the people'.[92] As many of the goldfields population frequented illegal sly grog tents, many were outside the law's protections and at the mercy of the police. All manner of crime was hushed up at sly grog tents, as patrons were acting illicitly by being there and had no wish to implicate themselves by reporting what they had witnessed.[93] This failure of the police to recognise the socially acceptable nature of drinking struck many as betrayal by the government. Instead of protecting the community, the police were apparently there to control it.

We are now back at those familiar grievances that miners levelled at the police – that the authorities failed to go after the 'real' criminals – but in this context, William Douglas was among the persecuted. When drinking water was not an option, and the social significance of alcohol was so great, it is easy to understand Douglas's crimes. The real William Douglas most often encountered the law for offences that were not deemed criminal by the majority of the goldfields population. And yet, in colonial reminiscence and contemporary reportage, he was cast beyond the pale of goldfields society.

*

William Douglas – the drunken yet legally astute ex-convict who had a way with words – was intimately a part of goldfields society, and represented the mining population more closely than stories about him allow. This is something Douglas himself appears to have concluded. In 1853, the 'somewhat celebrated Black Douglas' was arrested for drunkenness, but he did not go quietly. At his hearing, he 'complained that the police were always pouncing on him and that he had a bad reputation without a cause'. Although he was eventually discharged, the mayor (serving as magistrate) did not let Douglas go without reminding him of the old English proverb 'Give a dog an ill name and hang him', signalling that Douglas's plight was hopeless, as he had lost his reputation.[94] It did not matter that Douglas did not commit the heinous crimes he was accused of or that in many ways, he was a representative figure of the goldfields population as a whole. He had a bad name, and that proved his undoing, and until now, his sole legacy.

# CHAPTER 2

# THE LIFE AND TIMES OF WILLIAM DOUGLAS

## PART 1: THE VOYAGER

On Sunday 5 July 1835, 320 male convicts on board the *Marquis of Huntly* reached Sydney Cove after 100 days at sea.[1] Although this voyage from England to Port Jackson was short by 19th-century standards, the prisoners had nevertheless spent over three months in undesirable conditions.[2] The *Marquis of Huntly* was by far the oldest ship to reach the colony of New South Wales that year, having been constructed over three decades previously.[3] Although the ship's surgeon recorded only one fatality, there were many cases of general illness and debility among the convicts on board.[4] This, combined with the absence of female company and the changeable nature of the sea, must have made many convicts eager to leave the vessel; however, there was to be no immediate transition from sea to land.[5] Before they were permitted to leave the ship, each convict had to endure a thorough interrogation by a colonial clerk.

The government required that a detailed description, known as a 'convict indent', be taken of every prisoner upon entry to the new colony. Twenty-four to forty-eight hours after a ship's arrival, the clerk and the Principal Superintendent of Prisoners would finally have ascended the gangplank to the vessel, and the clerk was then tasked with recording the intimate details of every criminal soul on board. The convicts were questioned on a range of topics including their previous occupation, place of birth, religion, literacy, crimes and sentence but their answers were not the only information that was recorded. Convict registers were already partially filled by the time convicts were confronted by government clerks, both to expedite the process and deter convicts from giving a false account of themselves.[6]

After this interrogation came the physical examination. While we have no firsthand account of this process in Australia, the words of Canadian convict William Gunn provide a sense of this invasive colonial procedure:

> We were ... stripped of our clothing, and a minute description
> of every scar, blemish or mole on our persons, placed on record.
> There was another officer who eyed us most searchingly, and who
> also put on record a faithful description of our features, the color
> of our hair ... eyes ... nose, ears, chin, mouth &c., together with
> our height ...[7]

In July 1835, the passengers on board the *Marquis of Huntly* endured a similar examination, and it is lucky for us that they did. For among the 320 convicts to make it to New South Wales on this voyage was William Douglas, the man who would become 'Black Douglas', the terror of the Victorian goldfields. Douglas's convict indent from 1835 is the richest source on his life that remains. From this information, we know that he was sentenced at the Rye Quarter Sessions in England to seven years' transportation for larceny.[8] The register describes an eighteen-year-old, 5ft 8in in height, with curly brown hair and brown eyes. His complexion was 'mulatto' though he was pale enough for freckles to be seen on his skin. His nose was broad, and his breast covered in numerous scars. William Douglas was a Protestant originally from Philadelphia, USA, who could read and write, was single and marked by several tattoos. He had a half moon and three dots on his lower left arm and an anchor etched on to the back of his left hand.[9] This description of Douglas is worlds apart from that of the previous chapter. In the Gold Rush material, Douglas appeared an amorphous, shadowy figure as there was no indication of his appearance apart from the colour of his skin. The William Douglas of this 1830s indent is vividly described and while this helps us to picture him as an individual, this source was not intended to humanise him.

Although convict indents provide more information on working-class people than almost any other source in the world, the reason for this is far from benign. From the 1820s, British officials envisaged New South Wales as a colony built on convict labour, but convict men and women often had other plans. Despite the new environment, many left settlements and pastoral runs to take their chances in the bush. The longer the colonisers remained in the colony, the more knowledge about the contours of the landscape as well as its flora and fauna grew, and the more emboldened convicts were to embrace the bushland that was meant to contain them.[10] Some of these escapees were the first bushrangers, as many turned to theft to survive. Such convicts needed to be caught, and so these indents served as a 'written mugshot' to identify absconding prisoners and bring them back under official control.[11] Recognising convict indents' coercive, criminal framing is crucial if we are to push beyond it.

Although we often have scant information about William Douglas, knowing where he was and when allows us to piece together the worlds he lived in and the opportunities available to him as well as the obstacles barring his way. Informed imagination, probability and educated guesswork are less than ideal forms of history making, but they are often our only way to see people like Douglas who hover precariously around the margins of published sources. From these traces, we know that William Douglas was a well-travelled man. He was born in the United States, in a state still reeling from the impact of slavery. He was in Rye, Sussex, at a turning point in local government and the height of British transportation to the Australian colonies, and he was in New South Wales and Van Diemen's Land (Tasmania) at critical junctures in their dealings with convicts. At various points in his life, William Douglas was a convict, a sailor, a prize-fighter, a recidivist, a phrenologist, a beggar and a bushranger, as well as the man behind the Black Douglas legend. The Gold Rush myth forms only one small episode in Douglas's history, and it pales in comparison to his epic life story.

## PHILADELPHIA, USA

The only evidence of Douglas's origins are his year and place of birth that are listed in his convict indent. Although slim, these details are enough to provide us with a sense of his early life. When Douglas was born in Philadelphia, Pennsylvania in 1817, he entered a United States that was still marked by slavery.[12] It would be another thirty years before the American Civil War brought about complete emancipation, and even though Pennsylvania was a state that supported abolition, its steps to curtail slavery were far from complete. In 1780, Pennsylvania's *Gradual Abolition Act* decreed

> That all persons ... born within this state from and after the passing of this act, shall not be deemed ... slaves; and that all servitude for life ... is utterly taken away, extinguished and for ever abolished.[13]

But there were conditions on this newfound freedom that would have affected Douglas's black family. Free black people were still in the minority at this time, not only in Philadelphia but nationwide, and this strongly suggests that Douglas had slave ancestry.[14] Any slave born prior to 1780 was exempt from the *Gradual Abolition Act* and, given the date of Douglas's birth, this means that if his black grandparents were slaves, they would have remained enslaved. Children born to slave mothers were forced to work for their masters until they were twenty-eight years old, effectively buying their freedom with twenty-eight years of unpaid labour.[15] Douglas's age suggests that his black parent would have fallen into this category, and that he was one of the first generations of black people in Pennsylvania to have been born completely, legally, free from enforced labour, thanks to the *Gradual Abolition Act*.

Slavery was not the dominant form of labour in Philadelphia, even before this legislation was passed. Unlike their counterparts on the infamous plantations of the American south, most Philadelphian slave owners had only one or two men or women at their disposal, and this fundamentally changed aspects of the slave experience. The slave trade had declined by 1773 in Philadelphia, when a high-duty tax was levied upon each person purchased. Although slaves were useful in times of labour shortages, they were never the region's sole form of labour. Indentured, free wage and bonded workers toiled alongside each other as labourers and domestic servants.[16] The small numbers of slaves increased the proximity between slaves and their owners, and this relationship continued well after the *Gradual Abolition Act* was passed. Forty years after the act became law, 75 per cent of black boys and men and 58 per cent of black girls and women aged between fourteen and twenty-five continued to work for whites.[17]

This makes it likely that Douglas's black parent, if not Douglas himself, was a well-known member of the household staff. Being one of a few workers often fostered a greater intimacy between slave and master, and it was not uncommon for masters to have sex with their slaves (and later, their black 'employees' after the passing of the *Gradual Abolition Act*). While there were many cases of rape and coercion, there were also instances of affectionate, loving relationships between whites and blacks from all classes.[18] We have no way of knowing which group Douglas's parents belonged to, but their relationship was not the only factor to have affected Douglas's upbringing. The political context in Philadelphia was just as important in shaping Douglas's future.

Philadelphia was the centre of the abolition movement in the United States and the first city in the world to attempt state-enforced emancipation.[19] While the *Gradual Abolition Act* did not immediately release slaves from bondage, it was a trailblazing piece of legislation. Even the British (who would later contrast their benevolent liberation of slaves to the tyrannical oppression of the United States) would not bring about the formal abolition of slavery until over fifty years later, in 1838.[20] In words as well as deeds, the reform-minded citizens of Philadelphia worked to liberate, protect and support the black population. From the 1810s, Philadelphia became a hub for runaway slaves trying to flee bondage in the American south. Individuals smuggled black men and women into the city and hid runaways, while Vigilance Committees provided housing, food and basic assistance to newcomers in the area.[21] By 1830, Philadelphia had a black population of about 14 000 and the largest number of free black people in the United States.[22]

Education and cultural opportunities grew for the free black population of which Douglas was a part. As a port city, news and ideas from all over the world flowed through Philadelphia and gave shape to new schools of thought.[23] For whites, emancipation became a test to see whether Africans were 'degraded' by nature, and education and religion spearheaded attempts to remedy years of oppression:[24]

> From Philadelphia's narrow alley's [sic] and cramped courtyards came men and women who established many of the first northern black schools; literary, musical, and historical societies; and black newspapers. Here the first Negro convention met in 1830.[25]

From the late 1820s, Philadelphia was also home to thriving black literary societies that provided their own schools, libraries and rhetorical education.[26] This was a remarkable feat considering that at this same time, reading was viewed as a seditious skill for slaves in the American south. By 1834, Louisiana, North and South Carolina, Alabama and Georgia had passed laws that prohibited anyone from teaching slaves to read or write, while the latter three states also penalised anyone who taught free black people these skills.[27] William Douglas appears to have benefitted from Philadelphia's unique educational advances. They could explain his literacy, and the fact that he possessed notable advocacy skills by the time he faced the magistrate's bench in 1850s Victoria. Because of the fortitude and perseverance of black men and women as well as white sympathisers, 'Philadelphian abolitionists grappled with the broader meaning of black freedom earlier and more consistently than perhaps anyone else in American culture'.[28]

But not all Philadelphians supported the growing black population. Racial hatred grew as the 19th century progressed. Anxious questions were raised about the place these newly freed slaves would hold in 'civilised' society, and whether they should live among whites. In 1832, a group of Philadelphians brandished weapons to prevent a ship carrying ninety-two former slaves from landing on their shores.[29] In 1838 the right of free black people to vote was revoked by the state parliament.[30] And in 1850, the federal government strengthened laws making it illegal to assist runaway slaves.[31] So while Douglas might have been a part of the most prosperous, well-established free-black community in the United States, he was not wholly accepted by his white peers. He is likely to have experienced racial intolerance and might have predicted its increase. This may have been why he decided to travel to England.


## LIFE AT SEA

In January 1835 William Douglas was brought before the Rye Quarter Sessions in Sussex, and so sometime before this date, he must have made the 5600-kilometre journey to the British Isles. The most likely way that Douglas could have made this trip was by working for his passage onboard a trading vessel. Seafaring was the most accessible job open to African Americans. Maritime historian W Jeffrey Bolster describes how:

American shipping expanded during the early nineteenth century, employing more than 100,000 men per year [and] ... black men ... filled about one-fifth of sailors' berths ... [B]lack sailors established a visible presence in every North Atlantic seaport and plantation roadstead ...[32]

Philadelphia was no exception. Between 1810 and 1838, 16.6 to 22.4 per cent of berths in Philadelphia were held by African Americans.[33] As Douglas would have travelled before he was eighteen, he was still young for this type of trade. Only 8.9 per cent of black seamen from Philadelphia were under nineteen years old.[34] But his youth does not appear to have stopped Douglas from identifying with this profession. By the time he reached New South Wales in 1835, Douglas had an anchor tattoo on the back of his left hand.[35] Although anchors were symbols of hope and common tattoos for convicts, they were also closely associated with a seafaring life.[36]

Perhaps Douglas believed he had found freedom at sea. A ship's crew were not bound to their masters through slavery, patronage or fealty but by contracts. During times of high demand, the crew had a great deal of bargaining power. They could negotiate for higher wages, and if they had objections to their lot on board a ship, they could always look for work elsewhere. Ships also 'offered more equality and liberty to those whose skin colour marked them out for oppression and enslavement on land'.[37] For centuries, seafaring was an international profession as ships were composed of motley crews from all over the world.[38] Sailors were more likely to be organised by ability than race as collective labour was essential to many tasks: men were often 'pushing or pulling in unison' and gave rhythm to their labours through songs or chants.[39] Distinctions between crew members broke down even more in times of impending disaster (from stormy seas, pirates, a sinking ship and so on) when 'all hands' were needed to protect the vessel. This not only brought seamen into close contact with one another but fostered a collective maritime culture where sailors asserted their rights to liberty and freedom from tyranny.[40] Black seamen such as Douglas were more likely to have been accepted as part of this multiracial collective than they were as individual black men on land.[41]

But people of colour were still not free from racial prejudice. Not all crew members saw black seamen as their equals, and there was a tension between sailors' rights and racism. Black seafarers were often designated the lowest ranked positions. Even if they proved their maritime prowess, black crew members had virtually no chance of being elevated to officers, while white sailors could racially abuse black 'ordinary seamen' to emphasise their inferior position in the ship's hierarchy.[42] Many black sailors were 'consigned to particular roles upon the ship such as musicians, servants or cooks' and Douglas appears to have been one of these men.[43] In his convict indent, he is described as a 'cook/servant'.[44] Captains and their crew often hired free black people as domestic servants when they entered Philadelphia and these African Americans could then be recruited for the next voyage.[45] Servants on ships were also usually young men or boys, making this an ideal job for someone Douglas's age.[46]

The value of Douglas's work depended on his location. By the time he reached the Australian colonies in 1835, his experience as a 'cook/servant' might have worked in his favour. The Lieutenant-Governor of Van Diemen's Land, John Franklin, believed that convicts prized domestic work above other employment, and free colonists were only too eager to secure a servant with experience to enhance their own status and comfort.[47] However these same skills could have forced Douglas out of work when he reached England. The 19th century saw a contraction in the labour market that affected black, male domestic servants and seamen alike. In this period, domestic service was changing. Rising numbers of middle-class employers preferred female servants to men, and so, despite the cultural cachet attached to black domestic servants, many black men were pushed out of the profession. The demobilisation of the navy after the Napoleonic Wars also placed black seafarers in a precarious position. Sailors lost much of their bargaining power as competition for employment increased dramatically. When Douglas was at sea, black seamen had to vie with white sailors for a dwindling supply of jobs.[48] This may explain why, by the time he faced the Rye Quarter Sessions in 1835, Douglas had left seafaring behind and was working as a labourer.[49]

Labouring was low-skilled work, especially compared to the specialised work that Douglas would have performed on a ship, but it did have its advantages. As a casual labourer, Douglas would not have been beholden to the arbitrary power of his superiors in the same way that he was on a ship. Admiralty law put sailors under the authority of high-ranking officers who could inflict corporal punishment for any misdemeanour. The logic behind this approach was that hierarchy, obedience and absolute authority were necessary to maintain order, and by extension, the safety of the ship. In reality, this system was based on an officer's discretion and open to abuse.[50] In his writing on naval vessels, cultural historian Greg Dening eloquently described the intimate encounters that shaped power and authority at sea:

> ... so many trivial decisions taken in the course of ordinary living were subject to violent reprisal on the personal interpretation of what a superior thought a particular social situation meant ... The ordinary right to negotiate what words, gestures, actions mean was taken out of the hands of the participants and given to one man or a group of men who could impose a particular interpretation violently.[51]

Seamen's experiences on board a ship often depended on the disposition of their superiors, and black seafarers suffered disproportionately from arbitrary punishments due to their race.[52] Flogging was the most common form of punishment on board a ship, but superior officers could inflict whatever punishment they deemed necessary. Perhaps this is how Douglas received the scars on his breast that were recorded by the colonial clerk in New South Wales in 1835.[53] It was certainly an environment where he would have experienced intense discipline. But if Douglas hoped to find more liberty on land, he was mistaken. New forms of confinement awaited him in England.

## THE TOWN OF RYE

Seven January 1835 was market day in the port town of Rye in Sussex. Every Wednesday vendors sold their wares on the bottom floor of the Georgian town hall that stood in the town centre, and the stock sold each week alternated between corn and cattle.[54] On this day it is unclear which goods were for sale but either way, the market's presence would have disrupted the courtroom located on the second floor of the building. The call of sellers touting their wares could not have been shut out from the hallowed halls of British justice, and perhaps even the lowing of cows and the smell of their excrement wafted up the staircase to where the representatives of the British justice system presided over the day's trials.

Despite the irreverence of this scene, for William Douglas and John Smith, their presence in Rye Town Hall was no laughing matter. The men faced the magistrate's bench charged with stealing 'two woollen cloth coats of the value of four pounds of the goods and chattel of one Charles Taylor'. Although seven witnesses were called for the prosecution, none came forward for the defence. Both men were found guilty and sentenced to seven years' transportation.[55] On first inspection, this appears to be a common tale of misfortune. Larceny was the crime that most often sent convicts to Australia, and according to the indictment, the two men were caught red-handed in the middle of the theft. Douglas's race is not recorded in this court document, and the fact that he received the same sentence as his white accomplice seems to belie any racial power imbalance.[56] Four pounds was a lot of money in 1835. It was the equivalent of almost £200 in today's currency and more than the average craftsman builder would earn in two and a half weeks.[57] After spending seven days in Rye Prison, the men were transferred to the *Fortitude* prison hulk in Chatham where they awaited their voyage to the colonies. It seems to have been a clear-cut case, but there is more to this story than meets the eye.

Transportation was a common punishment in Britain in the early 19th century and in 1834, 4920 convicts, the largest number to ever leave Britain for Australia, set sail for the colonies.[58] But in Rye, this punishment was not the norm. Between 1788 and 1834, only one person had received this sentence in Rye prior to Douglas and Smith. From 1789 to 1867, almost the entire period in which convicts were transported to Australia, only seven men, including Douglas and Smith, were ever sent to the colonies.[59] As a port town Rye had been known for centuries as the home of nefarious characters, smugglers and illicit trade, but by 1833 amateur historian JD Parry could not help but describe the town as 'tolerably built ... but rather dull'.[60] Tales of skirmishes, carousing and lawlessness had long since passed, and a majority of early 19th-century offences were for misbehaviour in workhouses, vagrancy and the occasional assault.[61] In an 1834 Inquiry into local administration, commissioners declared that in this town '... all, except trifling cases, are sent for trial at the [Sussex] assizes' and yet Douglas and Smith were exceptions to this rule as they were tried at the Rye Quarter Sessions.[62] Clearly, for this port town in Sussex, transportation was an unusual punishment. We need to delve deeper into the history of the town to understand William Douglas's sentence.

\*

The town of Rye lies ensconced between river and sea 63 miles from London on the south-east coast of England.[63] In Douglas's time it was a trading port, a site of exchange that saw domestic products swapped with imports from the Netherlands, Norway, America and France.[64] In 1831 the population of Rye was listed as 3715, but in reality its numbers ebbed and flowed along with the ships that moored on its shores.[65] There were of course many such towns splayed across the United Kingdom's coast, but Rye was unique. Centuries before Douglas's birth, Rye had been designated as a 'Cinque Port', which meant that it had special powers to control its internal affairs. Tax, trade and criminal justice, including capital offences, could be dealt with at the local level instead of placed at the mercy of men in London.[66] It was the granular texture of local justice that shaped Douglas's sentence and by extension, the course of his life.

By the time of Douglas's trial in 1835, Rye was undergoing a significant change in government. Prior to the 1820s, the Lamb family had retained the office of mayor for almost a century.[67] For decades the number of men eligible to vote had been kept low to ensure voters were family or friends of the mayor, and this affected everything from the day-to-day workings of the town to the administration of justice.[68] The mayor was the chief magistrate, and he chose up to twelve enfranchised men of the town to assist him on the bench. Professional lawyers were not employed often, and the mayor was known to take evidence, charge the juries and examine witnesses from the depositions. In Rye there was no separation of powers, as the legislature and judiciary were composed of the same men, who relied on elections for their power. The people of Rye were not happy with this state of affairs. In 1832, a government report on the administration in Rye admitted that this system created 'great dissatisfaction … jealousy and discontent' among the population and 'diminished the confidence which ought to exist towards the magistracy in the town'.[69]

Only a couple of years before Douglas's arrest, the wealthy men of Rye moved against the Lambs and a new mayor named William Ramsen was appointed in 1833. This was literally the end of an era as it was the last time any Lamb held this office, but the change brought about by this election was far from absolute.[70] Although Ramsen and succeeding mayors expanded the franchise so more middle-class men could vote, new voters needed to be elected by existing voters. This meant that issues of patronage and favouritism continued to plague all levels of local administration. To make matters worse, the composition of the courts remained the same, leaving judicial power at the mercy of local politics. Ramsen was elected to power on the understanding that he offered an alternative to the Lambs' self-interested rule, and so he needed to convince his constituents that he represented their interests.

The local aristocracy was evidently on the decline and the middle class on the rise at this time, and one man to benefit from the change was David Taylor. Taylor gained the status of freeman (one who could vote) in 1830.[71] He was also brother to the victim of Douglas's theft, Charles Taylor. Born in Chiddingstone, Kent, in the late 1700s, the Taylor brothers were established men of Rye by the early 19th century.[72] David Taylor was a bookseller, binder, stationer, library owner, local fire office agent, letterpress printer, perfumer and stamp office agent, and in 1836 he also became one of Rye's twelve councillors.[73] Certainly David Taylor was a well-known man about town. Although Charles Taylor was less socially engaged than his older brother, he was also a part of the town's burgeoning bourgeoisie. He was a banker's clerk (most likely for Curteis, Pomfret, and Co., the town's local establishment), and also an insurance agent.[74] It was unfortunate for Douglas and Smith that they stole from a man who was so well connected at a time when the mayor was trying to re-establish his electorate's faith in the criminal justice system. Given these circumstances, it is likely that Douglas and Smith were punished severely as an example of the new government's robust stance on crime. All seven men sentenced to transportation in the history of Rye were convicted for property offences.[75] They could have been sent to the Sussex Assizes to be tried, as residents accused of indictable offences usually were, but instead they were tried and convicted in Rye.[76] The government in Rye clearly wanted to be responsible for exacting justice in these cases and went to great lengths to be seen to protect its wealthy constituents' possessions. Catering to the wants of the electorate was, after all, the most surefire way to receive votes.

Conflicts of interest did not end there, as witnesses at the trial also had a stake in seeing Douglas and Smith punished. By using censuses, directories and local guides, we can access biographical data for four of the seven witnesses present in court, and this reveals how intimate the trial really was. Unlike the transient population of sailors, traders and merchants who streamed in and out of the area, these four men were all residents of the town. And while the district of Rye sprawled far beyond the walled remnants of the ancient city, by the 1841 census three of these men lived close to one another in the heart of the town. Charles Taylor (as well as his brother) and James Newbery lived on High Street by that decade.[77] James Newbery was the local tailor, and so it is possible that Newbery had originally sold the coats to Charles, or else provided expert testimony at the trial about their make and worth.[78] He was also a man who relied on local clientele. Thomas Hearsfield lived in Watchbell Street and ran a pub there called the *Jolly Sailor*. This establishment was known to house sailors, drifters and the like due to its proximity to the harbour, and Douglas may have stayed in this accommodation. Like Newbery, Hearsfield had his own reasons to appease the magistrate's bench. It took him two attempts and a large public petition to gain his publican licence in 1832, and the men presiding over the trial had the power to take away such hard-won favours.[79]

Whether against transient outsiders or competing classes, the enfranchised men of Rye were prepared to close ranks to protect their interests. Intimate, quotidian encounters in the heart of the town as well as the new government desperate for their constituents' support ensured that loyalty and patronage were of the utmost importance to Rye's inhabitants. All these webs of self-interest and connection could not have worked in Douglas's favour. On 7 January 1835, they culminated in his conviction for larceny and his sentence to seven years' transportation to New South Wales.

# PART 2: THE CONVICT
## NEW SOUTH WALES

William Douglas had plenty of time to process the court's verdict and wonder at what his Antipodean life might bring before he arrived in New South Wales. From the courthouse in Rye he was escorted across the cobblestoned streets of the town and imprisoned in the remnants of a medieval castle that served as Rye's gaol. After suffering almost a week in a circular stone cell in the dead of winter, Douglas was ferried 75 kilometres across the country to a ship serving as a floating prison in Chatham, where he remained for over two months.[80] It was only in March that he ascended the gangplank of the *Marquis of Huntly* and joined 319 fellow prisoners in sailing from England to New South Wales. William Douglas had suffered almost six months of confinement before he caught even a glimpse of Sydney. International travel was by no means new to Douglas – by the age of eighteen when he entered New South Wales, he had a wealth of experiences and interactions with people from all over the world. But this voyage from England to Sydney was clearly different. Before 1835, Douglas appears to have travelled in search of greater freedom, but after his conviction at Rye, his movement was coerced. He did not choose to be transported to New South Wales, or to be sent from Sydney to the St Vincent district on the south coast of the colony, where he was assigned to work for a free settler named DW Kellar.[81] Sentences of transportation had not always curtailed convicts' freedom in New South Wales. It was unfortunate for Douglas that he arrived in the colony after a series of penal reforms increased the authorities' control over convicts' lives.

Prior to the 1820s, convicts enjoyed a relative degree of freedom and status in New South Wales. The sentence of convicts shipped to New South Wales was deemed to be exile from their homeland, and there was originally no provision for auxiliary punishment. In fact, New South Wales was unique in that all discipline, even flogging, could only be meted out if it was sanctioned by the law. If convicts refused to work, ran away, or were insolent or disorderly, they had to face a magistrate who would then decide their sentence for this new offence. They were not to be punished twice for the crime that led to their transportation, and there were originally no convict indents. Convicts were not distinguished by the nature of their offence in Britain or the duration of their sentence but were employed according to their skills. Incentives were offered for convicts to live on the land and off the public stores and in this early period, convicts were encouraged to become settlers. John Hirst and Grace Karskens are among historians who have shown that in the colony's formative years, New South Wales is best thought of not as a penal outpost but a 'colony of convicts'.[82]

By the time Douglas arrived in New South Wales in 1835, changing ideas about crime and punishment worked against this more integrated society. The British Government's interest turned towards the reformative and deterrent aspects of punishment, over the mere eviction of criminals from the British Isles. To this end, a Commission of Inquiry into New South Wales was conducted by John Thomas Bigge in 1819. One of the explicit aims of this commission was to investigate whether transportation deterred crime effectively. Rather than encountering a scene of horror, Bigge entered a society where convicts were land and stock owners, occupied important, respectable trades, were elevated to positions of authority and not even the doors of high society were closed to ex-offenders. Although scandal and gossip infiltrated Bigge's Commission, its report remained decisive.[83] It was no longer enough for convicts to be exiled from their country. They needed to be subjugated in the colonies too. Convicts were assigned to settlers in isolated areas and forced to work for the duration of their sentence. From 1823 penal policy 'assumed an increasingly military, authoritarian and anti-philanthropic character'.[84]

William Douglas entered New South Wales after this policy had been in place for twelve years, but for him, life in the colony appears to have been a rude awakening. He refused to abide by the rules of this new system. In his six years in New South Wales, he endured 336 lashes and spent twelve months working in irons.[85] In the early 19th century, flogging was a typical punishment for convict offences, 'offences ... which only became such or were punished in this way because of the need to discipline forced labour'.[86] In his first five years in the colony, Douglas was solely convicted for these offences. Between 1835 and 1841 William Douglas received lashes for being absent without leave, highly disorderly conduct, insolence and neglect of work. However, his misdemeanours only increased in frequency and seriousness over time. By 1840, he was sentenced to work in irons for assault.[87] Douglas's sentencing pattern suggests that he found the restrictions of convict life increasingly unbearable. And from a master's perspective, this meant that he was a liability as a worker.

It was not in masters' interests to send their convicts to the magistrate to be sentenced to a flogging. While the disposition of each master varied considerably, their main concern was that their convicts were working. If convicts were incapacitated due to the lash, this cost valuable time. Masters overlooked many offences from minor infractions to direct insubordination so long as their convicts were good at their jobs, and this reluctance to use the lash is borne out by statistics.[88] Stephen Nicholas has calculated that the probability of a convict being beaten every year of their sentence for transportation was only 0.001.[89] William Douglas was flogged on seven occasions, and from 1839 at least once per year, so he was in the minority. It seems that his masters repeatedly placed reprimand (and its intended, corrective effects) above the value of his labour. Douglas's repeated infractions would have made him 'incorrigible' in the eyes of his superiors as flogging was not enough to mend his behaviour, but he was not just punished to force him to work more effectively. He was also flogged to mitigate the threat his actions posed to convict society. By refusing to work on his master's terms and being 'insolent', 'highly disorderly' and otherwise disruptive, Douglas undermined the convict system.[90] His physical and vocal resistance to colonial authority might have become an example for other convicts to follow, and so he was also punished to deter his convict fellows from following in his criminal footsteps.

Although flogging was meant to dissuade convicts from committing crimes, a convict subculture evolved in which repeated flogging could confer status upon an offender. The iron-willed convict who refused to scream and silently suffered their sentence could be a source of inspiration to their associates.[91] Scars physically distinguished convict offenders from law-abiding convict workers, and the meaning of these marks changed according to context. The lacerations on Douglas's back marked him as a repeat offender to any employer (and a potential danger to any peace-loving convict), but they could also serve as a sign of strength and resistance to other convicts. As a 5ft 8in tall black man, Douglas would have already stood out among the majority of his white fellow convicts – who were on average 5ft 4in in height – and his flagellation marks would have made him attract even more attention.[92] William Douglas was a physically imposing, striking convict figure. For better or for worse, he was already making a name for himself in 1830s New South Wales for upsetting the colonial order.

By 1841, it appears that William Douglas was so unsatisfied with his place in the convict system that he tried to leave it. Less than two months after completing his sentence to work in irons, Douglas absconded and on 2 July 1841, he became a bushranger. This was the kernel of truth behind the later goldfields myth. William Douglas *was* a bushranger, but at a different time, in a different place from that of the Black Douglas legend, and there was certainly nothing spectacular about his bushranging career. William Douglas made only one attempt at bushranging. His haul was not a mound of gold but a bundle of goods and provisions. The real bushranging story was as short-lived as it was anticlimactic as Douglas was captured soon after:

John Wood and William Douglas were indicted for assaulting
and robbing Thomas Healey, at the Seven Mile Hollow [near
present day Croydon], of his blankets, some tea, sugar and
other property, while returning to his residence. The prisoners
were assigned to Mr. Prout, and ... part of the property was
subsequently found in the hut occupied by the prisoners, in
which some other assigned servants were also lodged. The Court
found both the prisoners guilty, and sentenced each of them to be
transported to a penal settlement for the period of [ten] years.[93]

In this instance, the colour of Douglas's skin was used to identify him
as one of the perpetrators. According to the *Sydney Monitor*, Thomas
Healey:

... was going home in his cart with his wife and daughter,
when two men stopped the cart at the seven mile hollow. He
recognized Wood, but Douglas, who is a man of colour, had a
black handkerchief over his face, but prosecutor [Healey] knew
him to be a man of Colour [sic] by his hands.[94]

Unlike the panic caused by Douglas's fictitious bushranging crimes
in Victoria in the 1850s, this case went largely unremarked. These
newspaper articles were the most extensive reports on the case, and
the two men were moved from Darlinghurst Gaol to Cockatoo
Island awaiting their second bout of transportation without apparent
incident.[95]

Although this one, real instance of William Douglas as a bushranger was unspectacular, it was representative of bushranging in the
colony in the early 19th century. Most bushrangers during this period
were convict bolters as opposed to free men.[96] Some bushrangers like
'bold Jack Donohoe', 'The Captain', William Geary, and Edward
the 'Jewboy' Davis achieved status and fame during this period, but
these men were the exceptions and not the rule.[97] Most bushrangers

committed small-scale robberies. While some made grand moral claims about their turn to bushranging, stating that they intended to punish bad masters and redistribute the colony's wealth among the deserving poor, this appears to have been a plea for public sympathy more than a reflection of reality. Most bushrangers did not see their actions as part of a noble quest to right the social order, but as a way to gain freedom and advance their immediate interests. For convicts, absconding often necessitated bushranging.[98] As a witness told the New South Wales Committee on Police in 1835 '[convicts] ... cannot be expected to have any honest means of support in the wilderness'.[99]

In light of this, Douglas and Wood's bushranging exploits were not unusual. In the 1830s convict bushrangers largely robbed to survive, and we can see this reflected in the items that Douglas and Wood stole from Thomas Healey: blankets, tea, sugar and 'other property'.[100] Blankets would have been particularly important to Douglas and Wood, as their robberies took place in one of the coldest months of winter. It was similarly common for witnesses to recognise convict bushrangers, as local robberies were the norm.[101] While we do not know where Douglas and Wood's master lived, it appears to have been close to their hold-up location as Wood was immediately identified by his victim. It seems that Douglas only took longer to recognise due to his mask.[102] Douglas was also in the majority with this disguise, as most bushrangers wore masks or blackened their faces in an attempt to remain anonymous.[103] William Douglas and John Wood were by no means exceptional bushranging figures.

Although the pair's return to their convict quarters (which they shared with other assigned servants) after the robbery might appear an ill-conceived move, it too was a typical bushranging strategy. Douglas and Wood might have been able to buy their comrades' silence with the goods they procured as this was the most common way bushrangers secured the loyalty of their harbourers. Convicts and small landowners were often open to such incentives due to their own precarious finances, but they also assisted bushrangers out of fear for their personal safety, greed or their belief in these convicts' quest for freedom.[104] Once they had entered into this arrangement, harbourers found it hard to rescind their support. They were immediately compromised by their actions and following the introduction of the *Bushranging Act* in 1830, the repercussions of bushranging crime had never been more severe.

New South Wales lawmakers believed that local support was essential to the success of bushrangers like Douglas and Wood, and so this Act went to great lengths to divide and conquer the population. Police search and seizure powers expanded under the *Bushranging Act* so that with only a general warrant, the authorities could force their entry into any property to pursue bushranging crime. They could remove any potentially stolen goods, and arrest anyone believed to be harbouring bushrangers. The *Bushranging Act* also sought to shift the balance of power by making it every colonist's duty to assist the police in their endeavours. If they neglected to do so, settlers could be fined a maximum of £5. We do not know what happened to the assigned servants who resided with Douglas and Wood, but as the *Bushranging Act* was in force during this time, it is unlikely that they emerged unscathed. If they were not the ones who reported the pair to the authorities, they would not have escaped lightly.

Douglas and Wood became bushrangers at a time of perceived crisis. This sense of emergency ensured that the *Bushranging Act* did more than punish bushranging supporters: to stem the tide of criminals, the legislation disregarded foundational tenets of British law. Under the Act, any citizen could lawfully detain any person they suspected of 'being a transported felon, unlawfully at large'.[105] This disregarded the legal safeguard of warrants for arrest.[106] The burden of proof was also reversed in these cases. Suspects were not innocent until proven guilty but needed to prove their innocence to a Justice of the Peace, and could be detained for as long as was necessary to ascertain their identity.[107] No one was above suspicion. It appears that even the Chief Justice of New South Wales, Francis Forbes, was apprehended as a potential bushranger and made to give a full account of himself.[108]

As long as there were convicts in New South Wales, there were concerns that the unfree population would revolt and take power from the government, and so convict bushranging was easily conflated with convict uprising. It was not only in the colony that the precariousness of British authority was felt keenly. In 1831 Viscount Goderich of the British Colonial Office wrote to Governor Darling of the need to guard against the bushranging danger. He was anxious that 'should these Bands [of bushrangers] encrease [sic] in strength, they will direct their first efforts to the chain Gangs [iron gangs], by a union with whom they would be enabled to threaten the very existence of the constituted Authorities'.[109] Not only were iron gangs composed of incorrigible convicts, they were some of the worst forms of punishment. The actions of desperate men who were forced to work in shackles were hard to predict, and their primary goal was often escape. Douglas's convict experiences align with Goderich's concerns. It appears that Douglas worked in an iron gang for a year and just two months after his release from working in irons, he bolted to become a bushranger.[110] Evidence like this exacerbated the fear of a convict uprising. While Douglas and Wood faded into relative obscurity in New South Wales, their bushranging crimes were part of a much larger, dangerous story. Douglas and Wood's sentences of ten years' transportation ensured the New South Wales government at least had two fewer convict bushrangers to worry about. They were then the responsibility of authorities in Van Diemen's Land.

## VAN DIEMEN'S LAND

In 1842 William Douglas was escorted on board the *Marian Watson* and forced to sea once more. This time he was bound for Van Diemen's Land – a place of secondary punishment, filled with convicts who had committed new crimes in the Australian colonies. By this time Douglas was twenty-five years old, and on the verge of experiencing the supposed cutting edge of penal discipline.[111] In 1840 Lieutenant-Governor Arthur introduced a new scheme termed 'probation' to replace the system of assigning convicts to work for settlers. Informed by Benthamite penal theory in Britain, this system aimed to punish and reform offenders through surveillance and strict regulation.[112] This approach diverged not only from that of New South Wales, but a centuries-old, European tradition of corporal or capital punishment instead of rehabilitation.[113] On arriving in Van Diemen's Land, convicts were forced to undergo a period of confinement and hard labour at a designated station. Offenders were grouped according to their crimes to contain their corrupting influence to those of their own 'criminal class'.[114] After progressing through 'several stages of decreasing severity, convicts received a probation pass and became available for hire to the settlers'.[115] This incremental approach was meant to discipline convicts at the same time as providing incentives for their rehabilitation.

Although the probation system was promising in theory, William Douglas's conduct record shows that it could not ensure a convict's reform. In his nine years on the island, Douglas was punished for thirty-two separate offences. As in New South Wales, his crimes in Van Diemen's Land increased in severity over time. Douglas was originally convicted only of misdemeanours: disorderly behaviour, drunkenness, misconduct and using obscene language. But after 1848 he was also convicted for absconding, using 'threatening language', 'riotous' behaviour and two assaults. This escalation in Douglas's crimes occurred despite the fact that he was sent almost the entire length of Van Diemen's Land in his nine years in the colony and experienced probation stations as distant as Fingal, Oatlands and Port Arthur. It also occurred despite Douglas enduring a new form of punishment: solitary confinement.

Douglas suffered eight bouts of solitary confinement in Van Diemen's Land, totalling fifty-nine days and twelve hours in isolation.[116] This punishment was meant to remove offenders from the corruptive influence of their peers as well as give them time to reflect upon their crimes and open their hearts to God and moral reform.[117] But solitary confinement often had unintended consequences. Convicts like Douglas could find the isolation debilitating, and we can see this most clearly when we look at this punishment's extreme form in the United Kingdom. Many convicts' experiences of the probation system actually started in Britain, as men and women intended for Van Diemen's Land served a period of their sentence in solitary confinement in one of England's new penitentiaries before they left for the colony.[118] Months and sometimes years in complete isolation from their fellows had a discernible effect on the prisoners, and the words of John Hampton, surgeon on board the *Sir George Seymour* on this matter are telling in the extreme. In his view:

> the sudden change from extreme seclusion to the noise and bustle of a crowded ship [as convicts boarded vessels to Van Diemen's Land] produced a great number of cases of convulsions, attended in some instances with nausea and vomiting, in others simulating hysteria, and in all being a most anomalous character.[119]

It was not only the convicts' bodies that were affected, but their minds. Another surgeon remarked how convicts' 'power of thinking, their common sense, and in a particular degree their *memory*, appeared to have been left behind them, buried in their cell'.[120] While some convicts might have been 'reformed' after this treatment as they did not commit any further crimes, physical and mental debility were common effects of solitary confinement.[121]

In Van Diemen's Land itself, solitary confinement was never so long nor so absolute as that experienced by inmates in the penitentiaries of England. An overpopulation of convicts, poor administration, lack of government funds, and an economic depression made strict standards of regulation impossible to maintain.[122] But solitary confinement was still greatly feared by convicts, in part because isolation was so different from their daily experience. Offenders in Van Diemen's Land usually slept, ate and worked with their criminal counterparts.[123] They often suffered punishments together. Hard labour was the most common punishment for convicts in Van Diemen's Land and Douglas was no exception.[124] He served forty-nine months and fourteen days' hard labour both with and without chains.[125] Hard labour was designed to combat the perceived idleness of the criminal classes, but it also allowed prisoners to work alongside their fellows.[126] In Douglas's criminal record, he may appear as one man resisting the convict system, but apart from spells in solitary confinement he was never alone. Isolation stood in contrast to the communal nature of convict life in Van Diemen's Land and meant convicts despised solitary confinement all the more.

For their part, colonists were more concerned with overcrowding than they were with offenders in solitary confinement. After transportation to New South Wales ended in 1840, Van Diemen's Land was used almost exclusively as the site for transported convicts in the Australian colonies until the 1850s.[127] When Douglas arrived in Van Diemen's Land, free settlers were not only incensed that they were flooded with convicts, but that these men and women were 'delayed in becoming useful employees' as they needed to work through several stages of government service before they received probation passes and could be hired by private employers. Colonists were similarly incensed that convicts needed to be paid for their labour as they had been forced to work for free under the assignment system.[128] Quite apart from these economic issues, the fact that outstations such as Port Arthur were 'places of closer confinement, harsher discipline and more primitive living conditions than were the seats of Government' worsened colonists' fears about the immorality of the convict population.[129] There were concerns that probation stations were 'breeding grounds for idleness, vice, and "unnatural crime" (homosexual acts)'.[130] Such was the scandal that these complaints generated that Arthur's successor, Lieutenant-Governor Eardley-Wilmot, was recalled by the Colonial Office in 1846 for failing to adequately address settlers' allegations of misconduct.[131]

While it is impossible to know whether William Douglas's pro-bation experience aligned with colonists' fears about 'moral contagion', he was part of a male-dominated society. Not only were there large numbers of men, with men composing over 85 per cent of the convict population in 1847, but masculine pursuits like prize-fighting attracted wide and eager audiences.[132] To the lower orders prize-fighting epitomised masculine daring, pride and power, and among William Douglas's many activities in Van Diemen's Land, he was a famous prize-fighter.[133] Although illegal in the colony, prize-fighting contests were an important part of convict culture. Manly strength, physical prowess and endurance affected the course of convicts' lives as they spent day after day toiling away in hard labour, and the 'ring' became a miniature of this reality – albeit one more happily cast in the guise of entertainment.

Prize-fighting gave men like Douglas a chance to make a name for themselves and we can see this celebrity status most clearly in 1850 when Douglas fought his most memorable fight, against Bob Fee of Sheffield. In three hours and twenty-nine minutes, the men battled it out, using bare fists, agility and raw strength in an attempt to get the better of their opponent. By this year, both men had already achieved a degree of fame, as sporting newspaper *Bell's Life in Sydney* remarked that, '[t]he known capabilities of these men rendered the ... event of no slight degree of interest'. This statement carried even more weight considering that the match itself took place in Hobart, miles away from where the paper was published in Sydney. Douglas actually identified as a Sydneysider in this particular bout of fighting, but this was not as unusual as it sounds.[134] Prize-fighters commonly used their home country or locale to gain support from those with similar origins.[135] This sport not only required fighters to prove their own manly mettle, but the strength and valour of the people they represented. It made more sense for Douglas to identify as a Sydneysider than a Philadelphian as the colonial association was more likely to rally support. Douglas was not the only felon facing secondary punishment in Van Diemen's

Land, and it was more than likely that fellow Sydneysiders formed the ranks of spectators.[136]

Prize-fighting was an elusive sport in Van Diemen's Land. Although it was popular throughout America, England and the Australian colonies during this time, in Van Diemen's Land 'only a few prize fights took place ... for modest purses' because of its illegality.[137] The police were usually quick to pursue any would-be combatants and Douglas's fight was typical in this sense, as the 'Blues [police], unluckily, were on the alert, and a shift was compelled to be made for fear of ulterior consequences' before the match could start. Fortunately, the organisers 'sequestered [a] bit of turf on Clarence Plains, where the roped area was put up, long before the unlucky toddlers could find out the whereabouts'.[138] The exclusive nature of the sport in Van Diemen's Land may have enhanced Douglas's fame, as he was one of only a few fighters there.

The prize-fighting ring may actually have been where the Black Douglas legend was born. References to 'Black Douglas' first appeared in Van Diemen's Land as William Douglas's prize-fighting name. Although it carried the most weight on the Victorian goldfields in the 1850s, goldminers did not create the moniker 'Black Douglas'. And it was not originally a derogatory term. In contrast to later, racist depictions of black men on the Victorian goldfields there appears to have been little explicit racism among convicts themselves and the authorities often treated these men and women in the same manner as their Anglo peers. 'Black' was not necessarily a derogatory term among convicts, but a description of appearance.[139] Although this sporting title may have been bestowed upon William Douglas, he could have invented the name 'Black Douglas' himself, owned it and embraced it.

*

Although white colonists' power was immense, they were never in complete control of William Douglas's life or his story. This is nowhere more apparent than at the end of Douglas's days, when the tables turned, and he was the one using colonists' ideas about race to his own advantage. After completing his convict sentence in 1852, Douglas travelled to Victoria where he remained until he died of 'old age and senile debility' in Bendigo Gaol in 1892.[140] After his goldfield adventures in the 1850s, he was constantly in and out of gaol for vagrancy and drunk and disorderly conduct. Douglas lived his life in prison, on the streets, in benevolent institutions, or in the pub. A pub may not appear to be an obvious place to challenge colonial ideas about race, but it was here, late in life, that Douglas became a phrenologist. Phrenologists believed that by studying the size and shape of a skull, they could divine information about a person's character and intelligence.[141] Although phrenology was 'the most popular mental science of the Victorian age', it was also deeply intertwined with racial theory.[142] The majority of white, male phrenologists used their findings to justify their position at the top of the racial order. And yet, at the same time William Douglas, a black man in a pub, was 'reading' white people's skulls in exchange for a pint.[143] White patrons may have come to Douglas for a reading because of the absurdity or novelty of the experience, but in this encounter, Douglas was the one decreeing the character and racial worth of white men.[144] Even as an old man, William Douglas confounded colonial expectations. He was a man who resisted any attempt to confine or define him. Including ours.

# CHAPTER 3

# THE MANY HISTORIES OF SAM POO

On 4 February 1865, Mr John Plunkett and his family, of Talbragar New South Wales, sought to ease the suffering of a dying man. They barely knew the ailing Senior Constable John Ward, as Plunkett had found him shot and bleeding in the bush only the previous day (see Plate 7).[1] Plunkett took the wounded officer to his homestead, and while they waited for the closest doctor to travel some 72 kilometres, he recited the Church of England service for the sick and dying as his wife and children knelt down beside him and offered their own prayers.[2] Unfortunately for Senior Constable Ward, neither the family's assistance nor the medical expertise of Dr William King could save him from the fatal gunshot wound he had sustained to his pelvis. At thirty-two years of age, John Ward died at four o'clock that February afternoon.[3] Even before Ward drew his last breath, men were on the hunt for the culprit of this unexpected murder. For although the 1860s 'became known as the "bushranging decade" because of the number and exuberance of the ... crimes committed', the man accused of this felony was apparently the first of his kind.[4] This case of bushranging was one of more than 300 in 1860s New South Wales when bushranging was at its height, but it was the only one to have a Chinese man accused of such crimes.[5]

Sam Poo was said to have bailed up travellers and robbed shepherds' huts for just a few days in 1865. It was also insinuated that he tried to rape a white woman and her young daughter, although charges were never brought against him.[6] The ill-fated Senior Constable Ward only became a part of this history because he heard that there was a Chinese bushranger in the Mudgee area, spied a suspect and was shot while trying to apprehend him.

Newspapers wasted no time in lamenting John Ward's violent death. He was said to have been 'a most efficient, intelligent and active officer':[7]

> A gentleman by birth and education ... He entered the police, and hoped by devotion to his duties to obtain advancement. That his conduct at Coonabarabran, where he was stationed, was appreciated, will appear from a subscription having started not long since, with the purpose of presenting him a purse of money and a testimonial; but he instantly vetoed it when he heard of its being afoot. And now poor fellow, he is dead. He died unflinchingly performing his duty – could the greatest hero that ever breathed do more?[8]

To news reporters at the time, Ward was all things good and honourable. He epitomised the ideal police officer. He would be missed by his loving wife and six children as well as by the community he died to defend.[9] In this unusual episode of Australian history, the police officer and not the bushranger is cast as a frontier hero. Ward's death was made all the more poignant by the fact that he was not meant to be in Mudgee on that February summer's day. The *Maitland Mercury* reported how the Senior Constable was stationed in Coonabarabran, almost 200 kilometres away. He was only in Mudgee to deliver a criminal to the courthouse for trial. Duty called him to Mudgee, and he appeared to have died there for the same cause.[10]

It would be easier to write the history of Senior Constable Ward, the benevolent squatter John Plunkett or well-travelled bush doctor William King, than it is to write the history of Sam Poo. In part, this is because Sam Poo's career as a bushranger and murderer was a brief one, lasting only twenty-five days. But what they lacked in duration Poo's bushranging escapades made up for in their impact. During that time in early 1865, he threatened the security of white settlers, obtained incredible notoriety and became more than just an armed criminal – he became emblematic of the 1860s bushranging crisis. Although brief, Sam Poo's criminal career is important.

The other barrier to Sam Poo's story lies in the material we have left to piece it together. Once again there are issues with the archive. On first inspection there appears to be a wealth of information on Poo's life. Physical and digital archives are teeming with sources – from black-inked newspaper articles to hand-scrawled court documents, police records and gaol logbooks – that chart his descent into crime. But this abundance of material conceals as much as it describes. While salacious details about his alleged crimes abound, very little can be divined from colonial sources about who Sam Poo was as a person or his life before he was branded a criminal. This makes his distorted colonial image easier to recover than his substance as a man. Reams of paper also stand between us and the awareness that Poo's perspective is missing. When you are drowning in documents, your first instinct is not to look for more material. But we need to look for more material, just as we need to challenge, interrogate and question the evidence we have. Only then can we access the multilayered, multiracial history of the 1860s bushranging crisis, and put Sam Poo back into the centre of his own story.

## COLONIAL VIEWS

The *Maitland Mercury* was the closest major newspaper to the scene of Ward's murder, and it bore the heavy responsibility of informing local readers about the crime and the perpetrator who remained at large. Although Ward's bloody death was certainly newsworthy, the paper opened its reporting of the case with an apology to its audience. 'As bushranging is now confessedly one of the institutions of New

South Wales', the Mudgee correspondent lamented, 'I do not suppose another case of its happening … will occasion much astonishment'.[11] The correspondent was correct in this appraisal. Bushranging was at its peak in 1860s New South Wales. It was not simply local hysteria that drove the reporter to describe bushranging as endemic to rural colonial society. Even historians cannot help but describe bushranging by this time as a 'settled institution'.[12] The numbers are astounding, and an estimate of more than 300 bushranging cases in this decade only represents the number of people who were convicted for bushranging crimes.[13] There were many more cases that never made their way to court or where there was insufficient evidence to secure a conviction.

While bushranging was a common feature of the Victorian gold-fields in Black Douglas's time, its form had changed by the 1860s in New South Wales. Although immigrants still flocked to New South Wales where new goldfields were being discovered well into the 1870s, the main bushranging threat did not come from ex-convicts or immigrants but 'native' New South Welshmen, who had been born in the colony.[14] These were meant to represent the 'coming man', the new colonial type upon whose shoulders the colony's future rested.[15] While some looked upon these white men as a new, robust and admirable breed, the fact that they composed 67.7 per cent of bushranging offenders between 1862 and 1867 seemed to belie this more favourable view.[16]

Earlier episodes of bushranging caused panic and disruption in the colony, but they could be more easily explained as originating beyond New South Wales' borders. The original convict bushrangers had already been tarred by their criminal actions before they set foot on the colony's shores. That some reoffended often came as no surprise to free settlers.[17] Ex-convicts who travelled to the goldfields in the 1850s and became bushrangers could be explained in the same manner, while Gold Rush immigrants from overseas who turned to bushranging were an external menace.[18] Although these bushrangers were greatly feared, they did not challenge the colony's future prospects in quite the same way as bushrangers who were born on colonial soil.

In colonists' eyes, the rural, white, 'native' youth of the 1860s who turned to bushranging were different from their predecessors.[19] By the middle of the decade, half of the population of New South Wales was colonial-born.[20] Many were related to convicts but had been born free and so had a unique connection to the land. For this generation, the home of Mother England was an image conjured from conversation with their elders, while the only home that they had ever truly known was the bush.[21] But official recognition of this connection, in the form of land ownership, was often difficult for these men to achieve. Colonial policy 'kept the price per acre so high that the average member of the working classes could only dream of land ownership'.[22] Instead, land policy favoured wealthy immigrants who disparaged local bush life and culture, and this was a source of great resentment among colonial-born men and women. The new free selection system that was meant to address this class issue would only become operational after the threat of bushranging was largely over.[23] There was no formal recognition of the colonial-born's connection to the bush.

In response to this exclusion from land ownership, itinerant, 'native' men honed a different set of skills. The bush-born became bushmen. From the 1860s, an increasingly romantic, mythic tone inflected depictions of these men. They were meant to know the lie of the land, its gullies, ravines and plains. They apparently knew how to ride a horse along rocky outcrops and loose roads, how to muster thousands of heads of cattle; how to make the bush an ally. In reality, the range and depth of experience varied from person to person and place to place, just as the bush encompassed a vast array of vegetation, landscapes and geography.[24] But overall, colonial-born men possessed many of the same skills as bushrangers. Practised bushcraft alongside local support meant that even the most short-lived and opportunistic of bushrangers posed a deep threat to colonial society. They added a new criminal stain to the colony's character, just as that of the convict era was slowly fading away. They jeopardised lives and property, and they threatened to further contaminate the communities in which they operated. The editor of the *Sydney Morning Herald* felt that:

> ... we have the proof that there is something socially rotten amongst a too considerable portion of the community in the fact that men who ought everywhere to be regarded as ruffians, as outcasts, as curses to the country, have a circle of colleagues, a large circle of sympathisers, a still larger circle of admirers, and a still larger circle of those who take a romantic interest in their achievements.[25]

The original Mudgee correspondent was correct, then, in declaring that another instance of bushranging would be of no surprise to his readers. But he was also correct in asserting that Sam Poo's case had 'peculiarities to distinguish it above ordinary ones'.[26] Not only was Sam Poo a Chinese man, but according to the *Sydney Mail* he was 'unfriended, on foot and ignorant of localities'.[27] 'Elite' bushrangers – those long-term, successful desperados who newspapers were used to describing – often had a large support base.[28] Although tales of men and women riding out to join bushrangers were the dramatic encounters that captured public attention, the extent of local support varied considerably.[29] Historian Susan West's meticulous research on rural banditry suggests that many settlers assisted bushrangers by simply ignoring their activities, or were compelled to provide food or shelter for fear that their own properties would be compromised.[30] But this did not sell newspapers in the same way as networks of informants and supporters (dubbed 'bush telegraphs'). Papers alternated between bewailing the extent of popular support that bushrangers received and giving a sly nod of approval when a white bushranger achieved a brave or daring feat.[31] And into the middle of this established print culture came Sam Poo.

While certainly different from their regular bushranging report-age, descriptions of Sam Poo being alone and 'unfriended' did have its advantages. It could suggest that he posed a limited threat to the colony and be used to more fully condemn his actions. Here was a man adrift from all society – both from his own race and the labouring classes to which he belonged. Colonial sources offered no reason for Sam Poo's crimes. There is no evidence that he righted wrongs or defended the oppressed as some white bushrangers claimed to have done in this period.[32] In popular depictions, Sam Poo offered nothing to colonial society, and in return society offered no assistance to him.

Reports of Sam Poo's isolation might have minimised his menace to white colonists but for the unfortunate circumstance of his arrest. Poo was eventually captured by three police officers and an Aboriginal tracker, fourteen days after Ward's death. After shooting a police officer Sam Poo remained free, unscathed and at large for two weeks, and the words of the *Sydney Mail* gain new meaning in light of this situation. What did it say about the security of white society if 'a Chinaman, unfriended, on foot and ignorant of localities' was able to remain at large for two weeks after committing murder?[33] When it was reported that the 'residents assist the police energetically, the ground of the bushranger's concealment is comprised in a radius of four miles; the troopers engaged are instantly on the alert, in disguise and well mounted', how could Sam Poo have remained on the run for so long?[34]

In responding to these questions, colonists chose a different explanation from the one they offered for Aboriginal bushrangers. To make sense of how an Aboriginal person could outwit white residents and police, colonists declared that they possessed innate bush skills. Unlike the hard-earned skills of the Anglo bushman, these instinctual attributes were seen to require no talent. According to white settlers, it was an Aboriginal person's primordial traits that kept white authorities at bay.[35] Chinese men, on the other hand, were not supposed to possess any bush skills at all, innate or not. The question of how Sam Poo could overcome such a 'superior' white force was explained by an alternative view, one that revolved around the power of the bush.

The Talbragar correspondent for the *Maitland Mercury* believed the land itself had a hand in preventing Sam Poo's capture. 'Although intelligence was received almost daily of … [Sam Poo's] presence in some part or another', the correspondent wrote that 'the bush is here chiefly of so scrubby a nature that it has constantly afforded him safe hiding places'.[36] Here, the bush replaced settlers as the source of a bushranger's concealment, but this still did not erase the danger that Sam Poo posed. While bushranging supporters could turn against their heroes, the bush had no such capacity. Although in these types of articles, the bush was given a certain agency – to hide, to conceal – this was indiscriminate, 'a natural opportunity' offered to all.[37] In the bush, Sam Poo found a 'colour blind' ally, and a resource to keep white justice at bay.

*

But depictions of Sam Poo were not only a product of the bushranging era. If we go back to 1861, four years before his crime spree, it is clear that Poo's portrayal in the colonial press was also shaped by years of intense opposition to the Chinese presence in the Australian colonies, as well as dramatic changes to law and policing. In 1861, the Lambing Flat Riots occurred. On the goldfields of Burrangong, over ten months, there were six riots against the Chinese. The largest of these involved 2000 diggers.[38] Miners' opposition to Chinese men was passionate, vitriolic and broad in scope, and they targeted practical as well as cultural concerns. Chinese diggers were said to use an excessive amount of water to find gold when this resource was in short supply.[39] They were accused of 'dirty habits' and spreading disease. And they were said to undermine the moral standing of the goldfields. Chinese men were condemned as heathens and bearers of drugs, gambling and sexual vice.[40] The following attack from the *Bathurst Free Press* was by no means alone:

The Chinese are, in every aspect we view them, an inferior race
... Murder is winked at by the authorities in China ... Unnatural
crimes are looked upon with a lenient and an approving eye by
the great majority of their [Chinese migrants'] countrymen.
Gambling is a national passion with them. Under these
circumstances, will the people of these colonies stand quietly
by, and see their country overrun with those 'human vermin'
and their mothers, wives and daughters exposed to their
contaminating influence [sic] Heaven forbid. Let them, then, rise
up as one man throughout the length and breadth of the land and
demand that these 'outcasts of humanity' shall at once and for
ever [sic] be prohibited from landing on the shores of Australia.[41]

This venomous account reflects the low position the Chinese held
in the eyes of many settler Australians. White colonists believed the
Chinese to be barbarians and incapable of any form of civilisation. The
*Free Press* went as far as to describe them as a 'race with whom ... [the
white diggers] have little more in common than with a race of baboons
or a tribe of ourang-outangs [sic]'.[42] To many colonists, the Chinese
could not be reformed or civilised any more than such animals. This
placed them precariously on the fringes of colonial society.

Yet their numbers continued to grow. In the 19th century, the
largest arrival of Chinese migrants to the Australian colonies came
with the Gold Rushes.[43] From 327 Chinese men in New South Wales
in 1857, the population rose so quickly that they numbered around
13 000 by April 1861, and formed nearly a quarter of all diggers in
the colony.[44] At this time the Chinese population was at its most
visible. Chinese people were renowned for congregating in groups
on the goldfields, bringing with them their unfamiliar attire, joss
houses, ceremonies, customs, food, languages and mining practices.[45]
There was fear and suspicion among white diggers of these men who
seemed so remarkably different to themselves. Although the goldfields

were constantly changing and cosmopolitan spaces, 'the definition of "colonists" could … never include Chinese'.[46] In many miners' eyes, they lacked 'the right to share in the wealth of the colony'.[47]

Chinese residents of New South Wales did, however, have the right to protection – at least according to colonial authorities. The 1842 *Treaty of Nanking* (Nanjing) explicitly stated that Chinese subjects were to receive 'full security and protection of their persons and property' in all British dominions, and this included the Australian colonies.[48] In response to the Lambing Flat Riots, the New South Wales government similarly declared that 'the Chinese must have the same justice and protection extended to them as other people'. But securing this protection proved more difficult than anticipated.[49]

There was great trouble assembling an adequate police force at Lambing Flat. In June, 'demonstrators moved into the Chinese area, demolishing tents, beating up Chinese miners and burning their property'.[50] According to one eyewitness, Chinese men 'were knocked down with clubs; and their tails [pigtails] cut off with tomahawks and butcher's knives; one man was shot in the thigh; several were hamstrung and several were murdered'.[51] In July, after the death of a miner in a pitched battle, the police retreated to a nearby town and left the field in possession of the rebels.[52] They were disorganised and unprepared to combat such a large-scale attack on the Chinese population. 'Twice at great expense and political embarrassment troops had to be sent to maintain order' and almost six months after these violent outbursts began, on 17 July, martial law was declared.[53] The Lambing Flat Riots not only brought anti-Chinese sentiment firmly into the public arena, but threw the inadequacies of the police force into stark relief. And here the riots connect to another thread of Sam Poo's history. This large-scale protest led to the creation of a new police force, of which Senior Constable Ward was a part.[54]

*

The year 1862 saw the most dramatic change to the police force that the colony of New South Wales had ever seen. Virtually overnight, the system used to enforce the law was unrecognisably altered. Six police forces – the Sydney Police, the Mounted Police, the Sydney Water Police, the Border Police, the Native Police and the Rural Constabulary – were amalgamated into one central body. The Rural Constabulary had been the main force dealing with bushrangers in the rural districts of New South Wales, and it underwent the greatest changes. Members of this arm of the police had been chosen by local magistrates but this did not prevent it from having a chequered past. Many convicts, ticket-of-leave men and emancipists had swelled its ranks. Corruption was rife and although these men mingled easily with their local communities, respect for their office was low. The new system sought to break these communal bonds. The Rural Constabulary was absorbed into the New Police Force and reported to the Inspector General of Police. 'New chums' were brought across from Ireland to fill the majority of police positions, while the few old officers who remained were moved to new areas in the hope that this would prevent their collusion with local criminals.[55]

Although the New Police Force was intended to be more efficient and practical than its predecessors, it was poorly equipped to deal with the conditions of rural New South Wales. In 1863, an *Empire* reporter bemoaned that:

> The new system was adapted to cope with insurgency but
> not with bushranging. The system which it had displaced
> had been accommodated to this purpose by a long course of
> gradual adaptations … it had grown out of the penal times,
> and it embraced the matured art of thief catching in the bush
> of Australia, as practised by experienced officers who, in their
> respective districts, were like spiders in the centre of their webs,
> cognisant not only of every illicit movement, but of every

flutter of their lawful prey. But all this having been swept away, bushranging became rampant at once.[56]

Unfortunately for the new force, riding in military formation and sporting polished sabres also did little to command the respect of local communities.[57] While the New Police achieved considerable success against bushrangers, their embarrassing blunders were emphasised by the press and 'elite' bushrangers alike.[58] Stories of police guns misfiring, bushrangers striding confidently past search parties and taunting officers with their missteps helped to undermine the prestige of the force and garnered support for their more talented foes.

But by the time of Senior Constable Ward's death in 1865, an alternative narrative about the police was beginning to unfold. By 4 February 1865 when John Ward was shot, residents of New South Wales were morbidly familiar with policemen who died attempting to catch bushrangers.[59] Ward was the fifth police officer in less than a year to have been killed by a bushranger in New South Wales.[60] The most recent murder was that of Constable Nelson, committed just over a week before Ward's fatal encounter with Sam Poo, and this connection was not lost on the press. In its coverage of Ward's death, the *Western Post* reported that '[s]carcely have the public recovered from the shock of the intelligence of Constable Nelson's death, than they are alarmed by the news of another brave constable being assassinated, not this time by Hall's Gang [of bushrangers], but by a single armed Chinaman'.[61] These murders could never make settlers forget the police force's many blunders, but they did open space for a different perspective. Although these men failed to apprehend their suspects, they died honourable deaths in pursuit of this end. Death was the ultimate test of an officer's character, a personal sacrifice that proved his intention to perform his duty and protect the community at all costs. This redeemed these policemen in some colonists' eyes, and newspapers were willing to make concessions for these fallen representatives of the law.[62] Four days after

FIGURE 2. Oswald Campbell, *Ben Hall, John Gilbert and John Dunn hold up the mail at Black Springs, New South Wales*, 1865.

*State Library of Victoria Pictures Collection, 49368311.*

Ward was attacked, for instance, the *Sydney Morning Herald* conveyed to its audience the hardships that police were forced to undergo in the name of their office:

> [D]escriptions of the ravages of the bushrangers are commonly followed by some reference to the police which reads like a sneer, and probably often is intended as such. Yet no man who knows the country, and the conditions under which these persons act, has the right to sneer.[63]

While this made officers' failure to catch bushrangers understandable, it did not lessen the threat bushrangers posed to law-abiding colonists. Sam Poo's murder of Senior Constable Ward heightened the sense that New South Wales was experiencing a bushranging crisis. Concerned colonists not only used the number of murdered police, but the unique features of Sam Poo's case to promote tougher measures to apprehend bushrangers. A Sydney newspaper declared that after hearing how Sam Poo remained at large without skills or resources, it 'becomes intelligible how well mounted men, familiar with the country and secretly assisted by troops of friends can so long evade police'.[64] White bushrangers became even more dangerous by comparison. If an armed Chinese man could remain at large and be so destructive, one could only imagine the damage that a skilled, reckless, young white 'native' could do.

Sam Poo's turn to bushranging added a sense of urgency to legislative debates about bushranging crime. It is striking that two months after Ward's death, in April 1865, the *Felons Apprehension Act* was passed in parliament after months of heated discussion. According to the Act, bushrangers who committed murder and did not surrender themselves to the authorities were outlawed. As such, police officers and ordinary citizens were given the power to stop these criminals by whatever means necessary. This included killing bushrangers if they resisted. Without a trial and the opportunity for legal defence, these men could be summarily executed.[65] For a colonial outpost that supposedly prided itself on the British rule of law, this suspension of British justice speaks volumes about the anxieties of the time. Proponents of the new law argued that it was unconventional, but necessary. The bushranging epidemic had moved so far beyond the pale of British civilisation that regular standards no longer applied. The Crown had to take extraordinary measures and temporarily suspend the safeguards of British justice to restore order.[66]

## TRIAL AND EXECUTION

Tuesday 19 December 1865 was the day of Sam Poo's execution. He had already been through a lot before that day. While a vortex of rhetoric swirled around the colony, bringing Sam Poo's image into parliamentary chambers and courtrooms, urban and rural dwellings, he was held first in Mudgee Hospital, and then in Bathurst Gaol. Poo had not been expected to recover from the injuries he sustained during his capture. Constable Miles Burns had smashed Poo in the head with his rifle so hard that its stock had shattered to pieces (see Plates 8 and 9).

But, somehow, on 10 April, Poo appeared before the court and faced the first of three trials. Since his arrest he had not spoken to anyone, and so his first trial was to determine whether he was mute by malice or divine intervention. Although Sam Poo could not stand and appeared 'very weak and emaciated',[67] 'his face bore the marks of the shot and only one of his eyes was partially open', the *Maitland Mercury* was relieved that his injuries 'were not nearly as dangerous as was first imagined' and so that he might 'live to meet the death he so richly deserve[d]'.[68] The men of the jury appeared indifferent to Sam Poo's 'emaciated' state. With no reference to his injuries, the jury swiftly decided that he was guilty of deliberately holding his tongue, and the next trial was ready to proceed.[69]

In the second trial, Sam Poo was accused of shooting with the intent to kill Harry Hughes, the Aboriginal tracker who helped the police apprehend him. This case was more complex than the first. Aboriginal evidence was not admitted in New South Wales unless it was corroborated by white witnesses. Legal experts and politicians contended that even though Aboriginal people were British subjects, 'admitting the evidence of a witness "acknowledged to be ignorant of a God or a future state would be contrary to the principles of British jurisprudence"'. Although this law did not change until over a decade after Sam Poo's case, Hughes made his deposition.[70] He opened with the fact that he lived with white people, that he was christened and understood the nature of an oath. While it fell on Constable Burns to support Hughes's declaration, the leading evidence at this trial was the tracker's own.[71] Despite legal opinion about Aboriginal evidence, prosecutors and courts made exceptions when it suited them. Rigid racial categories became malleable when it served the settler state. At this trial, Sam Poo was found guilty and sentenced to ten years' imprisonment with hard labour.

Finally, on 10 October 1865, Sam Poo stood before Bathurst Court for his third trial, this time for the crime that made him a colonial sensation – the murder of Senior Constable Ward. This trial had been months in the making. Originally, the prosecution did not have enough evidence to proceed with the case and witnesses were sought from around the colony.[72] In October, one by one these men (and one woman) made their way to the witness box, giving testimony against the accused. No one came forward in Poo's defence and he remained silent. The odds were not stacked in his favour.[73] The citizens of Bathurst, from whose numbers the jury was comprised, had already gained a reputation for their hardline policy on bushrangers. Only three years before, they had petitioned for a gang of bushrangers to be tried in their town as opposed to Sydney for fear that city-dwellers would be too lenient.[74] After only a 'short interval', the jury found Sam Poo guilty of murder.[75] The following day, Justice Hargrave sentenced him to death.[76] According to the *Illawarra Mercury*, the judge was almost moved to tears by his ruling, but these were not the final words at Sam Poo's trial. The last remarks were in Chinese, as a court interpreter translated the verdict in the hope that the newly convicted felon would understand.[77]

Sam Poo was hanged on 19 December 1865 (see Plate 10). While Poo's alleged crimes were used to make grand arguments about the state of bushranging, law and policing in the colony, only the *Bathurst Free Press* concerned itself with writing an original article about his fate.[78] The paper reported that he:

suffered the extreme penalty of the law ... within the precincts of the gaol. In the absence of any of his countrymen from outside the prison walls, three Chinese prisoners, who are at present confined in Bathurst gaol, were brought out to see the end of Sam Poo ... The wretched man, who, ever since his apprehension, has been quite weak in intellect, appeared perfectly unconscious of his fate and until his arms were pinioned by the executioners, stood at the door of his cell clapping his hands. The ceremony of pinioning over, he was led to the gallows without speaking a word, or even lifting up his head. The rope was fixed, the bolt drawn and the soul was ushered into eternity. The unfortunate victim of crime struggled convulsively for about a minute, and then all was still.[79]

'Sam Poo ceased to exist.'[80]

## WHO WAS SAM POO?

'Australia's only Chinese bushranger' may have died on that day in 1865, but this is not where his story ends.[81] The colonial history is not the whole truth, but one group's version of it. We cannot take anything for granted. We cannot even be sure that the man who was executed for Senior Constable Ward's murder was actually his killer.

Although Sam Poo remained silent at his trial, he had legal representation and to the chagrin of the prosecution it appears that his lawyer, JL Innes, was rather zealous in his defence. While witnesses stated that they had encountered Sam Poo with guns in his possession, Innes suggested that the Chinese man may have had a reason to carry them. John Clough, an employee of John Plunkett, had seen the accused the day after Ward was shot. Apparently after coming through the scrub, Clough:

saw him [Sam Poo] covering me with a gun. He asked me where I was going, and on my telling him I was going to Mr Plunkett's, he said, 'Go on, or I will give you one too,' pointing to the gun and a pistol that was lying near him on a log.

Although this evidence made Sam Poo appear menacing, Innes deftly queried who the victim was in this situation. Under cross-examination, he asked Clough if it had ever occurred to him that the prisoner might think that Clough intended to rob him.[82] In the court records, there is evidence that Innes took this line of defence one step further. He claimed that even if Sam Poo had shot John Ward:

> ... it was not shown in the evidence that Ward had any right whatever to molest the prisoner. In order to justify an arrest by a constable, he must be armed with a warrant, or have reasonable suspicion of felony having been committed. Now, it was not shown that Ward had a warrant, or that he suspected the prisoner had committed a felony.[83]

Innes's interpretation is supported by legal evidence. Ward may have heard of a Chinese bushranger in the Mudgee area, but this did not mean that the bushranger was Sam Poo. Although Sam Poo was labelled a bushranger by the press, he was executed for murder and never convicted or even charged with any bushranging crime.

This attempt to paint Sam Poo as a victim acting in self-defence would have resonated with audiences and spectators at the time. Bushrangers were notorious for targeting Chinese people, especially Chinese miners on the goldfields. They were seen as easy targets for men in pursuit of a quick buck, and fair game because of their race. To name just one example, bushranger John Vane's entry into the criminal world was the result of what he saw as a 'prank' on a lone Chinese man. While carousing at a pub, one of Vane's mates spied a Chinese man and declared that if he had a revolver, he would rob the man. In what

FIGURE 3. Unknown Artist, *Morgan Sticking Up the Navvies,*
*Burning their Tents and Shooting the Chinaman*, 1865.

*State Library of Victoria Pictures Collection, IMP25/01/65/9.*

appears to have been a fit of male bravado, Vane immediately stole a gun
from the bar and robbed the Chinese man himself. Neither the man
he accosted nor the police saw any humour in the situation. Pursued
by the authorities, Vane turned to bushranging to survive on the run
from the law.[84] From 1860 to 1869, 4.7 per cent of all bushranging
victims in New South Wales were Chinese.[85] This was high considering
that the Chinese population declined after the introduction of the
*Chinese Immigration Restriction Act* in 1861.[86] From 3.7 per cent of
the population of New South Wales in 1861, the number of Chinese
people dropped to 1.4 per cent of the population of New South Wales
in 1871.[87] At the time of Sam Poo's trial, goldfields were still operating,
white bushrangers were still at large, and animosity towards Chinese
people was yet to subside. It is likely that Sam Poo was personally
threatened and experienced discrimination, violent or otherwise,

during his time in the Mudgee district. Innes's interpretation of Sam Poo's actions had a solid foundation in local experience.

Although this defence ultimately failed, it need not have been the only line of inquiry that Innes pursued. From the court documents, it appears that Sam Poo's lawyer missed a glaring opportunity to question his client's involvement in these crimes. Witnesses' reasons for identifying Sam Poo as the Chinese man they encountered around the time of Ward's death relied solely on his general appearance. He was Chinese and apparently 'dressed as a Chinese man'. Long descriptions of Sam Poo's attire fill the depositions. But the items listed are not consistent and, as Ward himself stated to John Plunkett before he died, this would 'be of no use for the Chinaman would change his clothes'. None of the witnesses listed any distinguishing features of the man who was hostile towards them except for his race.[88] This is problematic as Sam Poo was not the only Chinese man in the area. William Pitts deposed that he had seen another Chinese man only three to four hours before he saw Sam Poo.[89] Given the mobility of Chinese people moving between goldfields, it is likely that even more Chinese men walked through the town on their way to and from the diggings.[90] Although the number of Chinese people in New South Wales declined after 1861, there were still 7220 in the colony in 1871. There were far more Chinese men than Sam Poo traversing the land.[91]

The witnesses at Sam Poo's trial could only prove that they had encountered a Chinese man who threatened them with violence. He did not steal their possessions. Even if this was the same man who later resisted arrest, there was no direct evidence that he shot Senior Constable Ward. The medical examiner stated that weapons similar to those possessed by Sam Poo *could* have made the wounds that Ward sustained.[92] But the only witness to the crime was Ward himself, and the only evidence left was his dying declaration. Knowing himself to be 'dangerously ill and at the point of death', the officer declared: 'To the best of my belief, the Chinaman was a short little cranky old man'.[93] Sam Poo was only thirty-five years old.[94] The *Western Post* thought he looked even younger and stated that in court he appeared 'rather a well built man, of about four and twenty'.[95] John Clough declared that the Chinese man he encountered was not 'an old man. He was stouter than he is now'.[96] There was originally controversy about whether Senior Constable Ward's words could be admitted in evidence, but Justice Hargrave ruled that as Ward declared them at the point of death, they had the same validity as any evidence provided under oath. The voice of the only witness to this crime was admitted to the court. It was just not used to interrogate most of the evidence.[97] From the standpoint of the present looking back into the archive, there is doubt as to whether Sam Poo was the murderer of Senior Constable John Ward.

*

At this point, we can see clearly how inadequate colonial represent-ations of crime can be. While white bushrangers' place in our histories is largely the result of their criminality, other information about their lives also remains. Whether to push for social reform to prevent more offenders, or to defend a bushranger's character or actions, white bushrangers were cast as individuals. It was not only their actions that were significant, but their life stories.[98] The evidence that remains about Sam Poo almost completely overlooks his origins. In nearly all the surviving documents, he only exists from that moment in 1865 when he first engaged in crime. On the rare occasion that later histories make any reference to Sam Poo's life, he is assumed to have been just one of the thousands of Chinese people who came to try their luck on the goldfields in the 1850s.[99] But this was not when Sam reached the Australian colonies. In one prison register from 1865, an official scrawled Sam Poo's city of origin alongside the details of his crimes. The register states that Sam came from 'Amoi' [sic] in China (see Plate 11). And this changes everything.[100]

The Chinese miners who came to Australia during the Gold Rush were largely from Guangdong province in the south of China and sailed to Australia from Hong Kong.[101] The migrants who came from the treaty port of Amoy in Fujian province were part of a very different story. After the end of convict transportation to New South Wales in the 1840s, squatters with large tracts of land started to energetically look for a new, cheap labour force to replace their dwindling supply of convict workers. After initially looking to India, the landed classes turned their attention to China. While indenture was technically illegal under the Qing government of the time, the coastal city of Amoy provided a way around these rules.[102] For centuries the people of Amoy had travelled to distant lands to engage in trade and to sell their labour as workers. In the 19th century, Amoy was one of the ports open to foreigners by the *Treaty of Nanking* (Nanjing), and Chinese officials chose to turn a blind eye to the recruitment of labourers from the city's shores. Colonial powers other than the British recruited Chinese workers during this time, but from 1848 to 1852 when indentured labourers were sent to Australia, the majority of migrants came to New South Wales. Of the 4840 men who left Amoy during these years, 2738 were bound for Australia.[103] Although several rich and detailed histories have been written about this episode of Australia's past, the experiences of these indentured labourers remain on the periphery of the national story. This is despite the fact that the experiences of these Fujianese men were very different from those of their goldmining countrymen who followed them.

Most stories about Sam Poo assume it was a lust for gold that drew him to New South Wales. Although 'gold fever' was said to have affected all miners to varying degrees, white diggers believed Chinese men to suffer the extreme of this affliction.[104] This persistent emphasis on gold is misleading. Not only does it play into colonial stereotypes, but it obscures the complex motives that led Chinese indentured labourers to leave their homes. Amoy was one of the poorest areas in southern China. It had very little fertile land, and was plagued by ongoing clan feuds, banditry, overpopulation and famine.[105] In many villages, people would 'talk of [a] twenty, thirty or forty crop, or a nobody crop' – meaning the crop was so poor that a number of their clan would have to emigrate, or so good that nobody had to leave.[106] Sam Poo may have volunteered to work overseas to escape this abject poverty and support his family, for it appears that he did have a family. In contrast to colonial accounts of Sam Poo as a lone bandit, his death certificate reveals that he had a wife in China.[107] It was not unusual for citizens of Amoy to travel overseas in search of work and to send what they could back to their families struggling at home. This practice was a significant part of their culture and had been carried out for hundreds of years.[108] From two brief administrative notes about his place of origin and marital status, we already have more details about Sam Poo's life than in newspaper articles and court documents combined. Already we can see Poo was part of a social landscape that forced him to respond to very real pressures and make decisions that would affect his life and that of his family.

While he may have been one of hundreds of Chinese workers who left willingly for New South Wales, Poo could equally have been one of hundreds more who were forced to leave their homeland. After the first labourers arrived in New South Wales in 1848 the demand for indentured workers only grew, and so British agents in Amoy and their Chinese underlings increasingly engaged in 'crimping' to meet their quotas.[109] The aim of crimping was to force unsuspecting Chinese into labour contracts by whatever means necessary. By gambling or receiving goods they could not afford, many people became indebted to crimps and lost their liberty in order to repay this debt.[110] Others were deceived, believing they were about to engage in 'employment in a foreign firm or on a foreign ship on highly advantageous terms'.[111] Still more were lured to areas where ships were waiting and they were swiftly kidnapped.[112] Procuring workers for indenture became a lucrative and notorious trade. In contrast to anti-Chinese sentiment and the idea that 'no one' wanted Chinese people to come to Australia, many squatters were desperate for them.[113] And although some labourers from Amoy wanted to take up this work, others were deprived of the choice. Colonists were clearly wrong in framing Sam Poo's story solely in terms of race, gold or greed.

There is no trace of Sam Poo in records before 1865, but this need not stop us from piecing together his life before he was accused of crime. We can use common experiences under indenture to envisage what might have happened to him. Most Chinese indentured labourers were employed as shepherds on vast pastoral stations, and this was hard and isolating work.[114] Day after day shepherds would lead huge flocks of between 100 and 300 sheep out to pasture.[115] Long hours out in the elements left them vulnerable to illness, and as historian Richard Waterhouse has written, some shepherds 'overwhelmed by their lives of absolute solitude, degenerated into alcoholism and insanity. So common was this that shepherds generally were assumed to be "dotty", as mad as the proverbial hatter'.[116] Here, Waterhouse is referring to white men. Chinese men had the added disadvantage of language and cultural barriers. Workers from Amoy spoke Hokkien, which was a completely different dialect from the Cantonese spoken by goldminers from Guangdong.[117] Although these Chinese shepherds could have learnt English over the five years of their indenture, when they arrived in the colony they would have been incredibly isolated and restricted to communicating with their fellow Fujianese workers.[118]

Miscommunication was a feature of indenture from the very beginning. Illiteracy meant that many workers could not read their labour contracts.[119] They could easily be duped, lied to or misled with virtually no way to prove that anything underhand had occurred. To make matters worse, indentured workers had to sign two contracts, one in Chinese and the other in English. Even if a labourer was literate in their mother tongue, they were rarely able to read English and so many would sign English contracts completely unaware of their contents on arriving in New South Wales. In some instances, the Chinese agreement offered far better terms for the employee than the one subsequently signed in the colony (see Plate 12).[120] Even though colonial law upheld the Chinese contract, most contractual issues never reached the magistrate's bench.[121] Ignorance of their rights under the law as well as poor English language skills meant that many Chinese men could never bring such matters to court. The system was open for Chinese indentured labourers to be 'beguiled … into agreements by attaching marks, by proxy, to documents which were not read nor explained to them, or which, if explained, they did not understand'.[122]

Although contracts were important, Chinese labourers' experiences in New South Wales largely depended on their employers and superiors on the station. And while some squatters treated 'their men' well, it was their encounters with the law that left records and there is ample evidence that employers abused their power. Some would overcharge their workers for goods, ensuring that they became indebted and faced the severest penalty under the *Masters and Servants Act* (of three months' hard labour) if they left before their contract ended. Despite these penalties, a number of Chinese workers still refused to work and absconded. Some were found by the court to have legitimate grievances, but the majority were imprisoned and then forced to resume their work. This not only ensured that the squatter got his money's worth out of his employee but acted as a deterrent to any worker contemplating a similar dash for freedom.[123]

Sam Poo would have fitted somewhere along this broad spectrum of experiences, but it is safe to say he would not have had an easy life. After their five years of indenture, some workers' contracts were renewed or they stayed on working for their original employer on a casual basis.[124] Some made the long journey back to China, while others stayed in the colony and left the site of their indenture far behind.[125] If Sam Poo was an indentured labourer, after his initial contract ended he would have spent another seven to twelve years in the colony before the tragic events of 1865. This means that witnesses were likely correct in stating that Sam Poo spoke English well in 1865, for by that time he seems to have been in New South Wales for between twelve and seventeen years.[126] Sam Poo was no ignorant 'new chum' by the time he encountered the law in the 1860s. He was not one of the many Cantonese migrants who had lately flocked to the colony's goldfields. He appears to have worked on a pastoral station, helping to turn the land from a supposedly uncivilised wilderness into a thriving pastoral empire. Historian Margaret Slocomb has called for indentured labourers such as Sam Poo to be regarded as 'pioneers' alongside their white counterparts, as many went out beyond the boundaries of settlement, cleared the land and brought livestock to new areas.[127] This also means that Sam Poo was complicit in the dispossession of Aboriginal people. From this material, we can see that this man who was supposedly an outsider to colonial society had likely lived and worked in the colony for over a decade. And willingly or not, he had helped to make colonisation possible.

*

This tells us something of Sam Poo's world, but not the way he understood his place within it. It is one thing to chart the course of someone's life, and quite another to see it through their eyes. We know it is unlikely that Sam Poo murdered Senior Constable Ward, and that he had lived in New South Wales far longer than colonial accounts suggest. But how would Sam Poo have understood the bushranging crimes he was accused of committing? It is possible that Sam Poo actually saw these crimes as acts of bushranging. He could easily have heard stories about bushrangers during his time in the colonies, or even encountered these criminals himself. But it is unlikely this was the only experience to shape his worldview. If we turn our attention to Poo's Chinese origins, another possibility comes to light.

White bushranging men are said to have their roots in the British tradition of highway robbery that goes back to medieval stories of Robin Hood, but there were other traditions of outlaw heroes.[128] In China, a celebrated outlaw tradition goes back to at least the 12th century (with some scholars proposing an even earlier date between 475 and 221 BCE).[129] This was not some obscure legend as stories of outlaw heroes, their codes of conduct and exploits were (and remain) a pervasive aspect of Chinese culture. The compilation of stories *Outlaws of the Marsh*, also known as *Water Margin* and *All Men Are Brothers*, is the most famous narrative about Chinese rebels. Written in the 14th century, this text features 108 different characters and charts their lives of crime and adventures on the run.[130] These stories were not restricted to the wealthy and literate members of Chinese society, as they were also recounted orally, portrayed in dramas and passed down in local lore. Like their Western counterparts, these Chinese figures were heroes when they observed a certain moral code and were seen to be fighting injustice. But the foundation of these ideas rests in Confucian ethics, notions of 'Yi' (honour), brotherhood and political revolution, as opposed to Sherwood Forest.[131]

It is likely that Sam Poo had knowledge of this outlaw tradition from growing up in China, and as a resident of Amoy the dimensions of this alternative outlaw tradition expand again. Quite apart from mythic outlaw heroes, Sam Poo would also have been exposed to 'pure bandits': men and women who became outlaws for practical reasons and took no interest in the outlaw code.[132] Banditry increased in relation to social unrest, famine, natural disasters, overpopulation, clan feuds and corruption. Amoy was plagued by all of these destabilising factors.[133] There was almost no government support in times of need or unrest. Corrupt officials would turn a blind eye to most depredations if they were paid enough money. Pressure for basic necessities like food, work and money drove many to become 'floating people', drifting from place to place in search of sustenance, and it was these people who were the most likely to become outlaws.[134] As writer Xu Ke has written of bandits from Guangdong, 'living in hunger and cold, they were sure to die, while being bandits, though violating the law, not everyone is captured'.[135]

Secret societies and brotherhoods were intimately associated with Chinese bandit culture. Organisations provided a new level of stability and security for individual drifters. Many had internal hierarchies that delegated their members into set positions and were able to recruit scores of supporters. These groups also provided a bond to replace that of family, family being a sacred and driving force in Chinese life.[136] Given this background, it is likely that Sam Poo would have felt his isolation in New South Wales. While there were occasionally bandits who, like him, operated alone, groups, clans, societies and brotherhoods were the norm in China, and the standard against which other bandits were judged. Banditry changed a great deal over the thousands of years it existed in China, especially when there were shifts in politics.[137] To date, China has experienced over 500 different regimes and as scholar Ye Zhang writes, 'in the transition period from one regime or dynasty to another, values changed radically. The lawful to the previous regime or dynasty might be unlawful to the new one; the outlawed now could come back inside the law'.[138] And so it was not only the colonial context of white bushranging, policing and legal change that defined Sam Poo's story. The instability of the Chinese context and very real struggles for survival would have affected how Sam Poo saw his alleged crimes in New South Wales as well as his place in the colony.

*

Given the different geographical and cultural worlds that Sam Poo came from, should we even call him a bushranger? Describing him that way allows us to uncover the beliefs, motivations, fears and desires held by colonial Australians, but it is also dangerous. If we take this approach alone, we naturalise colonial ways of seeing the world. We blind ourselves to different experiences and different perspectives, and deafen ourselves to different voices. Sam Poo was never just a 'bushranger' – and according to colonial law, he never was one. There are many histories of Sam Poo. Even though we see him first through colonial sources – through white people's eyes – it is important to remember that Sam Poo was his own person. Buried below the surface of these historical papers lies the simple fact that Sam Poo was never a colonial puppet. And it was his agency that made him a threat.

# CHAPTER 4
# THE MAKING OF MARY ANN BUGG

On Thursday 30 March 1865, Sergeant Cleary and Constable Byrne were on the hunt for bushrangers. They had been called to the station of Macleay, Little and Co. on the Culgoa, about 100 miles from Bourke, New South Wales, after it was stuck up by a gang of men four days previously. While one of the owners, Mr Beaumont, had been inclined to 'show fight', he had not found the station workers quite as keen to risk life and limb to resist the marauders. This lack of enthusiasm led to the theft of firearms, ammunition and two pack horses heavily laden with supplies, and had lost Cleary and Byrne a comparatively peaceful Thursday back at Bourke police station. Catching armed bushrangers was unpleasant and risky business. With Mr Beaumont and an unnamed Aboriginal man, the officers scoured the bush from 'the Brie and across the country to the Bokarra, from thence to Narran'. The bandits were four days in advance of their pursuers, had burnt the grass for miles around to obliterate their tracks and crossed a lake to further confuse the authorities. After days of false leads and travel through harsh country, the search party finally found fresh tracks and followed them to the bushrangers' camp.[1]

The male bushrangers were gone and only one heavily pregnant woman and two small children remained in the clearing, surrounded by incriminating stolen property.[2] This was not the prize the search party was hoping for, and it was only after unsuccessfully lying in wait for their prey to return that the officers decided to apprehend the woman and her children instead. Sergeant Cleary and Constable Byrne may have been quietly relieved that they missed the gun-toting gang, but if they expected the danger to be over then they were sadly mistaken. The woman 'twitted them on their want of success, and was particularly severe on Mr Beaumont, who, she said, was only showing off at the station when he wanted to show fight'. If this retort was unusual from a woman, what happened next was even more unexpected.[3] According to the *Maitland Mercury*, the female captive suddenly became a 'perfect amazon, who sprung like a tigress upon one of the police, ribboning his uniform, and taunting him with cowardice for seeking her apprehension instead of [the bushranger] Thunderbolt's'.[4] The *Empire* continued that 'with her passion she brought on, or feigned to bring on labour'. The police were forced to leave their prisoner at a nearby pastoral station for her to give birth while they continued to hunt the male bushrangers.[5] But upon the officers' departure the woman's contractions appear to have miraculously ceased. When Thunderbolt called by the property she and the children swiftly escaped.[6]

This remarkable woman's name was Mary Ann Bugg (see Plate 15). She was born in 1834, the daughter of James Bugg, a convict assigned to the Australian Agricultural Company (A. A. Co.) and Charlotte, a Worimi woman from the Hunter Region of New South Wales.[7] Between 1863 and 1867, Mary Ann lived with Frederick Ward, alias Captain Thunderbolt, one of the longest operating bushrangers in Australian history.[8]

Ward was one of those elite, white, gentleman bushrangers upon which the bushranging legend relied. He fashioned himself in the manner of a dashing British highwayman, achieving a reputation as something of a colonial Robin Hood among his supporters. Thunderbolt was handsome, gallant and courteous to women. He took great care to entertain his 'hostages', regaled his victims with tales of police ineptitude and injustice, and in many (although not all) instances, he refused to steal from the poor.

Mary Ann is unique in this book of other bushrangers as she, too, is remembered as a part of the bushranging legend. Given the demonisation of William Douglas and Sam Poo her inclusion in this heroic tradition is clearly exceptional, but it is also completely dependent on 'her man'. In popular histories and local lore, she is described as Ward's helpmate and loyal 'gin'; a sidekick in the background of the action.[9] In one well-known version of Ward's escape from imprisonment on Cockatoo Island, Mary Ann even swam through the shark-infested waters of Sydney Harbour to free her dashing partner.[10] In this encounter Mary Ann plays a larger role than most, but she still only assists the Captain and never acts on her own account. To make matters worse, this famous tale is a complete fabrication, as Mary Ann was miles away in Dungog when Ward made his escape.[11] Few writers have made Mary Ann's life their focus or charted its course beyond her adventures with Captain Thunderbolt.

Mary Ann Bugg's story was far richer and more complex than these legends would have us believe. For four years her life was intertwined with Ward's, but as more than a mere helpmate. She accompanied him around the colony, acting as his scout, informer, lover and confidante. She provided food and shelter, bore him three children, and at the time, many colonists alleged that she took part in the robberies herself. Mary Ann was also a brilliant strategist. She played with colonial expectations, leaning into them when it suited her and tossing them aside when they got in her way. Her public image was self-styled and intentional, but she never let colonists determine the course of her life. In previous chapters we have seen how colonial Australians misrepresented other bushrangers by stripping their personhood from the records, and putting forth colonial ideas in their stead. Mary Ann's case is different. Although material about her was shaped by white ideas and assumptions, her own actions and words have also left a mark on the archive. This chapter tells her story.

PLATE 1. Tom Roberts, *Bailed Up*, 1895, 1927, oil on canvas, 134.5 x 182.8 cm.

*Courtesy the Art Gallery of New South Wales. Photo © Art Gallery of New South Wales.*

PLATE 2. Ben Quilty, *Golden soil, wealth for toil*, 2004, oil on canvas, 145 x 200 cm.

*Courtesy the artist and the Art Gallery of New South Wales.*
*Photo © Art Gallery of New South Wales.*

PLATE 3. ST Gill, *Road in Black Forest*, 1852 (see page 13).

*National Library of Australia, PIC Volume 181 #S133.*

PLATE 4. ST Gill, *Zealous Gold Diggers*, 1852 (see page 18).

*National Library of Australia, PIC Volume 200 #U1034 NK586/10.*

PLATE 5. William Strutt, *Native Police Escorting a Prisoner from Ballarat to Melbourne*, 1859 (see page 24).

*State Library of New South Wales, BSMITH 994.5031 ST8V.*

PLATE 6. ST Gill, *Sly Grog Shop*, 1852 (see page 31).

*National Gallery of Australia, 86.634.*

Plate 7. Jason Phu, *The Ballad of The Widely Loved and Revered Aussie Bushranger Sammy 'Pooey' Pu: The Successful Great Revolt Against the Southern Crossers by L.H.C., The Shooting Death of S.C.J.W. by a Chinaman, The Great Chase and Final Showdown at Barney's Reef, The Trial of The Mute, The Execution by Hanging of Sam Poo* (detail), 2015, ink, texta, coloured pencil on Chinese paper, 60 x 1050 cm (see page 64).

*Courtesy the artist and The Hughes Gallery, Sydney. Photo: Document Photography.*

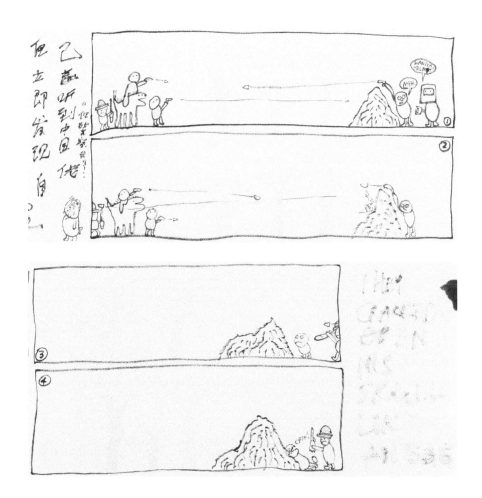

PLATES 8 & 9. Jason Phu, *The Ballad of the Widely Loved and Revered Aussie Bushranger Sammy 'Pooey' Pu: The Successful Great Revolt Against the Southern Crossers by L.H.C., The Shooting Death of S.C.J.W. by a Chinaman, The Great Chase and Final Showdown at Barney's Reef, The Trial of The Mute, The Execution by Hanging of Sam Poo* (detail), 2015, ink, texta, coloured pencil on Chinese paper, 60 x 1050 cm (see page 78).

*Courtesy the artist and The Hughes Gallery, Sydney. Photo: Document Photography.*

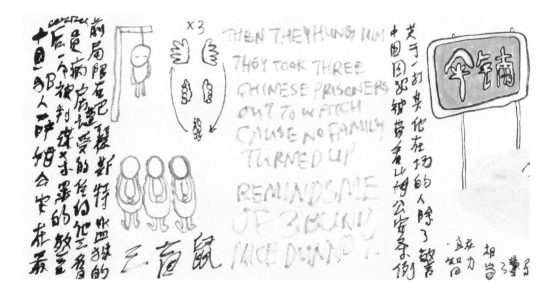

Plate 10. Jason Phu, *The Ballad of The Widely Loved and Revered Aussie Bushranger Sammy 'Pooey' Pu: The Successful Great Revolt Against the Southern Crossers by L.H.C., The Shooting Death of S.C.J.W. by a Chinaman, The Great Chase and Final Showdown at Barney's Reef, The Trial of The Mute, The Execution by Hanging of Sam Poo* (detail), 2015, ink, texta, coloured pencil on Chinese paper, 60 x 1050 cm (see page 79).

*Courtesy the artist and The Hughes Gallery, Sydney. Photo: Document Photography.*

PLATES 11 & 12. Jason Phu, *The Ballad of The Widely Loved and Revered Aussie Bushranger Sammy 'Pooey' Pu: The Successful Great Revolt Against the Southern Crossers by L.H.C., The Shooting Death of S.C.J.W. by a Chinaman, The Great Chase and Final Showdown at Barney's Reef, The Trial of The Mute, The Execution by Hanging of Sam Poo* (detail), 2015, ink, texta, coloured pencil on Chinese paper, 60 x 1050 cm (see pages 84 and 87) .

*Courtesy the artist and The Hughes Gallery, Sydney. Photo: Document Photography.*

PLATE 13. Jason Phu, *The 5th Reincarnation of Sam Poo, Infamous Bushranger and the Mustard Horde: The Last Stand*, 2018, type C photograph (see chapter 3).

*Image courtesy and © the artist. Photographer: Leanna Maione.*

PLATE 14. Jason Phu, *Waiting for the 6th Reincarnation of Sam Poo, Infamous Bushranger and End of the Mustard Horde*, 2018, type C photograph (see chapter 3).

*Image courtesy and © the artist. Photographer: Leanna Maione.*

PLATE 15. Unknown photographer, *Portrait believed to be of Mary Ann Ward (née Bugg)*, date unknown (see page 93).

*Courtesy of Uralla Historical Society and McCrossin's Mill Museum, Uralla, NSW, 2358.*

PLATE 16. Unknown photographer, *Ethel Page, who
became Mrs Jimmy Governor*, c.1900 (see page 127).

*Courtesy the University of Newcastle Special Collections, John Turner Collection.*

PLATE 17. AC Jackson, *The Hunt for the Governor Gang of Bushrangers. A posse of mounted police, Aboriginal trackers and district volunteers*, 1900 (see page 144).

State Library of New South Wales, BCP 03906. Courtesy the Mitchell Library, State Library of New South Wales and Scone Historical Society.

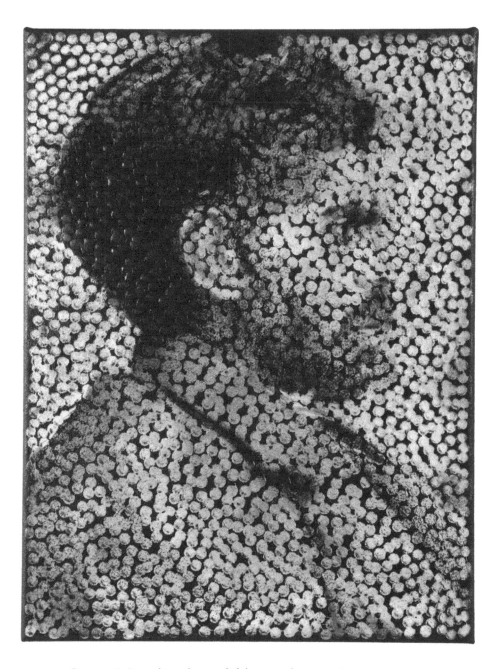

PLATE 18. Daniel Boyd, *Untitled (JG 26.II)*, 2016, oil, acrylic, pastel, charcoal and archival glue on polyester, 41 x 31 cm (see chapters 5 and 6).

*Courtesy of the artist and Roslyn Oxley9 Gallery, Sydney.*

PLATE 19. Daniel Boyd, *Untitled (JG 26.1)*, 2016, oil, acrylic, pastel, charcoal and archival glue on polyester, 41 x 31 cm (see chapters 5 and 6).

*Courtesy of the artist and Roslyn Oxley9 Gallery, Sydney.*

PLATE 20. Edward L Wheeler, *Deadwood Dick, the prince of the road*, 1899 (see page 165).

*Edward L. Wheeler, 'Deadwood Dick, the prince of the road', Deadwood Dick Library vol. 1, no. 1 (1899), p. 1.*

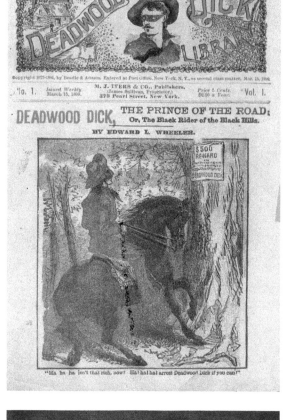

PLATE 21. Jamie Preisz, *Dreaming of Sidney*, 2019, oil on canvas, 183 x 122 cm.

*Image courtesy and © the artist.*

## 1866: 'THUNDERBOLT'S GIN' IS CHARGED WITH VAGRANCY

Almost a year to the day after Mary Ann encountered Cleary and Byrne, on Saturday 31 March 1866, Thomas Nicholls made himself ready for a day of legal proceedings as magistrate for the bench at Stroud, New South Wales. This township was an old one as far as the Northern Districts were concerned, having been established by the A. A. Co. in 1826, but its residents had experienced a number of set-backs since the boom years of the 1830s. A decline in the A. A. Co.'s profits in the depression of the 1840s led the Company to sell large tracts of land, and by the 1850s the business retreated from the remnants of its inland estates and moved its headquarters to Sydney. Once the nerve centre of the greatest private agricultural enterprise in the country, Stroud became a small and quaint rural town, a relatively unremarkable dot on the colony's ever-expanding map.[12] Perhaps Nicholls' magistracy was popular among the remaining residents, as the court provided a renewed sense of purpose and importance to the town. When the notorious bushranger Captain Thunderbolt's 'half-caste woman' graced their courthouse with her presence, the colony's attention focused on the town of Stroud once more.[13]

As Mary Ann was called to approach the bench, onlookers saw a 'dark sallow' woman with black hair and brown eyes walk into view. She was not particularly tall, being only 5ft 2½in in height, and her nose was 'slightly cocked'.[14] Holding her infant child in her arms, Mary Ann was charged with 'being an idle and disorderly person and a companion of reputed thieves, having no visible means of support or fixed place of residence'.[15] Only a few days earlier another posse of police had come upon her camp in search of Frederick Ward and had missed him again.[16] Tales of police incompetence were becoming a common occurrence in the metropolitan and local press, as weary colonists noted that several years had elapsed since Thunderbolt's first bushranging spree. Guns misfiring, slow horses and officers' inexperience in the bush had repeatedly allowed Thunderbolt to escape from the clutches of the New Police. Loath to return to 'civilisation' empty-handed, on this occasion Senior Sergeant Kerrigan arrested Mary Ann on a charge of vagrancy.[17] Vagrancy was a common offence in this period, as the *Vagrancy Act*'s wide discretionary powers allowed the police to arrest almost anyone they considered a nuisance.[18]

Mary Ann took an unusual approach in her defence to these charges. She declared to the courtroom that she was no vagrant, as her husband, Frederick Ward, 'kept her'.[19] To try to escape a conviction for vagrancy, Mary Ann openly claimed a man who was one of the most notorious white bushrangers in the colony. When Mary Ann stood before the court she was charged as 'Mary Ann Ward'. All depositions, gaol logbooks and court records referred to her by this name. It was the name she gave when arrested by Senior Sergeant Kerrigan, the way she was introduced to the court and her only defence to vagrancy charges.[20] While declaring yourself the wife of a fugitive may appear counterproductive to escaping a charge of 'being in the company of reputed thieves', Mary Ann made this association very deliberately. We know this because there is no evidence that she ever married Ward. Although Mary Ann claimed that she was married by a travelling minister, no such person, or record of her wedding has ever been found.[21]

Mary Ann's claim to be Ward's wife was a savvy move. At a time when reporters referred to her by racist slurs such as 'Thunderbolt's half cast [sic] gin', it gave her greater social standing.[22] Marriage was a bond that legitimised her relationship with Ward, as their union had been sanctified before God and the community. As historian Ann McGrath describes, 'marriage confirmed public recognition and acceptance of a couple's intimacy' as the performance of a ceremony and the presence of a legal contract moved the relationship from a matter for individuals to a matter of the state.[23] In the 19th century, marriage also enshrined a wife's dependency on her husband. According to the law, husband and wife were one legal entity, a husband had the right to act on his wife's behalf in official matters and a woman's property became that of her husband upon their union.[24] By drawing on ideas of marriage that the colonial courtroom would know well, Mary Ann made it appear natural that Frederick Ward 'kept her' and provided for his family. If this meant that Mary Ann was living off the proceeds of crime, then she made it clear that this was her partner's misdeed and not her own. Mary Ann's words suggested that like all dutiful, lawful wives, she was guilty of relying upon her husband, and nothing more.

Mary Ann could very well have believed in the importance of marriage, despite not having married Frederick Ward. Her white father had petitioned the church in New South Wales for seven years to be allowed to marry her Aboriginal mother, and Mary Ann had been married herself, becoming the wife of an emancipist named Edmund Baker at the age of fourteen.[25] Baker apparently died a few years after their wedding, but Mary Ann's youth suggests that her father arranged or at the very least actively supported the match.[26] The marriage of a minor, below the age of twenty-one, almost always required the consent of the child's father at this time.[27] While it would have been to the family's advantage if Mary Ann married well and she might have been pregnant to Baker at the time, marriage was clearly valued in Mary Ann's family. Its importance had been instilled in her upbringing.[28]

This is the intimate context, but Mary Ann's claims to have married Frederick Ward were also part of a larger, colonial story. Marriage had a particular resonance in 1800s New South Wales. From its very inception, the colony suffered from a chronic imbalance of the sexes and over eight decades had yet to amend the high ratio of men compared to women.[29] White women were deemed to be the only appropriate wives for white men but the realities of life in the colony meant that exceptions had always been made. The government feared that the absence of white women would lead to homosexual acts and insidious moral decay. At the founding of the colony in 1788, Governor Phillip had even suggested fetching women from the Pacific Islands to remedy the stark imbalance of the sexes.[30] Phillip's proposal never came to pass, but it reminds us that issues of sexual and moral deviancy occasionally pressed more strongly than race on the minds of those in government.

Sexual unions between Aboriginal women and white men were as old as the frontier itself, but the experiences of Aboriginal women were wide and varied. Some Aboriginal women offered themselves to white men willingly, acting as emissaries for their clan and hoping through sex to incorporate the invaders into their world as kin.[31] This appears to have been how Mary Ann's mother first encountered her father, as the Worimi had a long tradition of this diplomatic practice.[32] James Bugg was the overseer of shepherds in the Berrico area, a man of authority and power over his immediate peers: a man seemingly worthy of such diplomatic efforts.[33] However, there were also countless cases of white men capturing, abducting and raping Aboriginal women for lust, intrigue or sport.[34] To justify these heinous acts, colonists habitually cast Aboriginal women as debased prostitutes and Aboriginal men as unworthy partners. Such men were either portrayed as pimps, willing to sell their wives for a touch of tobacco, or barbarians who brutalised their own women. White men cast themselves as superior to the First Nations people they colonised. To their minds this superiority not only entitled them to the land, but sex with the Aboriginal women they sought to dispossess.[35]

This leads us to the other advantage of Mary Ann claiming to be 'Mrs Frederick Ward'. Only certain, 'civilised' people were actually allowed to marry. The marriage of Mary Ann's parents was forbidden for seven years due to this belief. In response to James Bugg's petition to wed Charlotte, William Broughton, Anglican 'Bishop of Australia', declared that the marriage could not take place as Aboriginal people were heathens.[36] To marry, a person was meant to possess a certain degree of enlightenment and moral understanding. They were supposed to be educated in the ways of the church to ensure the spiritual integrity of the union. Marriage was one way to police who was inside or outside of respectable society; it demarcated civilised from 'savage'. Instead of being hampered by these racist ideas, Mary Ann recognised them, appropriated them and used them to advance her own interests. In claiming to be married, she claimed this degree of 'civilisation' as well as entitlements as a wife.

But for all of its appeal, Mary Ann did not refer to herself by her married name alone. She also described herself as the 'Captain's Lady'.[37] 'Lady' was not some quirky moniker in the 19th century. It carried a great deal of power. The word 'lady' gave a woman social standing and authority as she had apparently reached the pinnacle of refinement, culture and feminine delicacy. In the 1800s, there was also a revival of the term 'lady' in a chivalric sense, as a woman who was the object of a gallant, courtly love.[38] Newspapers could have used the term seriously or ironically, to illustrate the absurdity of applying that status to an Aboriginal woman, but Mary Ann went to great lengths to associate herself with its respectable meaning. By fabricating her marriage and insisting she was dependent on her husband, Mary Ann's status as the 'Captain's Lady' would not appear out of place.

Considering the battle for hearts, minds and support that Thunderbolt was then waging, he was lucky that Mary Ann's image as the 'Captain's Lady' reflected well on him too. In the 1860s, white, male bushrangers were not understood as national heroes the way that they are today. These men were described as dastardly villains as well as with admiration. Their networks of harbourers and supporters were challenged by informers and local volunteers who hunted bushrangers down. This made bushrangers' public image all the more important. From local, opportunistic desperados with short-lived careers to intrepid, calculating bandits who possessed guile and success – image mattered. In public statements, many armed robbers claimed that they had never 'bailed up' a poor man, used violence or assaulted any of the 'fairer sex'. Whether these claims were true was another matter, but they helped to elevate bushrangers above common criminals.[39] 'Gentlemen of the bush' such as Ward had apparently not lost their moral feeling in the pursuit of their criminal ends, and Mary Ann's position as the 'Captain's Lady' enhanced her husband's status as a gallant 'man of the road'.[40] By fashioning their relationship as one of chivalric love, Mary Ann made Thunderbolt appear nobler and more constant than his itinerant life might suggest. Just as Robin Hood had Maid Marian to illustrate his tender, gentlemanly side, Thunderbolt had Mary Ann.

*

Back in that courtroom in 1866, however, the image of Mary Ann as demure 'Mrs Thunderbolt' came under fire. The arresting officer, Senior Sergeant Kerrigan, had a different tale to tell. Far from a respectable woman who was dependent on her husband, 'the prisoner – I have no doubt has accompanied the man Ward and has assisted him to plunder as she has spoken of several robberies ...' Furthermore, the officer declared that 'they [meaning Thunderbolt and Mary Ann] used to kill ... cattle by having a shear blade tied to the end of a pole and hamstringing them ... [the prisoner] stated that when the police chased Ward she was dressed in men's pants'. It appears that the last two allegations proved too much for Mary Ann. Although her protestations in court were not recorded, Kerrigan's firm responses to them were. 'You did say that when the police chased Ward that you had pants on. You did tell me that you lived chiefly on beef.'[41] Kerrigan's claims were not alone. Only days before Mary Ann's capture, her Aboriginal midwife told the police that Mary Ann dressed and rode like a man and slaughtered cattle in the way that Kerrigan described.[42] Mary Ann not only engaged in these practices but volunteered that information to the police. She decided when her public persona had to be kept and when it could slide, and she did not always choose wisely. Standing before the court, baby in her arms, this thirty-one-year-old was sentenced to six months' imprisonment under the *Vagrancy Act*.[43]

But this was not the end of the matter. As Mary Ann adapted to the claustrophobic confines of Maitland Gaol, 'benevolent' white men were busily making motions in her defence. On Thursday 5 April 1866, David Buchanan, the member for East Macquarie, moved the adjournment of the house. It was his aim to bring to the attention of the government 'an act of most cruel injustice'. He described how the bench at Stroud had 'convicted an aboriginal woman under the Vagrant [sic] Act', an act from which Aboriginal people were explicitly excluded.[44] One of the reasons that the *Vagrancy Act* had been created in 1835 was to protect Aboriginal people from the nefarious influence of whites. The legislation made it illegal for 'every person not being a black native or child of any black native ... [to be] found lodging or wandering in company with any black natives of this Colony' if they could not prove they were doing so 'for some temporary or lawful occasion'. The Act aimed to prevent colonists from inciting Aboriginal people to violence, engaging in mixed-race relationships, or spreading discontent or disease. It was not intended to eliminate bush-dwelling ways of life.[45] With this legal history to support his claims, Buchanan went on to state that had they dragged an honourable member 'from his home, they could not have done a greater wrong than had been done in the case of this poor woman, for the wilderness was her home, and the wide bush the only residence she possessed'.[46] Other members of the house were quick to follow suit. John Dunmore Lang declared it was monstrous that 'a woman like this ... should be treated like a criminal', while James Hart believed it was a gross perversion of justice, all done 'because it was suspected that she was the paramour of the bushranger Ward'.[47]

In their attempt to release Mary Ann from prison, these parliamentarians labelled her a primitive woman. As several newspapers reported, 'the illegality consisted in the dealing with the prisoner as a civilised person'.[48] These men could only conceive of Mary Ann as an Aboriginal woman, 'living as her ancestors had lived' and not as the active partner or spouse of a white bushranger, let alone an educated, literate woman who had been 'brought up in civilised habits'.[49] In truth, Mary Ann was better educated than Ward and many of the rural population in New South Wales as she could read and write.[50] Education was another institution valued by her family, as Mary Ann's father had paid for her schooling in Sydney when she was a child.[51] These details about Mary Ann's upbringing were missing from legislative debate. Depositions claiming her active involvement in Ward's bushranging crimes were never cited. The possibility that she was married to Ward was never even alluded to. In one account, the innovative weapon Mary Ann and Ward used to hamstring cattle became an Aboriginal woman's spear.[52] From an articulate, educated and shrewd woman before the court, Mary Ann was rendered voiceless and described as 'an aboriginal savage of Australia'.[53]

This legislative intervention was heated, but it did not exist in a vacuum. Attorney General James Martin sent for the original court documents so that he could examine the legality of the case. The convicting magistrate, Thomas Nicholls, provided his reasons for sentencing Mary Ann and the case was reported in newspapers across the colony – where it received a very mixed response.[54] Some papers continued to refer to Mary Ann as a pitiable Aboriginal woman, while others stated that she was an exceptional, dangerous criminal.[55] In one of the more extreme articles, the *Sydney Morning Herald* reported

> So far from being the 'poor harmless creature,' who 'roamed through her native home, the bush,' she was Thunderbolt's chief lieutenant and right hand man ... turning her adrift to join him again would be far worse for the country than if half a dozen of the most hardened criminals on Cockatoo were granted permits for his gang.[56]

These disputes reached their height while Mary Ann was held in Maitland Gaol and Thunderbolt remained at large. We cannot know whether she had any idea that these debates were afoot, or that MPs were making an appeal on her behalf. We do know that the petition for her release was successful. On 18 April 1866, Mary Ann made her way through the thick sandstone walls of Maitland Goal and walked out of its doors a free woman – but not for the reason we might expect.[57] On reviewing the case, the Attorney General found that Mary Ann Ward *could* be charged under the *Vagrancy Act* as she had been educated, '… and acquired civilized habits'. It was a legal technicality that led to her release, as the charges against her had not been drawn up properly.[58] Even in the resolution of Mary Ann's case, public understandings remained at odds with the facts of her situation. As late as four months after her release, the *Empire* was still reporting that Mary Ann 'may have some black blood in her veins, but she is not darker than many European women who might easily be made amenable to the Vagrant [sic] Act'.[59] The issue of race could not be as easily dismissed as Mary Ann's charges. According to the white public, her release remained an issue of Aboriginality and not a technical problem with the indictment itself.

## 1788–1835: ABORIGINAL TRADITIONS

Even though colonists were obsessed with Mary Ann's Aboriginal ancestry, they never saw her actions in light of Aboriginal culture. Race allowed colonists to treat Mary Ann as if her destiny was biological and fixed, whereas culture muddied the waters. Culture is not inherent or static. It is learnt and powerful, often old yet also adaptive. It provides a way of seeing the world as well as our place within it.[60] At first glance it may seem right that colonists never understood Mary Ann in relation to Aboriginal culture. After all, she made very public appeals to white values and ideas. But in the context of the court or the popular press, it made strategic sense to adopt the colonisers' frame of reference. White culture was not the only one to influence Mary Ann Bugg. An incident from Mary Ann's family history in 1835 suggests that complex webs of Aboriginal resistance, kinship and tradition also shaped the course of her life.

Mary Ann was just twelve months old in 1835.[61] Her white father, James Bugg, was an overseer of shepherds for the A. A. Co., and the family lived on a Company station at Berrico in apparent tranquillity until 8 May, when James Bugg was attacked. On this day, ten Aboriginal men came to the station asking for provisions and received corn and tobacco from the Company stores. Bugg later deposed that he 'did not expect from their manner that they intended doing any mischief', but this false sense of security nearly proved his undoing.[62] After lingering about the station for several hours, two Aboriginal men took Bugg unawares and struck him senseless with their waddies. Shocked Company shepherds hesitated to come to his aid, apparently afraid that the attackers had taken possession of Bugg's firearms, and it was Mary Ann's mother, Charlotte, who drove the attackers away. She discharged a gun in their direction, causing the Aboriginal men to retreat from the scene. Only then did the shepherds overcome their paralysis and join in the station's defence.[63]

Despite Bugg's later claim that the violence was random, this was not an isolated attack. It was one of three such strikes on stations and shepherds' huts in the area in less than a month and not all white men were as lucky as Mary Ann's father. By 23 May, James Bugg had recovered enough strength to provide an affidavit to a visiting Justice of the Peace.[64] Around the same time, newspapers reported that five convicts from a neighbouring station had been killed by Aboriginal men.[65]

There is a certain symmetry between Mary Ann's depiction in the Thunderbolt myth and Charlotte's place in the official tale of the attack. Reverend William Cowper used the Buggs' story as proof that Aboriginal people were 'not insensible to kindness, nor incapable of gratitude and affection' when he stood before the Select Committee on the Aborigines Question in 1838. He countered the opinion of many of his contemporaries by suggesting that Aboriginal people had emotions and sensibilities of their own. While Cowper intended to praise the Buggs' union, he still cast their relationship as one of a loyal Aboriginal woman assisting a white man.[66] If our point of reference shifts from James to Charlotte, this story reveals so much more. Charlotte was not only loyal but active, daring and brave while the men of the station were initially scared, immobile and unwilling to put themselves in harm's way.[67] Charlotte defied colonial stereotypes by showing she was neither a delicate, fragile woman, nor an amoral, self-serving 'black'. And at the same time as saving James Bugg's life, Charlotte's actions likely influenced Mary Ann's time with Frederick Ward.[68]

Mary Ann was an active partner in life and in crime to Captain Thunderbolt. Although (as far as we know) Mary Ann never fired a gun in his defence, she fought for their life together in other ways, often at great personal danger to herself. She moved around the country with a known fugitive, berated and physically assaulted the police, fed the authorities and locals false information, assisted Thunderbolt after he was shot and nursed him back to health. All of this was done throughout Mary Ann's three pregnancies and while she provided for their children.[69] It appears that Charlotte and Mary Ann went to great lengths to support their families, and that mother and daughter were both courageous, resilient and audaciously bold.

While the connections between Mary Ann and her mother are clear, they may seem to be more personal and familial than part of any Aboriginal tradition. Not only at the time but in recent writing, Charlotte's defence of James Bugg is cast as her choice of the settlers over her own people. In her fictionalised account, historian Carol Baxter even suggests that when Charlotte fired Bugg's gun she put her own and Mary Ann's lives at permanent risk, as her actions declared her allegiance to Bugg over her Aboriginal kin.[70] This retelling might seem natural, with its neat division of loyalties – one was either with the white people or with those who were black – but we cannot take this version at face value. We need more evidence to know if it is true.

There is no proof that Charlotte fought off her own people as there is no evidence of the Aboriginal clan or band to which she belonged. Aboriginal people were never one homogenous group. We know that

Charlotte was from the Worimi language group from where she lived. Worimi lands extend 'from the northern bank of the Hunter to the Manning River and to Tuncurry along the coast; inland to about Glendon Brook and the head of Myall Creek and including the whole of Port Stephens', and Berrico was nestled in this area, to the north near Barrington Tops.[71] Within this language group there were many smaller groups, called clans, which had beliefs, law, stories, customs and territories of their own.[72] Aboriginal people habitually travelled in 'bands' composed of 'male members of a clan, their wives (married in from other clans) and children, and unmarried female clan members'. The multilingual, multi-clan nature of bands gave their members 'connections and rights to much broader areas than single-clan estates'.[73] Aboriginal group and kinship connections were intricate and complex.

Despite regularly lumping all Aboriginal people together with dehumanising terms such as 'blacks' or 'natives', the colonisers were not completely ignorant of group distinctions and recognised these differences when it suited them. From the earliest years of the A. A. Co., Company officials recorded that Aboriginal groups had different rivalries and animosities. Local historian Damaris Bairstow writes that in the district closest to the coast at Port Stephens, the 'Carrington Aborigines feared the northern tribe and took the opportunity to use A. A. Company intervention to settle old scores'.[74] The Karuah people and the Myall to the south-east of Port Stephens were also known to have no love for one another, and the hostility of the Myall people towards any outsider (Aboriginal or not) was made worse by the violent incursions of timber cutters into their lands.[75] In settlers' correspondence about the 'outrages' in 1835, similar clan distinctions were made between the Williams River and Manning River groups around the Berrico area. It is possible that Charlotte was not shooting at her own kin, but rather strangers or her traditional enemies.[76]

This reading is strengthened by Aboriginal kinship and clan responsibilities. When James Bugg entered a sexual relationship with

Charlotte, he was likely incorporated into her people's world as kin.[77] By 'making a place for strangers', Aboriginal people knitted newcomers into the fabric of their communities, forging a reciprocal relationship between them and the group.[78] It seems that Bugg fulfilled obligations to his Aboriginal kin. He was living with and supporting Charlotte and Mary Ann. Materially providing for Aboriginal kin was part of one's family responsibility, but it was also essential to the survival of many Aboriginal people after whites had taken their lands and resources. On the day of the attack, James Bugg had provided corn and tobacco to the ten Aboriginal men who asked for supplies.

Refusing Aboriginal demands for provisions often led to hostility and violence. In her research on the Worimi people around Port Stephens, Bairstow discovered that all Aboriginal attacks on settlers after 1829 'followed a refusal to hand over flour or blankets'. In the 1820s, the early years of the A. A. Co.'s advance into Aboriginal Country, it appears that the Company distributed provisions unevenly throughout the clans, privileging some Aboriginal groups at the expense of others.[79] By the 1830s, the Company tightened its distribution, providing its employees with enough supplies for their personal use alone. This effectively prevented stations from sharing goods with Aboriginal people.[80] In 1835, Bugg's actions were exceptional as he gave provisions to the Aboriginal men who visited his station. Bugg appears to have fulfilled his responsibility to provide for local Aboriginal people, yet he was the first white man to be targeted in a series of attacks. There must have been other issues at play.

An alternative motive behind the Aboriginal assaults may have had less to do with Bugg's actions than Charlotte's choice of spouse. By the 1830s the number of fertile Worimi women was falling. Aboriginal people often had no immunity to European illnesses and venereal disease was rife among A. A. Co. workers and the Aboriginal women they slept with. 'In the first three months of 1828, recorded cases of venereal disease had risen to 51.9%' of workers, with fifty-four cases of syphilis and fourteen of gonorrhoea. Later that same year the total had increased to 60.7 per cent of Company employees. Both diseases, if left untreated, could lead to infertility, and in 1828 prominent landowner John Macarthur declared that venereal disease in the A. A. Co. had 'already put a stop to the black population in as much as there is not a single black infant to be seen in the arms of his mother'. Although it is possible that Macarthur's definition of 'black infants' overlooked children of mixed heritage, his words suggest a marked decline in the number of childbearing Aboriginal women. The Company made some meagre attempts to separate its workers from Aboriginal women, but sex between the two groups remained commonplace.[81]

In such circumstances, competition for Aboriginal women was fierce, and for fertile women like Charlotte, possibly even greater. Whites frequently coerced, lured or convinced Aboriginal women to grant them sexual privilege at Aboriginal men's expense, and Aboriginal men fought back. Aboriginal masculinity was carefully cultivated in the 19th century.[82] In some areas of New South Wales, new practices that involved hypermasculine behaviour, rituals and magic developed in response to this sexual imbalance and the theft of women. Extreme attempts were made to reinstate patriarchal authority because Aboriginal society was changing so drastically.[83] Charley, an Aboriginal man from the Hunter Valley area and the only person to be convicted for the 1835 attacks, claimed that he murdered a white overseer named Alfred Simmons because he broke gendered law. Simmons apparently showed Charley's 'murai, muari', an Aboriginal amulet, to his female, Aboriginal partner when only men were permitted to view the talisman. According to Aboriginal law of the time, this meant death for both Simmons and his Aboriginal mistress.[84] In this context, it is more than possible that Bugg was attacked so that Aboriginal men could reclaim Charlotte as their own.

The *Australian* newspaper agreed that white men's treatment of Aboriginal women had led to the 1835 'outrages', but by using racist tropes, they were able to quash any sense of wrongdoing:

It may sound well to talk of the reasonable animosity which is raised by the white men taking their [Aboriginal men's] *gins* from them, and it may be asked with much appearance of truth, whether it is necessary to look for other grievances suffered by the blacks from these parties; those, however, who are at all acquainted with life and manners amongst the aborigines know that this is not felt very deeply by a people who scarcely rate the 'fairest jewel of their tribe' at any price whatever, and whose estimation of their partners is some degree below that which they hold their bomrings [sic] and nullah nullahs.[85]

The idea that Aboriginal men cared nothing for their women spared white colonists from reflecting on how their own conduct might have brought about the murders.[86] But for good measure, white men did not use this means alone. They also blamed bushrangers for instigating the attacks.

*

Here we come to another connection between the events of 1835 and Mary Ann's life: the relationship between bushranging and Aboriginal resistance. In the first few weeks after the attacks and murders in the Berrico area, several newspapers reported that Aboriginal people had been directed to commit the crimes by four white bushranging men.[87] For papers like the *Sydney Herald*, it was the collusion between Aboriginal people and white bushrangers that made the violence all the more threatening. '[T]he very fact of the existence of this combination, headed and guided by runaway Convicts, is most alarming to the inhabitants, who constantly expect a renewal of the attacks.'[88] Edmund Ebsworth, A. A. Co. accountant and the Justice of the Peace on the hunt for the Aboriginal suspects, was inclined to agree that there was at least some white involvement. In a letter to the Colonial Secretary, he disclosed that 'from this systematic organisation [of the Aboriginal attacks] I am induced to place some reliance on the report that a white man may be the instigator'. However, an Aboriginal constable named Williams was his informant and according to colonial law, 'the whole information [was] doubtful' as Aboriginal people were not permitted to take an oath.[89] Williams was the only one who claimed to know of a connection between the attacks and white men. While a party of five white bushrangers robbed a property on the Upper Hunter on 31 May, this was never linked to the Aboriginal attacks.[90] One white man named Harvey Henley was imprisoned in Newcastle Gaol on suspicion of his involvement in the Aboriginal crimes, but he was never convicted of anything other than 'failing to keep the peace'.[91] Witness testimony at Charley's trial referred to a white man ordering Aboriginal people to kill all the whites and bring him their possessions, but this was only hearsay.[92] This evidence is all that exists to suggest white men's involvement.

The idea of white leaders was so popular because it resonated with colonists' fears about bushranging, Aboriginal people and rebellion at this time.[93] In the 1830s, the New South Wales government and the Colonial Office in Britain believed that a convict uprising was a real and dangerous possibility.[94] Even though escaped convicts who took to the bush and survived through the proceeds of crime had decreased since the introduction of the *Bushranging Act* in 1830, colonists remained fearful for their safety. The isolation of many settlers, the numbers of transported felons in their midst and the opportunity for concealment in the bush meant that colonists felt vulnerable to attack. In response to the 1835 assaults, for instance, the 17th Regiment had to travel over 250 kilometres from their base in Sydney as there was no permanent force stationed in those outlying districts near Berrico.[95] If nefarious whites and Aboriginal insurgents joined together, there was no telling the damage they could do. A force of Aboriginal warriors at the beck and call of incorrigible runaway convicts could threaten the very existence of 'civilised society'.

The idea that these attacks were orchestrated by whites also aligned with colonists' ideas about the inferiority of the 'Aboriginal race'. Ebsworth clearly did not believe that Aboriginal people were capable of such organised and co-ordinated assaults. They were neither considered intelligent enough for such tactics, nor were they thought to have genuine grievances against colonists.[96] The fact that Aboriginal assailants stole from their victims also strengthened the idea that they were working for, or had learnt their skills from, white bushrangers.[97] Two months after Bugg was attacked, Aboriginal people on the Williams River engaged in activity that was described like a bushranging hold-up:

> On Friday last they [Aboriginal people] stopped our dray on
> its way from Clarence Town, with salt &c.; they knocked down
> the bullock driver ... the only articles the blacks took were a
> canister of gunpowder, and the shoemaker's box, containing his
> clothes. They have also robbed another dray of tea, flour &c., and
> yesterday, a party of them armed with muskets, went to a Settler's
> station, drove the men from their sheep, and robbed the huts of
> three muskets and everything portable. Now that the blacks are
> possessed of firearms, they are of course much more formidable
> than ever ...[98]

Despite the similarities to bushranging, these were common resistance strategies for Aboriginal people. Disrupting transports, taking whites' much-needed possessions and otherwise harassing colonists were tactics to push them out of the area and take back Aboriginal Country.[99] Stealing firearms was another effective strategy as Aboriginal people had long witnessed the power of guns in frontier conflict and had learnt to use them too. The A. A. Co. gave local Aboriginal people guns to help them provide food for the Company stores, especially in the organisation's early years.[100] This was not a case of Aboriginal people following white men or simply mimicking their actions. This activity that appears so akin to bushranging was, in fact, an Aboriginal mode of resistance, and an alternative tradition that could have informed Mary Ann's life with Thunderbolt.

It is important to recognise the stakes of recovering this Aboriginal perspective. If we fail to recognise bushranging's relationship to Aboriginal resistance, we privilege the colonisers' view of the world over that of Aboriginal people. Although the idea that bushrangers could use Aboriginal fighters frightened colonists, it was not as disturbing as recognising that Aboriginal people were capable of co-ordinated violence on their own, or that they were fighting to assert their sovereignty and extricate their land from white control. As the *Australian* saw it, colonists had two options when it came to Aboriginal people: they could either use force to counter Aboriginal resistance or remove themselves from the land. And as the newspaper pithily declared, 'few will be found whose unreflecting philanthropy will recommend the latter'.[101]

There were also connections between Aboriginal resistance fighters and legendary bushrangers like Frederick Ward. Both were ostensibly fighting for freedom from tyranny. Both represented an alternative system of justice at odds with that of white officials. They were both demonised by outsiders, while their actions resonated with the groups to which they belonged. Anthropologist Deborah Bird Rose's work with the Yarralin and Lingara people of the Victoria River District (Northern Territory) even suggests that the mythic type of the bushranger resonates with some Aboriginal communities today, as they draw strength and meaning from bushrangers' struggle against the authorities.[102] This is not to say that Aboriginal warfare and bushranging were the same, but that their intersections shaped the contours of Mary Ann's life. The frontier was not simply a site of colonial domination. Although unequal, power always flowed both ways.

## 1867–1905: MARY ANN BUGG
## FADES FROM VIEW

Mary Ann's family history was shaped by Aboriginal resistance, adaptation and exchange, but by 1866 when Mary Ann's conviction for vagrancy was overturned, frontier warfare had essentially ended in New South Wales. In this period, Aboriginal people were increasingly forced to live on the fringes of colonial society and Mary Ann was no exception.[103] Life after imprisonment was not easy for her. Upon regaining her freedom, she spent at least five months tracking down her fugitive spouse. Having left two of her older children with Ward's family, she took her youngest child with her as she moved from town to town hoping to find word of Captain Thunderbolt. By August, Mary Ann appears to have been close to giving up the chase, as in Tamworth she reportedly declared that if Ward did not come for her soon, then 'she would have to look for a fresh situation'.[104] Although she had previously told the court that her 'husband, Frederick Ward kept her', for these months Mary Ann was essentially an abandoned wife and had to rely on her own resources to survive.[105] There was no government welfare for the poor at this time, as poverty was seen as the sufferer's own fault – it was deemed to be the product of people's personal failings. Family and charities were often the only safeguards standing between people down on their luck and complete destitution, and even then, charities were largely based in cities and towns rather than the outer reaches of the colony.[106] We do not know how Mary Ann managed to survive alone during these months, but sometime between September 1866 and January 1867 it is clear that she found Frederick Ward. Police discovered her at his camp on 6 January 1867. Once again she was arrested, this time for being in possession of stolen goods. After her conviction on 24 January and more than a month in Maitland Gaol, Mary Ann was released upon proof that she had purchased her goods lawfully.[107] And from this point, she fades from public view.

The Thunderbolt legend picks up where the newspaper trail seems to go cold on Mary Ann's life. According to folklore, Mary Ann died that year in 1867, in poignant and dramatic circumstances. After leaving Maitland Gaol for the second time, she apparently re-joined her Captain and they lived together until Mary Ann became desperately ill. Near Muswellbrook, Thunderbolt spent several anxious days tending to Mary Ann, only leaving her side to visit a Mrs Bradford for much-needed supplies. As her condition worsened, Thunderbolt was forced to leave Mary Ann in the care of Mrs Bradford at whose residence, under the alias Louisa Mason (or Yellow Long), she died on 24 November. And that, so the popular tale goes, was the end of 'Thunderbolt's Lady'.[108]

Two recent findings reveal this story to be a complete work of fiction. In 2013 Lorraine Martyn, a resident of the Newcastle area of New South Wales, made a startling discovery about her family history. Her niece had accessed ancestry.com, the online genealogy database, only to discover that Lorraine was related to Thunderbolt and Mary Ann Bugg.[109] This was a shocking revelation. Until this time, Lorraine had been unaware of any Aboriginal heritage in her family, and her branch of the family tree dispelled the myth that Mary Ann died in 1867. Lorraine Martyn is descended from Mary Ann and Thunderbolt's son, Frederick Wordsworth Ward (Jr) who was born in 1868, one year after Mary Ann's supposed demise.[110] In 2013, the same year as Lorraine's discovery, historians David Andrew Roberts and Carol Baxter published an article that also challenged the common account of Mary Ann's death. With forensic attention to detail, Roberts and Baxter proved that the woman who died at Mrs Bradford's that day was, in fact, an Aboriginal woman named Louisa Mason, the wife of Robert Mason, a settler of Rouchel, near Scone in New South Wales. By trawling through birth, death and marriage records, the pair also proved beyond doubt that Mary Ann and Thunderbolt's son was born in 1868.[111] Together, family history and academic research have overturned the narrative of Mary Ann's death that was enshrined in folklore.

The question which naturally follows is why did Mary Ann's untimely death become a part of the Thunderbolt myth? Why did it spread so widely when Mary Ann was still very much alive? One answer lies in Frederick Ward's position as a bushranging hero.[112] If Mary Ann's role as Ward's 'lady love' illustrated his romantic, gallant and chivalrous side, then the story of her dramatic demise exaggerated this even more. It lent an element of tragedy to the tale of a daring highwayman, showcasing a more emotional and human side that might stir sympathy, pity or compassion in an otherwise cold-hearted public. This story could have enhanced Ward's appeal by ensuring that like all great outlaw heroes, he had a personal misfortune to spur him on with his criminal efforts. For now, with the loss of his love, he apparently had nothing left to lose.

That is one answer, but it is not the most compelling. We need to remember that Mary Ann was not just some character in a white man's story. This tale of Mary Ann's death was *essential* to Ward's image because in reality, their separation was far from romantic, fated or enforced. It was her choice.[113] It appears that after being released from prison in 1867, Mary Ann and Ward had one last, brief encounter, when Mary Ann became pregnant with Frederick Ward (Jr) before they parted for good.[114] Frederick Ward famously died at a shootout in the town of Uralla on 26 May 1870, and less than two months *prior* to Ward's death, Mary Ann gave birth to Ada Gertrude Burrows, the daughter of John Burrows, a labourer on the Liverpool Plains.[115] Mary Ann lived with Burrows for at least another two decades until he died at some point between 1887 and 1900. In that time, she purchased, improved and sold land, became a nurse and had at least four more children. In Mudgee at the age of seventy, Mary Ann died of natural causes in 1905.[116]

But it was not simply Mary Ann's life after Ward that complicated the idea of the pair as star-crossed lovers. Mary Ann had already given birth to six children before she lived with Frederick Ward. Her first child was to her first husband, Edmund Baker, while the next two were

FIGURE 4. Samuel Calvert, *The Death of Thunderbolt, the Bushranger*, 1870.
*State Library of Victoria Pictures Collection, IAN18/06/70/116.*

to John Burrows. Her relationship with Burrows later in life was clearly a reunion rather than a new partnership.[117] After her first encounter with Burrows, she bore three children to a James McNally and it was only following this that she met Frederick Ward. These aspects of Mary Ann's life were not remarked on in the press and were never incorporated into the Thunderbolt legend. They certainly did not align well with any chivalric ideal. But if we view this from the perspective of the working classes to which Ward and Mary Ann actually belonged, what we see is very different.

It was not unusual for women from these classes to engage in bigamy and adultery.[118] With no guarantee of charity, many women sought to support themselves and their children by finding a new partner. Women were still in relatively high demand, especially in rural areas in the 1860s, and many who found a willing spouse did not let social niceties get in the way of financial security. This approach to relationships was never celebrated; it never became the stuff of ballads or legends or songs, but it was a practical necessity for many women when survival trumped all else.[119] This did not mean that all such relationships were loveless: there appears to have been a deep affection between Mary Ann and John Burrows. After decades apart, they found each other again, lived as man and wife for over twenty years and had at least six children together. Mary Ann's relationship with Burrows was the longest of her life. It was clearly more than strategic, however it might have been rekindled by Mary Ann's need.[120]

*

Mary Ann's life confounded expectations for the spouse of an outlaw hero. And it forces us to question how central bushranging really was to her story. There is currently a movement to have Mary Ann celebrated as a bushranging hero in her own right. Lorraine Martyn would like to see a statue to Mary Ann alongside Thunderbolt at Uralla.[121] ABC's Radio National ran a program in 2016 labelling Mary Ann a 'bushranger and spy' and calling for greater attention to be paid to 'ratbag women'.[122] In 2018 I was asked to write an obituary for Mary Ann by the Australian Centre of National Biography to redress her absence from the nation's past.[123] All of this interest in Mary Ann derives from the four years she spent with Thunderbolt. While these years were clearly extraordinary, perhaps Mary Ann's biggest achievement was to survive and live peacefully, in obscurity, after such a turbulent time with Ward. For Mary Ann to have lived such a high-profile life and then fade from public view does not reflect a fall from grace but rather a level of freedom that she would never have known while in the public eye. Even though it was not as thrilling as her bushranging career, her life away from public view and institutional control was an achievement in itself, especially for an Aboriginal woman in this era.[124]

We need to remember this context as we face one last fabrication about Mary Ann. Mary Ann Bugg was a Worimi woman. In her lifetime, she was renowned for her Aboriginal heritage. But her death certificate states that she was born in the Bay of Islands in New Zealand and implies that she had Māori ancestry.[125] Back in the 1860s, well before her death, there was also reference to her having Māori heritage. This strongly suggests that Mary Ann chose this identity for herself.[126] This myth was even passed down in family lore. Lorraine Martyn was raised to believe that her great-great-grandmother was Māori, as her father had before her.[127] Claiming to be Māori may appear an odd choice for Mary Ann to make, but it proved another savvy move. Māori held higher status in British eyes than Aboriginal people.[128] Since the late 18th century, the British recognised Māori martial strength, agriculture, trade and settled communities and viewed them as signs of their capacity for civilisation and worthiness of respect.[129] Māori sovereignty was recognised in the Treaty of Waitangi, and by the 20th century, Māori had achieved the position of honorary white men in New Zealand public discourse.[130] Settler Australians similarly believed in the superiority of the 'noble savages' of New Zealand and had experiences with Māori themselves as Māori chiefs, emissaries and subjects had been travelling to New South Wales from as early as 1793.[131] Māori were afforded a greater equality with whites than were Aboriginal people, which likely made Māori status appeal to Mary Ann.

My interview with Lorraine Martyn reveals a more sinister and pressing reason why Mary Ann and her children might have attempted to pass as Māori and why in later generations, her family reinforced this myth. According to Lorraine:

[Mary Ann's Aboriginal heritage] was all kept quiet because I was born in the early forties. And then, they was taken off you

if you had Aboriginal in you, half caste and that and they would
be taken away or treated badly so I think that's why they never
mentioned it.[132]

The late 1800s saw the steady increase of white intervention into
Aboriginal people's lives. As the British consolidated their possession of
New South Wales there were fewer possibilities for Aboriginal people
to live outside of white society. By 1882 a government report estimated
that over half of the Aboriginal population of New South Wales
worked 'more or less permanently' for the whites.[133] This meant that
when drought, depression and economic uncertainty hit in the 1890s,
Aboriginal jobs were the first to go and many had to seek charitable
assistance and move to Christian missions or government-run reserves
to survive.[134] Before 1900, there had already been attempts to remove
Aboriginal children from their families, but these were more ad hoc
than government ordained.[135] In 1883, the Aboriginal Protection
Board (APB) was created ostensibly to 'protect' the 'remnants' of the
'dying race' of Aboriginal people in New South Wales.[136] In its earliest
incarnation, the Board had powers to remove Aboriginal children
from their families for 'educational purposes'.[137] By 1905 when Mary
Ann died, she would have witnessed officials' increasing power over
Aboriginal people's lives, and perhaps this prompted her to claim
Māori heritage – to protect her freedom as well as that of her large
family.[138]

After Mary Ann's death, white control over Aboriginal lives
only increased in breadth and intensity. As historian Anna Haebich
has written, by the turn of the 20th century, with the federation of
the Australian colonies and the advent of the White Australia Policy,
Aboriginal people:

were an anathema to the country's new modernising and
nationalising project. There was no place for them in the
emerging Australian nation. Instead they were to be swept

out of sight into remote 'gulags' or their 'mixed race' children absorbed into the lowest rungs of the colonial workforce or kept permanently in segregated institutions.[139]

In 1909 the *Aborigines Protection Act* gave the APB wide powers to intervene in Aboriginal life, but there were still conditions on when an Aboriginal child could be removed from their parents.[140] In 1915 this procedure was dispensed with as the Board was given the power to remove any Aboriginal child by virtue of their race.[141] Well into the 1960s this practice of removal continued, as children were forcibly taken from their families in the name of welfare, only for many to suffer physical, psychological and sexual abuse from the institutions in which they were raised.[142] In Australia, these Aboriginal children are now known as the 'Stolen Generations'.[143] If Mary Ann's family hid their Aboriginal heritage in the hope of avoiding discrimination and protecting their children, they were not the only ones. If a family looked light enough, they would often try to pass as white. When this option was not available, some families chose the same path as Mary Ann's.[144] By reframing her Aboriginality as Māori before draconian government policy tightened around Aboriginal people, Mary Ann seems to have saved her family from being broken up, her sons, daughters and grandchildren from being persecuted and her descendants from being stolen. Until the very end of her life, Mary Ann had a keen awareness of the power of popular opinion. By creating her own ancestral myth, Mary Ann was not necessarily repudiating her Aboriginal origins, but working to protect the ones she loved.

\*

Mary Ann's story pushes us to question who we celebrate as Australian legends and why. Typical outlaw heroes die extravagantly, in a blaze of glory: that is how they can best secure a place in the popular imagination.[145] But occasionally, bushranging supporters refuse to

believe that their heroes have died. An alternative mythology sometimes emerges, involving official conspiracy and cover-ups, a clever
escape, and an alternative life.[146] There is a group of Thunderbolt fans
today who believe that Frederick Ward escaped to Canada and that
another man met his death at Uralla. Fictional tales of bushrangers'
survival are influential as they enhance their legend and exemplify the
talent these men are supposed to have possessed.[147] But in reality, it
was Mary Ann who lived longer than the stories allowed. She is the
one who assumed a new name, a new life, and who lived in peace until
the end of her long days. In settler society, no one expected as much
of Mary Ann as they did of Thunderbolt. And ironically, that is what
ensured her survival.

FIGURE 5. Unknown Artist, *Jacky Porter, the boy Peter, and the wife of Jimmy Governor*, 1900.

'Jacky Porter, the boy Peter, and the wife of Jimmy Governor', Evening News *(31 July 1900), p. 3.*

# CHAPTER 5

# THE GOVERNOR FAMILY

On Monday 23 July 1900, nine-year-old Albert 'Bertie' Mawbey was called before an inquest in Breelong, northern New South Wales. At the crime scene that was also his home, the child explained all that he knew of his family's murder. Three days previously, at about half past eight at night, Bertie had awoken to 'the voice of a blackfellow singing out, "I will blow your brains out", and stamping his feet'. He 'jumped out of bed and came to the door, and saw a blackfellow standing in the middle of the sitting room'. The black man was 'belting into' his brother, Percy, 'hitting him with a rifle or a stick ... he hit Percy 10 or 12 times'. Albert 'was frightened and ran out over the creek' and this effectively saved him from the same fate as the rest of his household. There were two Aboriginal men in the Mawbeys' residence that night, and they attacked everyone they could find using a tomahawk and an Aboriginal club called a 'nulla nulla'. As Bertie ran three-quarters of a mile to raise the alarm, the screams from the house faded away, and Albert's mother, live-in schoolteacher, brother and two sisters were either dead or dying.[1]

Although Bertie could not identify his family's murderers at the time, he knew one of the culprits well. Jimmy Governor was an Aboriginal man who worked on the family property at Breelong. He had been employed by Bertie's father to put up a fence on the land, and along with his white wife, Ethel, and baby son, Sidney, he had camped on the Mawbeys' property while the work was underway. Jimmy Governor had bought supplies from the Mawbeys' stores, played cricket with the Mawbey boys and then, on 20 July, Governor and his

123

Aboriginal friend Jacky Underwood murdered five members of Albert Mawbey's family. Jimmy Governor's crime spree did not end there. While Underwood was captured soon after the Breelong murders, Governor's brother Joe joined him on the run. They committed countless robberies, murdered four more white settlers, including a pregnant woman and her young child, and evaded the police for three months. This was despite thousands of volunteers and police giving chase, resulting in one of the largest manhunts in Australian history.[2]

To survive on the run from the law, Jimmy Governor committed bushranging crimes – he and Joe were adept at robbery under arms. While these crimes mark him out as one of the bushrangers in this book, it was Governor's murders that caused a colonial sensation. Residents throughout the Australian colonies were gripped by the crimes as newspapers circulated explicit details of the 'Horror at Breelong':

> Hilda Mawbey [11 years old] ... bruise on forehead over left eye; skull broken in behind the ear ... Percy Mawbey [14 years old]: Cut through right ear; cut 8in wide across right side of neck, penetrating vertebrae column in neck; skull fractured across right ear, wound on back top part of head; fracture on crown of skull ... Mrs Mawbey [44 years old]: Brain matter protruding at back of head; hacked about the head and arms with tomahawk.

The list of injuries and victims went on.[3]

The violence of the crimes, the ages and genders of the victims, and the race of the culprits have ensured that the Breelong murders have not been forgotten, but they are no less distorted for that. Today, Governor is most commonly remembered through a work of fiction – Thomas Keneally's *The Chant of Jimmie Blacksmith*. Published in 1972, the book quickly captured the public imagination and was adapted into a film in 1978.[4] The novel won the Royal Society of Literature Prize in 1972 and the *Sydney Morning Herald* Literary Competition the following year, and Keneally's story is the subject of interviews, literary criticism and articles to this day.[5] Keneally's was not the first attempt to bring Jimmy Governor to a popular audience, but it is the most enduring.[6] As Jimmie Blacksmith, Governor became a vessel for Keneally to explore race relations in his own time of the 1970s.[7] *The Chant of Jimmie Blacksmith* was never intended to chronicle the real Jimmy Governor's life. Yet it remains the most pervasive representation of it. Scholars have been no less fascinated with Jimmy Governor and the Breelong murders. Governor has been the subject of local histories, biographies and academic journal articles, as many studies attempted to understand what triggered the Breelong crimes.[8] The massacre is commonly cast as the result of taunts by the Mawbey women about Governor's mixed-race marriage, or as Jimmy Governor's response to a labour dispute. But there has never been consensus as to the cause of the murders.[9]

Although Jimmy Governor's story seems familiar to us, there is much left to understand. For starters, research rarely recognises that the Governor brothers, Jacky Underwood and their victims were not the only ones to be affected by these crimes. Governor's actions forever changed the lives of his own family too. The impact of the murders on Governor's white wife, Ethel, and baby son, Sidney, as well as his Aboriginal relatives from the rural town of Wollar, remains to be told. At first glance it may appear appropriate to separate the Breelong murders from Jimmy Governor's family life. Governor's position as a husband and the head of a family appears at odds with his role as a mass murderer. But this separation is both artificial and ahistorical. It was made by colonists who refused to see Governor as anything more than a 'blood-crazed savage'. In 1900 these two facets of Governor's life existed side by side. And in family stories, their connection is remembered.

Aunty Loretta Parsley is a Yuin woman from the south coast of New South Wales and a direct descendant of Jimmy and Ethel Governor. In contrast to murder, crime and race, she sees her ancestor's life as defined by family:

> I believe that Jimmy had a strong connection to his country and a great loyalty to his family ... Ethel expected that Jimmy would be a loyal husband and a protector of her and their child Sid. Sid and Ethel were to become the most stable and grounding force in the events that led up to Jimmy's capture and consequent hanging in Sydney.[10]

Aunty Loretta's comments encourage us to push beyond colonial accounts and take seriously the connection that Jimmy Governor had with his family. They also help us recognise that the 'Breelong rampage' was always about more than three Aboriginal men. It was a story of Federation, of colonists reckoning with frontier violence and being made to face the survival of First Nations people in the wake of colonisation. In settlers' eyes, it was not only Jimmy Governor's crimes, but his intimate relationships that made him a threat.

## THE FAMILY MAN

In 1900, Jimmy Governor declared that the Mawbeys' ridicule of his relationship with his wife incited him to violence. He stated that the live-in schoolteacher, Miss Kerz, and Mrs Mawbey:

> ... were always poking fun and laughing at us [Jimmy, Ethel and Sidney] and Mrs Mawbey was always getting on to my wife for marrying me, my wife told me Mrs Mawbey said that any white women [sic] who married a blackfellow was not fit to live, and ought to be dead, this made me very wild, as I always worked hard, and paid for everything the same as a white man, and I reckon I am as good ...[11]

These lines are considered pivotal in studies of the Breelong murders as they seem to reveal Jimmy Governor's character. They have been used as evidence that Governor wanted to be a productive member of white society, and that he was indignant when colonists refused to treat him as an equal. They have been used to speculate on Governor's pride and sense of self-worth, his work ethic and position as a member of the working classes, but they have never been used to examine Governor's relationship with his wife.[12] The idea that Jimmy Governor intended to protect and defend his partner has been obscured by the violence that ensued.

But a strong and complex bond existed between Jimmy and Ethel Governor (see Plate 16). Ethel Mary Jane Page, aged sixteen, married James Governor, twenty-three, at the rectory of the Church of England in Gulgong on 10 November 1898. To look at the wedding certificate itself, nothing appears to have been particularly remarkable about this marriage. Although Ethel was young and needed her parents' permission to marry Jimmy, this was not unheard of at the turn of the 20th century.[13] The couple's fathers were both described on the certificate as labourers, and so in class terms, it appears to have been a suitable match. This legal document left no space to write the race of the consenting parties. The only hint that there was anything unusual is that the ceremony took place in the small stone rectory instead of next door, at the church in Gulgong.[14] While some historians have used this as evidence of early racial prejudice that the couple faced, there was another explanation for this peculiar venue. Ethel was already five months pregnant when she became Mrs James Governor.[15]

This piece of information did not just drop from the lips of gossiping locals, but was broadcast in the press almost as soon as the events at Breelong unfolded. It was six days after the murders had been committed, five days since Ethel and her eleven-month-old son Sidney had been captured by police and three days since the inquest into the Breelong murders had begun when the local papers turned their attention to Ethel's sex life. In an article entitled 'The Mysterious White Woman', the *Singleton Argus* presented an exclusive interview with Mrs Governor but laced her statements with local rumour and condemnation:

I have just interviewed Mrs Governor ... She tells me she
was married to Jimmy, who is undoubtedly the instigator
of this awful deed, at Gulgong some 18 months ago by
Rev. F. T. Haviland, Church of England. He only consented, it
is said, to perform the ceremony at the earnest solicitations of
the girl's mother, who, for reasons which may be understood,
wished to save her daughter's reputation. One naturally
wonders what manner of woman the mother was ... The fate
of this girl and her offspring seems more awful, if that may be,
than the victims of her husband's murderous rage.[16]

In a similar tone, the *Mudgee Guardian* reporter declared:

The idea of marrying this white child ... 'to save her name' is
really very, very funny, and ... more or less blasphemous ... it
would have been far better to leave her free to go and sin no
more than to perpetuate her prostitution by cementing it with
the sacrament of marriage.[17]

Despite these vehement statements, Ethel was not a 'prostitute'. She
may have had sex with Jimmy Governor before they were married, but
this was relatively common in colonial Australia. As historian Frank
Bongiorno has written, 'in the late nineteenth century, around a third
of children born in wedlock had been conceived out of it'. The sins of
premarital sex were commonly forgotten if the couple married before
the birth of the child.[18] The baby would not be a 'bastard' but entitled
to the same rights as any child conceived in wedlock.[19] The comments
of these newspapers clashed with common practice, and this is what
makes them significant. Ethel's choice of husband was so disruptive
that normal standards were not applied.

It would be easy to dismiss these articles as an obvious response
to the Breelong murders. Of course Ethel's relationship was ridiculed
– she was married to an Aboriginal mass murderer. But the reality was

not so simple. Strong emotional ties bound Ethel and Jimmy Governor. Even though Ethel publicly condemned her husband's murderous actions, when it came to their personal affairs, she was unswervingly loyal. When asked by a reporter whether it 'would have been better to remain single rather than marry an aboriginal', Ethel responded, 'You might think so, but I was very fond of Jimmy ... I don't want to give him up ... He was very good to me, he was'.[20] In court, when Ethel believed she was being asked whether taunts about her marriage affected her relationship with Governor, she was apparently indignant and bluntly replied, 'No ... not a bit'.[21] Even after the horrors described in the trial, after the judge donned his black cap and passed the sentence of death, Ethel still visited Jimmy Governor in prison until he was taken away and hanged.[22]

In response to these apparent contradictions, newspapers described Ethel as an aberrant woman, 'past comprehension'. Public responses dismissed her as a 'misled slatternly slut' and fixated on the apparent 'depravity of her nature'. White colonists were 'astounded and horrified' but neither they nor later historians have made any real attempt to understand Ethel Governor.[23] When we look at the traces of her life that remain, Ethel's choices appear complex, but not beyond comprehension.

Ethel genuinely wanted to be Jimmy's wife. Even after the murders, she unashamedly told the *Singleton Argus* that 'a lot of girls wanted to have' Jimmy when they lived in Gulgong. Ethel even went as far as to declare that Jimmy had been forced to leave his job as a tracker with the Cassilis police because a 'man threatened to shoot him if he did not marry his daughter'.[24] Decades later in 1960, a witness who knew the Governors was still supporting this view. In the *Coonabarabran Times*, Sam Ellis recalled that 'Jimmy's wife told me the history of their courtship and of how many white girls she beat to him and what a heroine she thought herself when she became legally married to him ...'[25] Ethel was proud that she had won the affection of such a desirable man. More than loyalty, desire or pride, Ethel was also connected to Jimmy through their children. Ethel became pregnant with their second child only weeks before the murders at Breelong.[26] This is a fact that no newspaper and very few history books make note of, but it could be a fierce motivator of her actions.[27] When Ethel gave evidence against her husband at his murder trial, and when she visited him on death row, she was between four and five months pregnant.

One pressing question for Ethel was how she and her children were to survive without the support of her husband. Four days after the Breelong murders, Ethel herself was arrested and imprisoned inside the red brick walls of Dubbo Gaol. She remained there for sixty-nine days without charge as the Attorney General and Crown Prosecutor deliberated what was to be done with her.[28] There is no record of what happened to Sidney while she was incarcerated. When Ethel was released from gaol on 1 October, Jimmy was still on the run from the police and on 23 October he was also declared an outlaw.[29] As such, all of his possessions and money were confiscated by the state, and Ethel was left destitute.[30] Although there had been a brief flourishing of government-sponsored welfare institutions in New South Wales in the 1890s depression, by 1900 these had largely disappeared. The main support came from charities and relied on the goodwill of individuals to provide for the 'deserving poor'.[31] Ethel travelled hundreds of kilometres to move to Sydney as the hunt for her husband escalated, and in November she was found by reporters to be living in one of these charitable institutions while she awaited details of Jimmy's whereabouts.[32]

Ethel had many good reasons to publicly condemn her husband's crimes. Quite apart from any revulsion she might have felt towards the murders, she now relied on the goodwill of white settlers to support her growing family. There is no evidence that Ethel interacted with any of Jimmy's Aboriginal friends or relatives, except for four who stayed with the couple for a short time at their Breelong camp.[33] Despite the *Mudgee Guardian*'s hysterical claims that Ethel had 'consented to live a black gin's life', she did not turn to Aboriginal people, but white society for help.[34] And with her Aboriginal, murderous husband and 'mixed race' offspring, the odds of white society supporting her were not in Ethel's favour.

These facets of Ethel's life did not feature in the press or the everyday gossip that circulated in Breelong because they challenged colonial ideas about race. Relationships between Aboriginal men and white women were almost unheard of in the 1900s. Colonists explained this by insisting that Aboriginal men were undesirable to white women – it was absurd that such men could threaten whites in the sexual or marital stakes.[35] Aboriginal academic Jackie Huggins and historian Thom Blake take this argument even further, revealing that had the tables been reversed and Ethel was Aboriginal while Jimmy was white, the couple would have had to apply to the New South Wales Aboriginal Protection Board (APB) for permission to marry. There were no restrictions governing who Aboriginal men could marry because 'it was inconceivable that a white woman would consent to marry an Aboriginal man'.[36] And yet, Ethel not only remained steadfast in her attachment to Jimmy but boasted that she had *won* her husband. She did not appear to be alone in finding Jimmy desirable. Other white women did too. Jimmy and Ethel Governor's relationship called colonists' beliefs about gender, race and sex into question. Irrespective of the murders, it would never have been accepted by colonial Australians.

\*

As if allegations of prostitution and promiscuity were not enough, colonists also undermined Ethel and Jimmy's relationship through the law.[37] In British law, a wife was never to give evidence against her husband. Eighteenth-century legal theorist Montague Lush went as far as to write that in 'common law, on account of their having the same "affections and interests," neither husband nor wife could give evidence for or against each other'.[38] If one spouse testified against the other it amounted to self-incrimination, as they were one legal entity.[39] In New

South Wales, these British principles were amended and applied in the *Criminal Law and Evidence Amendment Act* of 1891. According to section 6, the husband or wife of someone charged with an indictable offence should 'be competent, but not compellable, to give evidence ...' at their spouse's hearing.[40]

Despite the weight of legal opinion, Ethel stood before three separate hearings and gave evidence about the Breelong murders.[41] And even in the final instance, at Jimmy Governor's murder trial, the issue remained unresolved.[42] Facing a court full of journalists who documented her every movement, lawyers who cross-examined her testimony, hundreds of eager onlookers in the public galleries and a husband who 'never took his eyes off his wife's face', Ethel gave evidence in a highly charged environment.[43] She was well into her testimony before Jimmy Governor's barrister questioned whether she knew that she did not have to testify. Despite two previous hearings where she had given evidence, Ethel initially declared that she was 'not well enough educated to understand' her rights in the matter. It was only after the judge drew attention to Ethel's ignorance and addressed the subject in open court that she changed her mind and agreed to continue her statement.[44] This courtroom of learned white men saw no need to view Ethel as an extension of her husband, or the couple's interests and affections as bound together through matrimony. There was apparently no loyalty, affection, or respect between the two. In the eyes of the law, Ethel and Jimmy's relationship was found wanting.

\*

It is difficult to reconcile the image of Jimmy Governor as a husband and father with that of a murderer who killed women and children. There is an uncomfortable symmetry between Governor's pregnant wife and young son, and the pregnant Mrs O'Brien and her fifteen-month-old son whom Jimmy and Joe killed three days after the Mawbey murders.[45] But the brutality of Jimmy Governor's crimes should not silence his relationship with his family. In 1900 these apparently contradictory images of Governor existed side by side, and it was the strength of Jimmy and Ethel's relationship that made it a threat to colonial society. Its erasure does not reflect historical reality. And its absence from our history books is anything but benign.

## THE ABORIGINAL PEOPLE OF WOLLAR

While silences such as these still plague Governor's story, we are no longer completely blinded by colonists' views. After the 'Great Australian Silence' about white Australia's Aboriginal past began to break in the 1970s, historians and writers changed their approach to the 'Breelong tragedy'. Governor's actions were still condemned, but it was now commonly recognised that 'The murders that Jimmy Governor committed took place against a backdrop of [Aboriginal] dispossession, displacement, oppression and in many cases, the murder of now nameless Aboriginal people'.[46] Although white colonists were also killed by Aboriginal people, the number of Aboriginal victims since 1788 surpassed the number of whites by tens of thousands.[47] But in 1900, four decades after frontier warfare ended in New South Wales, the tables turned and three black men slaughtered whites.[48] This perspective is crucial for understanding the significance of the Governor murders, but it should not distract us from the fact that Aboriginal people were also affected by Jimmy Governor's actions. By moving from the experiences of Jimmy Governor's nuclear family to those of his extended, Aboriginal family at Wollar, we can not only see the impact of the 'Breelong rampage' on Aboriginal people, but how white settlers reacted when they were confronted with frontier violence once more.

*

Wollar is a country village about 50 kilometres from Mudgee, New South Wales. In the 1900s, it was described as 'an eccentric little place, which looks as if it fell into its present position on the flats ... and has been too languid ever since to climb out':[49]

> From the Mudgee side ingress is made through the Wollar Gap, a narrow, winding pass ... coming down this road one almost stumbles on the village as, 200 yards further back, the traveller would not suspect it was so near ... Wild as the country is on the Mudgee side that on towards Merriwa beggars description. For 13 miles to the Goulburn River the country is probably the wildest of any in Australia.[50]

In the 1890s, journalist Harold Mackenzie reported that it was rare to see a group of Aboriginal people, 'as most have long since died out in these parts' although at 'Wollar there are still a small number, who have cosy quarters on the creek bank, living peaceably and happily enough, and at times doing little jobs in the shape of "ringing," burning off, and other things'.[51] At the turn of the century Wollar had a population of only one hundred white residents and the *Daily Telegraph* bestowed it with the dubious honour of being 'one of the deadest [most uneventful] places in the colony' at ordinary times.[52] But in July 1900, 'the sleepy village' awoke to become a 'theatre of frenzied excitement'.[53]

Almost as soon as the authorities received word of the events at Breelong, it was believed that the murderers were making for Wollar and so police and civilians flocked to the town. Less than two weeks later, the *Dubbo Dispatch* declared that 'Wollar resembles a regular camp in time of war. Sentries are posted all round the town, and no one is allowed to pass without the password "Bobs." Men are constantly galloping in for or with instructions'.[54] Newspapers estimated that fifty police officers and over 300 bushmen had descended upon the village, more than tripling its previous population.[55] Despite the swelling number of people, communication was anything but easy. No telegraph lines reached this remote place, and so news of the Governors' whereabouts was often late and hard to disseminate. One reporter even brought his own carrier pigeons to combat this issue, but difficulties persisted.[56] Not only did search parties often return to find that the Governors had been spotted in a different area, but there was little by way of comfort in the town itself.[57] After a 50-mile ride through the scrub, the *Daily Telegraph* correspondent was upset to find that 'every available place [in the town was] crammed with humanity' and that he would have to camp on the floor. All dwellings were initially barred to him as no one had told him the password. And, to add insult to injury, the reporter discovered that the 'local supply of whisky had given out'.[58] These were trying times indeed.

Circumstances were worse for the Aboriginal community at Wollar. Extraordinary steps were taken in the name of protection. Quite apart from fortifying the town, one of the first measures that police and residents took was to relocate the town's small Aboriginal population. The women, children and elderly were taken from the creek into the town centre, where they were locked in the local hall after 7pm each night. This arrangement was maintained from 23 July until 22 August 1900. The young and able-bodied Aboriginal men were separated from the rest of the group and placed in the town's lockup.[59] From the records, it is impossible to tell the exact identities of all the Aboriginal people at Wollar, but a significant number were either Jimmy Governor's relatives or acquaintances. Nevertheless, the day after the Breelong murders, stories began to circulate that Governor intended to harm some of 'the Wollar Blacks'. News reporters and police had difficulty naming Jimmy Governor's intended targets and they were variously described as: 'Jimmy Coombes', three people who killed his father, 'all the blackfellows', 'Jimmy's brothers and sisters and cousins', 'all the blackfellows save … [Jimmy's] mother and uncle'.[60] Despite their inconsistencies, these reports unanimously declared Wollar's Aboriginal people to be in danger.

These newspapers cast the incarceration of the Aboriginal people of Wollar as a benevolent attempt to protect them from their blood-crazed brethren, and this aligned neatly with white understandings. At the turn of the 20th century, many believed that Aboriginal people would soon disappear from Australia. Colonists often remarked that 'in the South [of the country] the blacks ha[d already] practically disappeared' while old settlers remembered a time when Aboriginal people were an inescapable part of the colonial experience and declared how dramatically times had changed.[61] In the wake of Charles Darwin's bestselling work on evolution, it was easy for colonists to imagine the disappearance of Aboriginal people as inevitable.[62] Nature apparently decreed the 'survival of the fittest' – a position white colonists claimed for themselves – and the disappearance of those lower on the evolutionary ladder. As a 'dying race' it appeared that Aboriginal people were in need of settlers' protection.

At the centre of this 'logic' was a myopic view of who counted as a 'real' Aboriginal person. As Paul Irish has written of coastal Sydney, to some Europeans 'local Aboriginal culture was represented by a shrinking group of tribal celebrities with deep links to the local area'.[63] Aboriginal people who were born into a post-contact world were perceived to be less Aboriginal than their ancestors. The 'direct descendants and contemporaries of tribal celebrities were not considered to retain any knowledge or authenticity, especially if they also had European ancestry'.[64] While there may have been a decline in the number of so-called 'real' Aboriginal people by the turn of the century, there was an increase in the number of Aboriginal people of mixed parentage, who were pejoratively termed 'half-castes'. Colonists were particularly aware of this population as many sought colonial support in the wake of the 1890s depression, and anxiety about the 'half-caste problem' only grew alongside concerns about the declining birth rate among white settlers.[65] Although some colonists saw Aboriginal people as part of a vulnerable, vanishing race, others feared the growth of the mixed-race Aboriginal population of which Jimmy

Governor was a part. Colonial ideas about race could make menaces as well as victims of the Aboriginal people of Wollar.

Absorbing Aboriginal people into the white community (on unequal terms) was touted as one solution to this issue, but Jimmy Governor challenged this approach. His life before his crimes appeared to be a perfect example of successful assimilation. Governor attended various public schools until he was able to start working. He was an expert sportsman, and 'old Wollar residents recalled that "Jimmy was quick and intelligent and learned to read and write well" ... [he was] ... "well liked, handsome, strong, agile, sober, hardworking, honest and trustworthy"'.[66] Governor never seems to have aspired to transcend his class, but he took pride in his work and appealed to working-class respectability.[67] After the massacre at Breelong, it was Jimmy Governor's exposure to white culture that worried his Anglo contemporaries. 'It seems dreadful to contemplate that two men [Jimmy and Joe Governor], who have moved in the midst of civilisation from their cradle, yet are not civilised, can continue to go on to such desperate end' an *Evening News* reporter bewailed.[68]

To white observers, Jimmy Governor's actions seemed to prove that Aboriginal people were incapable of accepting the 'gift of civilisation'. Despite the appearance that Governor had assumed white ways, he turned his back on that life at the same time as destroying the lives of others. This had serious ramifications for the Aboriginal people of Wollar. While Governor's family was demonised in the press as 'loafers', many of his Wollar relatives also worked on local properties and had the same education.[69] There appeared to be nothing to stop Jimmy Governor's 'tribe' from following in his criminal footsteps. Only a small number of metropolitan newspapers ever painted the Wollar Aboriginal people as victims in need of support. The more powerful narrative, especially in regional Australia, was that the 'Wollar blacks' were dangerous and white people needed protection from them. There was a strong argument that if left to their own devices, 'the other blacks ... would be too eager to join the desperadoes in their ghoulish deeds'.[70]

The idea that the Aboriginal people of Wollar were confined to protect them breaks down even further when we recover the experiences of the five Aboriginal men who were imprisoned in the Wollar lockup. For approximately twenty-seven days these men were contained in a log cell 10 feet squared in size. They remained in this 'building' for all but four hours during the day, when they were allowed out for exercise. They were never charged for any offence during their incarceration.[71] While this arrangement must have been known to all within the small town, only the *Mudgee Guardian* and *Evening News* reporters felt inclined to mention the matter to their readers, and they did not condemn the situation. Although the *Evening News* reporter conceded that the 'blacks' had always been law-abiding members of the local camp and were now '... under lock and key, padlocked in a dungeon', he thought this was for the best. The correspondent believed that they were 'better where they then were ... [and] that they would only get into mischief if Jimmy and Joe Governor palled in with them'. The *Mudgee Guardian* reporter agreed.[72]

Far from questioning the legality of these measures, local residents pushed to get the Aboriginal men sent even further away. Senior Sergeant D'Arcy supported the move, not only because the men complained of their cramped conditions in Wollar, but because, by removing them, two dangers might be averted. Holding the Aboriginal men in a more secure facility would thwart their supposed desire to 'emulate the exploits of the brothers Governor'. Plus, the move might protect the Aboriginal men from the white residents of Wollar. D'Arcy wrote to his superior that 'the feeling of the residents is so intensely hostile to the Aborigines that in their own interests they should be sent away from here'. Superintendent Thomas Garvin deferred to D'Arcy's request and on 18 August 1900 five warrants were issued for the men's arrest. On 19 August they were shackled with leg irons and chained to one another as they entered Mudgee and proceeded to the town's gaol. The five Aboriginal men were then remanded for eight days although they had not been charged with any crime.[73] It was only at this point that the treatment of these men began to gain wider attention and divide public sympathies.

On Thursday 23 August, Legislative Council Member George Cox stood before the House and asked 'by what authority the blacks had been taken in charge and put in confinement at Mudgee, in view of the fact that no charge had been made against them'.[74] In parliament there was, for the first time, official intercession on these Aboriginal men's behalf, but interest in the matter was short-lived. While official inquiries were made, the press largely dismissed the issue. Most voiced the opinion that while 'the legality of this step has been questioned … the general feeling is that, under the circumstances, the step is a judicious one'.[75] The last public comment made on the matter was that of WH Suttor, who retorted on that same day that while 'due inquiries would be made … he wished to say that there was nothing unusual about blacks being arrested for having no visible means of support'.[76] He was, of course, correct in this appraisal. As we know from Mary Ann Bugg's experience, as early as the 1860s Aboriginal peoples' exemption from the *Vagrancy Act* was being eroded. As time progressed, the Act became a useful tool for authorities to move unwanted Aboriginal people and criminalise any nomadic way of life.[77] However, these Aboriginal men were never charged with vagrancy or any other crime. And regular vagrants were not transported almost 50 kilometres in leg irons and handcuffed to one another in the depths of winter. These arrests clearly did more than confine 'idle and disorderly persons'.[78]

One of the problems faced by the Aboriginal people of Wollar was the conflation of Aboriginal protection and colonial policing in New South Wales, and this was made painfully apparent on 30 August when Edmund Fosbery, the Inspector General of Police and Chairman of the APB, was asked about the chaining. The APB was a government-sponsored body responsible for Aboriginal welfare and, during one of its meetings, board member JM Chanter asked Fosbery whether there was any truth in the claims that some of the 'Wollar blacks' were chained. 'The chairman [Fosbery] said that he did not think that the statements could be true' to which Chanter expressed his relief as 'it would be a very extreme step to put those people in chains'. On hearing this, it appears that Fosbery felt the need to qualify his statement and he rejoined by saying 'that he would not absolutely say that it was wrong to do so, as ... it was just possible that for a short period the police might have to chain the prisoners'.[79]

This exchange reveals two competing responses to the Governors' time on the run. Chanter was the member for the Murray district in the Legislative Assembly, and although a pastoralist, his interests lay to the south of the colony and safely out of harm's way from the Governors.[80] His criticism of chains reflected the widespread, progressive view that they had no place in civilised colonies on the eve of Federation.[81] While frontier warfare in the north and west of Australia continued into the 20th century, in New South Wales, it had largely ceased by the 1860s and '[a]fter nationhood in 1901, Australian histories became clothed in the rhetoric of peaceful settlement'.[82] In this context, chains were associated with slavery, barbarity and backwardness.[83] The history of convict chain gangs gave them an unwelcome familiarity, and they appeared a shameful relic of a past that was better left buried.[84] By contrast, Fosbery positioned himself as a pragmatist. While he recognised that the use of chains was undesirable, he refused to say that it was unnecessary. Fosbery and Superintendent Garvin co-ordinated the efforts to catch Jimmy and Joe Governor.[85] Under Fosbery's watch, four more people had been killed since the Breelong murders.[86] With police efforts criticised by the public and the press, the strains on his department's budget and the body count rising, Fosbery could not completely prioritise progressive symbolism over public safety. The word 'completely' is important here. Fosbery was well aware of public perceptions, and we know this because at the APB meeting, he lied. He knew that the Wollar men had been chained. He knew this not only from the press or the eyewitnesses, but because his superintendent had ordered it.[87]

Fosbery truly believed that the colony was in a state of crisis and that unpalatable measures needed to be taken to restore order. In the

'Governor rampage', he saw reverberations of the past and glimpses of an apocalyptic future. Five days after the Mawbey murders the APB saw fit to comment on the attack. While the general consensus was that this was an isolated incident that stood in contrast to 'the generally peaceful character of the aborigines of the colony', Fosbery disagreed:

> Mr Fosbery ... could speak from personal experience of a time when the Aborigines in many districts were dangerous to white people. He recalled a period between thirty and forty years ago when the blacks on the River Murray had become so aggressive, attacking white people and spearing them, that a mounted party, of which he was one, had to be organised in order to put down the trouble.[88]

The Inspector General of Police and the Chairman of the APB had firsthand experience of frontier warfare, and he was not the only one to let memories of the past colour his vision of the present. Although the vast majority of newspapers depicted Jimmy Governor's mother, Annie, as a harmless woman and concerned mother, the *Singleton Argus* and *Northern Star* conjured up a monster. According to these papers, it was Mrs Governor who encouraged 'her sons to do acts of violence, as she states the Government took the poor blacks' country, giving them nothing in return'.[89]

In 1900, the colonists of New South Wales had not forgotten the violence of the frontier. There were many like Fosbery who had first-hand experience of frontier warfare, while others were privy to stories through word of mouth or popular culture.[90] Confident that Aboriginal people were disappearing, some colonists felt comfortable enough to acknowledge that 'there was more might than right about their dispossession'.[91] But as Jimmy and Joe Governor traversed the country, evading police and murdering white colonists, such admissions could not be made so freely. Significantly, the *Singleton Argus* and *Northern Star* were the only newspapers to make explicit reference to Aboriginal dispossession in their coverage of the Governor case. They demonstrate that at least some white New South Welshmen saw the Governors' actions as revenge for colonisation, and because of this, a combination of fear and guilt infused their words.

Inspector General Fosbery, however, felt no such compunction. Whether 'full blood' or 'half-caste', there were certainly enough Aboriginal people for him to fear an uprising in 1900:

> I am certain had police not taken the steps they did and matters had turned out as supposed there would have been a rising from one end of the country to the other ... I am quite aware that perhaps the police went further in this matter than they were legally justified in doing but there cannot be any doubt that it was far better that such a course be pursued than have further serious crime if not murder committed.[92]

Senior Sergeant D'Arcy at Wollar shared the Inspector General's opinion. Before the Wollar Aboriginal men were moved to Mudgee, D'Arcy wrote to his superior that 'sooner or later the Aborigines will have to be shifted from here otherwise the growing males are likely to cause a recurrence of the present trouble'.[93] The *Mudgee Guardian* and residents of Wollar took this one step further again. Residents lobbied Fosbery to move the remainder of the 'tribe' at Wollar while the *Guardian* labelled these people 'the problem of the future'.[94] With a frenzy of questions, the paper asked:

> What is going to be done with all these people? Is society, unmindful of the lessons of the past, going to permit the younger members of the Wollar tribe to grow up in the same surroundings and the same life led by Jimmy and Joe? Who is going to take up this question, and see it forced to an issue, free from the sentimental twaddle which some people are already talking about the rights of these people?[95]

At the turn of the century there was a pervasive fear that New South Wales had regressed to the warfare of the past, and that Aboriginal people were a threat to the burgeoning Australian nation. But alongside the panic about public safety, the Breelong murders also presented a unique opportunity. As early as the 1880s, there was nostalgia for the glory days of the Australian bush in the south-eastern colonies. The nomadic bushman was being revived as a national icon at the same time that these people were disappearing from the landscape. Advances in transportation, communication and the mechanisation of agriculture eroded the need for rugged men trained in the arts of the bush, and the ex-convicts who had been bushmen of necessity were growing old and dying. Progress and urbanisation bred nostalgia for a rougher but more honest bush culture; the pioneers were gone and contemporary colonials cherished their memory.[96] Or so it seemed until 1900. Jimmy Governor's crimes offered white men a chance to relive the danger and glory of the past. The frontier was a reality once more, and its challenges allowed Australian men to position themselves as the inheritors of the bush tradition at the same time as proving their manly mettle.

Letters flooded into the Inspector General's office from men seeking to assist in the capture of the 'Breelong Blacks'. There was correspondence from North Sydney, Neutral Bay, Paddington, Newtown, Darlinghurst, Redfern and myriad other metropolitan police stations from officers asking to be transferred to the case. Civilians from all over the country showed no less interest. They wrote to the Inspector General in their hundreds and their original letters are held by the State Archives and Records Authority of New South Wales. It is possible to get a sense of the vastly different backgrounds, wealth and education of their writers from the different quality and size of the paper, the clarity of their spelling and expression, and the legibility of their hand. To recommend their services, these men claimed to have various qualifications. Some had apparently grown up in the bush and had an intimate knowledge of the Governors' beat. Others claimed to 'know as much about the darkies ... as any one [sic] in Australia' and thought that they could put this knowledge to good use by tracking down the Governors. Despite their diverse backgrounds, there were two claims that dominated all others; that the volunteers were good shots, and excellent bushmen.[97]

Although many of these men wrote from suburban areas, they did not necessarily fabricate their bush skills. At a time when railway lines and improved roads facilitated greater movement between the city and the bush, the jobs once taken by rural swagmen were increasingly picked up by the urban unemployed who fled cities in search of work. Even though these men were not romanticised like the nomadic workers of old, they did have practical experience in the wilds of New South Wales.[98] Many policemen in search of the Governors also had years in the bush to recommend them, however, there was some distinction drawn between the two groups. While the civilians depicted themselves as the true heirs of an illustrious bush tradition, the police were often cast as outsiders. They were part of an organised, modern force that appeared to stand in contrast to the individual prowess and instinct of the expert bushman. Sometimes civilians joined police parties and they worked together to find the Governors (see Plate 17), but in general there was antagonism and rivalry between them.[99]

In reality, both parties could be as bad as each other. Superintendent Garvin complained that the civilians were 'doing mischief and working without system running over one another'. He went as far as to declare that 'I believe had the pursuit been left to police from the start offenders would have been captured before this – they [the volunteers] are far too noisy and many of them absolutely useless to us'. False reports of the Governors' whereabouts swept the country and the public was often blamed for misinforming the authorities. At the same time, the police were not beyond reproach. They roamed around in impractically large groups, left towns completely undefended to follow unsubstantiated leads, and in at least one instance, they were so poorly co-ordinated that two search parties nearly shot each other by mistake in the dark. In spite of the fact that both the authorities and the volunteers were far from ideal trackers, there was very little reference to the civilians' failings in the press. Internal police correspondence and the odd police press release were the only platforms used to complain about the volunteers, and so public condemnation centred almost exclusively on the police.[100]

More than simply denigrating the authorities, the widespread reportage of police ineptitude strengthened many volunteers' resolve to track down the Breelong murderers as well as solidifying their own sense of belonging and purpose. It is often said that nationalism is forged through war and that identity is articulated most clearly in the face of an enemy. In Australian history, the country's involvement in the First World War is usually depicted as the 'birth of the nation', but there were other instances of war before this.[101] While the search for Jimmy and Joe Governor was underway, thousands of Australian troops were fighting for the British in the South African War (also known as the Boer War).[102] Some servicemen returned from the frontline to join the hunt for the 'Breelong Blacks', and this search was itself a bloody national awakening.[103] In New South Wales, for the first time since frontier violence ended in that colony in the 1860s, there was a profound fear of uprising. While the frontier wars were tainted by the moral ambiguity of dispossession, in the chase for the Governors, men mobilised to defend women, children and the elderly, who were the brothers' victims. And so, with righteousness on their side, hundreds of men sought to protect their communities, display their aptitude as bushmen, and continue a noble bush tradition.

It was with great satisfaction to the volunteers, then, that civilians were the ones to bring the Governors' criminal careers to an end. On Saturday 27 October, a party of seven local men had captured Jimmy Governor at Bobin.[104] A few days later on Wednesday 31 October 1900, a grazier named John Wilkinson shot Joe Governor as he was roused from sleep near St Clair.[105] The end of the Governor brothers' 'reign of terror' quickly entered the popular imagination. In 1903, a bush ballad was created to commemorate the 'Breelong Rampage'.

Entitled the 'Ballad of the Breelong Blacks', the poem cast the hunt for Jimmy Governor as a victory for the white volunteers. After more than sixty stanzas describing the murders at Breelong, the ballad recounted the capture of the killers:

> It was the civilians who brought them [Jimmy and Joe] to justice,
> And not the troopers, I vow,
> For had they been left to the Johns,
> I think they would be out there now.

Ordinary white men had proven themselves by putting a stop to the Governors' depredations. The men of the new Australian nation had been tested and were not found wanting. But significantly, there was no mention of those months of anxiety when the Governors were on the run. The ballad spun the illusion that the Governors' crimes only affected white society and the 'Breelong Blacks' themselves.[106] The reality was not so simple.

While Jimmy and Joe were at large, the lives of the Aboriginal people at Wollar continued to change. After their arrival at Mudgee Gaol, the five Aboriginal men from Wollar were held in prison without charge for twenty-four days. This arrangement only ended because the presiding magistrate became frustrated with the Inspector General's insistence that the men remain indefinitely on remand. The police magistrate declared that 'if the Government intended that the men should remain in gaol until the Governors were caught, he thought they would remain there all their lives'. He recommended they be moved to Brewarrina Aboriginal Mission instead.[107] After hasty consideration, Fosbery sent the five men and the remnants of the group at Wollar to the mission. Technically, the APB did not have the legal power to move Aboriginal people until 1909, but with Fosbery in charge of the police, there was a force ready and willing to remove these people from their home.[108] All but four of the Aboriginal men, women and children of Wollar were moved to Brewarrina Aboriginal Mission on

23 September 1900.[109] Here, they were denied rations and clothing until at least mid-October.[110] The group were labelled 'indolent' by mission authorities and punished for refusing to work.[111] Jacky Governor, Jimmy and Joe's brother, escaped, and it appears that months later, at least some of the group found their way back to Wollar.[112] But the evidence here is too thin for their story to be told any further.

*

Jimmy Governor's family are critical to understanding his story. Ethel Governor and the Aboriginal people of Wollar had their freedom curtailed and became the objects of slander, speculation, fear, local gossip and condemnation in response to Governor's 'rampage' – but they did not suffer the same indignities. Although both were imprisoned illegally, Ethel was portrayed as unintelligent, promiscuous and degraded by circumstance (having married an Aboriginal mass murderer) rather than by nature, and this hastened her release from prison. There had been whispers that Ethel Governor was present at the Breelong massacre, but this evidence was never substantiated, and Ethel was released without charge after serving sixty-nine days in Dubbo Gaol.[113] She was condemned as a traitor to her race, rather than a criminal.

What the Aboriginal people of Wollar experienced was different. According to colonists, they were criminal by nature – fated to savagery by virtue of their race. Governor's crimes apparently proved that even a relatively 'civilised' Aboriginal person could not deny their true nature and would leap at the opportunity to shed blood.[114] This perverted view was used to justify colonists' intervention in Aboriginal people's lives long after Governor was executed in 1901. Jimmy Governor's crimes shook the Australian colonies and pumped fear through the nascent nation on the eve of Federation. They resonated with settlers' memories of frontier violence and bolstered their understanding of race as something fixed, immutable and static. And according to colonists, they tarred all First Nations people by association.

## CHAPTER 6

# JIMMY GOVERNOR
# THE BUSHRANGER

On Wednesday 8 August 1900, Jimmy and Joe Governor robbed the camp of an opossum trapper named Byrnes at Rockgidgiel.[1] This was by no means the first time the pair had stolen from unsuspecting settlers. It was then nineteen days after the Breelong murders, and either by stealth or by force, the brothers took everything they could to survive on the run from the law. Unlike white bushrangers like Captain Thunderbolt who came before them, the Governors did not have access to a 'bush telegraph' of supporters for information, or local harbourers to provide them with shelter and sustenance.[2] Murdering white women, children and the elderly did nothing to endear them to colonists, and their Aboriginal heritage only positioned them further outside of white society. For the Governors, living as outlaws required being constantly on the move as well as outsmarting and outlasting their pursuers in the elements. But the environment could be harsh and unforgiving. Food from the land was often seasonal, scarce or unyielding. Jimmy and Joe Governor traversed arid grasslands and thickly wooded forests, plunged down gullies and scaled rocky outcrops. They travelled hundreds of kilometres – far enough that even the dirt that caked their boots and feet would have changed hues, oscillating from browns to reds and chalky golds. Despite their bush skills the brothers did not always have the resources, and they certainly did not have the time, to live off the land alone. The Governors robbed to survive.

While it was not unusual for Jimmy and Joe Governor to steal, in this instance in August 1900, Jimmy Governor left something in exchange for the food, ammunition, cheque book, blue serge suit and boots that he and Joe had taken from their unwitting victim, Byrnes. About a mile from the camp, Governor left a letter addressed to the Inspector General of Police.[3] In this, he described himself as a bushranger, and provided a short list of grievances that had led to his turn to crime.[4] This was not the first nor would it be the last time that Governor claimed to be a bushranger. He had brought up bush-ranging before he broke the law and he persistently called himself a bushranger during his months on the run. This is one of those rare instances where the archive contains more than the chatter of white settlers. Here, we have the perspective of a person of colour – we have Jimmy Governor's words. In his own eyes, Governor was not simply robbing to sustain himself. He saw himself as a bushranger. He claimed a remarkably white, colonial, criminal persona as his own.

Although we have Governor's voice, it is important to remember who held the narrative power here. Governor might have committed 'robbery under arms' and identified as a bushranger but this was not enough to make colonists recognise him as such. White bushranging men were increasingly lauded as Australian legends at the turn of the 20th century, and no one wanted a black murderer in the pantheon of emergent national heroes. And so bushranging was written out of Governor's story by settlers after his execution in January 1901 and has largely been left out of histories ever since. This chapter is the first to take seriously Jimmy Governor's repeated assertions that he was, in fact, a bushranger.[5] This claim from an Aboriginal man would have been unusual at any time, but it was particularly so in 1900 when most colonists believed that bushranging was a relic from a bygone age. Bushrangers were perceived to be more folklore than reality, more romantic than any real, viable threat in 1900, although they did live on in people's imaginations. Thanks to popular culture, the impact of bushranging remained strong enough that in 1900, Jimmy Governor declared that white bushranging tales had inspired him to commit a slew of serious crimes. But this was not simply a case of mimicry or history repeating itself. The way Governor saw bushranging, the affinity he felt with past robbers and the grievances for which he sought redress were uniquely his own.

## RECOGNITION

Connections between Jimmy Governor and bushranging were made only seventy-two hours after the murders at Breelong, and they came from two unlikely sources. The first was hearsay testimony from two members of the Mawbey family, including Percy Mawbey, one of the murder victims. At the inquest on 24 July at the remnants of the Mawbeys' homestead, John Mawbey declared that his sons 'Percy and Reggie had heard Jimmy Governor say that he would like to be a bushranger as no police could ever catch him'.[6] In all probability the Mawbey boys thought that the statement was mere bravado, but this was not the first time that Jimmy Governor showed an inclination towards bushranging. We know this from our second source of information, Ethel Governor. At the same inquiry, at the scene of her husband's crimes, Ethel told reporters that two months after she married Jimmy in 1898, 'he said "I will be a bushranger before long"' and that Jimmy had been reading about bushrangers when he was a tracker in the Cassilis police, back in 1896.[7] Ethel Governor's words were also the first to explicitly connect Jimmy's desire to be a bushranger with the Breelong crimes. She told the inquiry that when Jimmy Governor and Jacky Underwood came back from the Mawbeys' house on the night of the attacks, Jimmy declared 'we are bushrangers now'.[8] From this point on, allusions to Jimmy Governor and bushranging flitted in and out of coronial inquiries, court records and newspaper articles. On the rare occasion that newspapers referred to bushranging, they were usually reporting statements that Jimmy or Ethel Governor had themselves provided.[9]

The *Clarence and Richmond Examiner* was one of the few exceptions. The paper was published in Grafton – a rural area so far north-east in New South Wales that it never felt the sting of the Governors' crimes personally. Yet its residents were apparently no less interested in the Governors' case and its reporter felt qualified to argue passionately against Jimmy Governor ever being seen as a bushranger. According to this journalist, race was not the issue. It was cowardice:

> ... if he had been a bushranger who had stuck up coaches in a dramatic manner, or if in the commission of his crimes he had displayed great courage, the court would have been rushed to see him at the dock. But there was nothing heroic or picturesque about the man. On the contrary, he was the most cowardly murderer that has ever been tried in this country. He attacked people when they were defenceless and his scheme of murder embraced women and children as well as men.[10]

Bushrangers had always needed to adhere to a code of conduct to secure public support. Bravery and daring were prized in this heroic tradition as they showed that bushranging men possessed the resolve to fight for their freedom.[11] But it was not just pluck that made a bushranger worthy of assistance and praise. It was their values. Following a moral code ensured that bushrangers were not seen as 'real' criminals by their supporters, even though they acted outside of the law. A crucial tenet of the bushranging code was the protection of the weak and vulnerable, and Jimmy Governor completely disregarded these rules.[12] He targeted women, children and the elderly, the three groups that were most in want of protecting. There was no prowess required to cut down people perceived as defenceless innocents. To colonists, Governor could never be a bushranger as his actions were too dishonourable. He could not be described with a term that so often elicited praise.

But the reality was never as clear-cut as the *Clarence and Richmond Examiner* suggested. The most celebrated Australian bushrangers of all time, the Kelly gang, plotted a similar attack that targeted civilians as well as the authorities. Although at the time these men were not unanimously seen as heroes, they had a groundswell of support that the Governors did not enjoy.[13] In 1880 after two years at large, Irish-Australian bushranger Ned Kelly and his gang attempted to derail a special police train. The group forced railway workers to tear up a stretch of track, hoping to wreck the train as it journeyed to the rural town of Glenrowan in Victoria.[14] While the train contained police officers and trackers who were intent on the gang's demise, it also contained 'innocents': train staff, journalists, photographers and at least two female civilians. In the end, the bushrangers' plan never came to pass. The police were alerted to the death-trap that awaited them and the train stopped before the broken tracks. The authorities surrounded the Glenrowan Inn where the Kelly gang and the local townsfolk (their hostages) were hauled up, and a shootout began. This is where the Kellys donned their now-famous metal armour and had their last stand. The gang's plan failed, and their lives were forfeit as a result. But this bloody end should not distract us from the Kelly crew's murderous intentions. They may have failed to derail this train, but it was not for want of trying.[15]

This was not even the first time that Ned Kelly, the leader of the gang, had gotten blood on his hands. In 1878, he murdered Constable Lonigan, Constable Scanlan and Sergeant Kennedy at Stringy Bark Creek. Whether from remorse or recognition of the damage this might do to his reputation, Kelly attempted to justify the killings. For instance, he later claimed that he had first shot Kennedy in self-defence and then as an act of mercy as the officer was mortally wounded, however, new evidence suggests that his death was a deliberate execution. Ned Kelly followed the wounded Kennedy as he fled through the towering gumtrees at Stringy Bark Creek and shot him at point-blank range. His body was then stripped of all valuable possessions.[16] The most famous and beloved bushranging gang in Australian history committed murder and intended to kill more, including women and civilians. Clearly, murder itself was not enough to prevent criminals from being recognised as bushrangers, let alone bushranging heroes.

FIGURE 6. James Waltham Curtis, *A Strange Apparition –*
*Ned Kelly's fight and capture*, 1880.

*State Library of Victoria Pictures Collection, IAN17/07/80/120.*

Murder and cowardice are not the most compelling reasons why Jimmy Governor was rarely called a bushranger. More significant was the fact that times had changed between the bushranging decade of the 1860s and Governor's crimes in 1900. When white, male bushrangers operated in the 1860s, they had a distinct base of supporters. These men appealed to lower working-class, colonial-born white colonists who felt disenfranchised, exploited and forgotten by the well-to-do classes in society, especially the well-heeled British immigrants who disdained them.[17] By the time the Kelly gang were operating in late 1870s Victoria, bushranging was largely a thing of the past. Ned Kelly and his men were stragglers, almost a generation too late to be a part of bushranging's 1860s golden age.[18] After Ned Kelly was hanged in 1880, another two decades elapsed before Jimmy Governor's exploits.[19] In this intermission popular interest in bushrangers had only grown. Two decades were enough for these figures to have largely receded into myth. The bush skills colonists prized were exemplified by bushrangers who could evade police and survive in the bush.[20] Their escapades increasingly became titillating stories, based on real people but untethered from the messy, nasty and gruesome aspects of real bushrangers' lives. Although bushrangers were always depicted as criminals on the run from the law, the distressing details of their crimes faded from view.

Take for instance, Dan Barry's drama, *The Kelly Gang*. This 1898 play unashamedly rewrote history, insisting that the bushrangers were honourable men fighting against the tyranny of the authorities. The Ned Kelly of this play reveals his ardent belief that killing is wrong (unless in self-defence) when he stops the execution of Sergeant Kennedy. With the passing of time, details that clashed with bushranging legends (like the fact that it was Kelly who killed Kennedy) could be erased or forgotten.[21] In this play, as well as other forms of popular culture at the turn of the century, bushrangers were forced into their criminal situation by an unjust society, and their actions were informed by an unimpeachable standard of ethics that excused any recourse to crime.

Many of these bushrangers' original supporters believed this at the time they were roaming the bush, but by the 1900s this view was so pervasive that it had gained support from all manner of society.[22] This cult of forgetfulness allowed bushrangers to inform the ideal national type and provide an inheritance that the nascent Australian nation could gladly receive.[23] It was at the same time that bushrangers were being recast as romantic rebels fighting for justice that Jimmy Governor tried to claim the title as his own. From this perspective, Governor's exclusion from the bushranging tradition is easily explained. The threat he posed to colonial Australians was too real and pressing to be similarly repurposed or forgotten.

Despite its glaring absence from the *Clarence and Richmond Examiner*'s report, race was another issue that placed Jimmy Governor outside the emergent bushranging mythos. As we have already seen, Aboriginality and 'blackness' were closely associated with memories of frontier warfare in 1900, and colonial Australians were quick to revive these ready-made signifiers to pigeonhole Jimmy and Joe. The pair were referred to as 'black murderers', 'the black fiends', 'the Breelong Blacks' and 'the black terror'. Their barbaric actions became synonymous with the colour of their skin. Far from settler heroes or colonial poster boys, the Governors threatened colonists' lives at the same time as challenging their vision for the new nation's future. They were a terrifying reminder that Australia would never be white. Colonists could expel 'aliens' and prevent 'undesirable' races from entering the country once the Australian colonies had federated.[24] But Aboriginal and Torres Strait Islander people are *First Nations* people. They had lived for tens of thousands of years on the land the colonists had so recently claimed.[25] Despite frontier violence and disease and *terra nullius*; despite missions and reserves and white men carving up Country with title deeds and fences and houses; despite clearing and planting and 'taming the land' – Indigenous Australians survived. And they did not appear to be going anywhere.[26]

# GRIEVANCE

As much as this troubled colonists, race helped them here too. Attributing the Governors' crimes to their 'inherently savage' nature allowed colonial Australians to overlook any wrongdoing on their own part. And it had the added bonus of preventing the brothers from being seen as rational men acting in response to genuine grievances. This characterisation was critical because Jimmy Governor *did* have genuine grievances – he even articulated them in a manner familiar to colonists. Governor left notes and letters for the police when he was on the run, echoing the infamous Kellys. In 1879 Ned Kelly dictated a fifty-six-page letter at the town of Jerilderie in which he outlined the wrongs he and his family had suffered at the hands of the authorities and justified his resort to crime. At over 8000 words, it was a long statement, but it touched on well-worn bushranging themes: the need for the rich to share their wealth with the poor, the corruption of the police and the persecution the Kellys faced from representatives of colonial justice.[27]

Governor's letters are much less elaborate, the longest being only a couple of paragraphs.[28] On first inspection, they bear little resemblance to a justification for his actions. In the first letter Governor left for his detractors, for example, he wrote:

> I bushranger now; they would not register my dog or let me ride in the train free, and they all have a set on me at Dubbo. This is my horse now. I bushranger now ... Put this in the *Sydney Mail* so they can all see it – Jim Governor.[29]

Unsurprisingly, colonists did not view these as very compelling reasons for mass murder. On reading this declaration, a contributor to the *Mudgee Guardian* proclaimed that although 'sentimentalists' might offer excuses for Jimmy Governor's actions, Governor's own words proved that it 'did not take much to drive him to adopt a career of murderer ...'[30] Or did it? This letter was clearly important to Governor. He risked death or capture to write these lines, took pains for them to be found, and specifically demanded that they be circulated in the press. Dismissing Governor's words does not take us any closer to understanding his actions. But if we situate this letter in the world in which he lived, a rich and complex picture quickly comes into view.

Governor's claim that 'they would not register my dog ...' might seem trivial but it would have had a huge impact on his life and livelihood. In 1898, the appropriately named *Dog and Goat Act* was passed to consolidate legislation relating to dogs and goats in New South Wales. This Act required that all dogs within the boundary of any 'city, town, or police district' for more than fourteen days be registered with the authorities. A fee was required for registration, and the onus was on the owner to prove that their animal had been recorded. The *Dog and Goat Act* posed many problems for men like Jimmy Governor. For one thing, itinerant workers would have to register their dogs in multiple areas, incurring large costs and great inconvenience. Registration only lasted for one year, meaning that there were ongoing fees. And if the animals were not registered, the consequences could be dire. Not only were the owners fined, but if an unregistered dog was found by the authorities and unclaimed for twenty-four hours, it was killed. If a dog was 'at large', with no collar and not in the 'immediate custody' of their owner, then anyone was authorised to kill the animal. In fact, they were *encouraged* to do so. Police were fined for not reporting unregistered dogs, while rewards were offered to civilians who killed them. Provided that the executioner brought the dog's tail to a police magistrate or judge as proof, they would be paid for their trouble.[31] This meant that unaccompanied or lost dogs without collars could be killed on sight. Such wide discretionary powers also meant that this law was open to abuse. If you wanted to harass someone, killing their unregistered dog was a simple and effective way to go about it. Any of these situations could have occurred in Jimmy Governor's case. Even if his dog had not yet been killed, being denied registration would have put its life in jeopardy.

Governor's dog was clearly important to him. The strong connection between Aboriginal people and dogs has long been recognised, with even conservative estimates showing that Aboriginal people's relationships with dingoes (Australian dogs) reaches back around four thousand years.[32] Dingoes are important to Aboriginal culture and spiritual belief, while domesticated dogs were prized by Aboriginal people as soon as they were introduced by Europeans.[33] At the turn of the 20th century, dogs were still important to Aboriginal people and served a range of purposes. They were often beloved companions as well as 'bed warmers' on cold nights camping out.[34] Dogs could also help with hunting, allowing Aboriginal people to supplement expensive provisions and secure a staple diet.[35] Jimmy Governor would have felt any threat to his dog keenly.

The second point in Governor's letter – about being refused free train travel – is also more significant than it first appears. Historian Paul Irish has shown that Aboriginal people adopted train, tram and steamship travel to meet up with other Aboriginal groups around New South Wales almost as soon as this transport was introduced. Some journeyed to reconnect with kin, others to attend ceremonies and use these new technologies to travel routes that their ancestors had before them. While Irish's work concentrates on the east coast of New South Wales and Jimmy Governor's people lived further inland, it is very likely that Governor and his Aboriginal family used trains in the same way.[36] For a seasonal worker like Governor who moved from job to job, trains also enhanced his ability to find work.

While train travel in New South Wales was never officially free for Aboriginal people, it appears to have been common for rail authorities to let them ride without a ticket. In 1900 two members of the Aboriginal Protection Board (APB) raised this issue, with EM Clark of St Leonards declaring that 'the general public was under the impression that an Aborigine could jump on a train ... without any charge being made', while JM Chanter of Deniliquin acknowledged that 'some years ago the aborigines had the right to step on to a ... train when they thought proper and travel about'.[37] But the the Board was not happy with this state of affairs. They soon saw Aboriginal people 'travelling all over the colony ... to the great annoyance of everybody else' and so took active steps to prevent them from using trains. New South Wales government railways were informed that the APB wanted to prevent Aboriginal people from using their services in 1892, and 'rail passes' were brought in to regulate Aboriginal people's travel in 1890. From this time, Aboriginal people had to apply to the Board for a pass to use the trains and this was far more than a formality. The APB would not approve this request until a police magistrate had verified that the journey was a 'legitimate' one.[38] This was a clear attempt to curtail Aboriginal people's freedom of movement. And the new cost disproportionately affected poorer families who could not afford the expense. Jimmy Governor spoke for many Aboriginal people when he decried the end of free train travel and labelled it a particular grievance.

The final issue that Governor raised in his letter was the most personal: 'they all have a set on me at Dubbo'.[39] Dubbo is a regional centre almost 400 kilometres north-west of Sydney that currently sits at the junction of three highways. Today it is a 'city' surrounded by open plains, grasslands and paddocks, and its weather is one of extremes. In summer, the heat can be oppressive and often soars over 40 degrees Celsius, while in winter it can plummet to close to zero. Nowadays it is renowned for its impressive zoo.[40] In 1900 Dubbo was different – less developed and less populated but still a bustling regional outpost by early 20th-century standards. It was also an area with which Ethel and Jimmy Governor had strong connections. Dubbo benefitted from the magnetic pull of the railway as it had a train station – a station that was by far the closest to where Jimmy worked in Breelong.[41] This would have been the gateway to Jimmy's much-maligned train travel.

Ethel had links to the area too. She went back and forward to Dubbo as she originally left her son, Sidney, there with her parents while she and Jimmy set up their Breelong camp.[42] Ethel's parents had only recently moved to Dubbo in the two years after she and Jimmy had wed, and local historian Maurie Garland believes that this move was driven by necessity. It is his contention that the Page family relocated to flee the scandal caused by Ethel and Jimmy's marriage in their old home of Gulgong – about 100 kilometres east of Dubbo.[43] These connections between the Governors and Dubbo are important. Given their presence in the town, the scandal surrounding Ethel and Jimmy's interracial marriage and the vocal disapproval they received (from the Mawbey women before the murders and in the press afterwards), it is likely that the pair were well known and slighted in Dubbo too. If that was the case, then Governor's remark that 'they all have a set on me at Dubbo' could mean that the town's inhabitants were 'set against' him for trying to reach above his station and presuming to marry a white girl.[44]

## HONOUR

The idea that Jimmy Governor fought to defend his and Ethel's good name saturates material on this case. It was even Governor's official defence to the charge of murder. In November 1900 Governor stood before the Supreme Court in Sydney. The public gallery was crammed with curious onlookers waiting to be further scandalised by the notorious outlaw, and court reporters sat with pens poised to capture the confession of a murderer. The following account is from the *Australian Star* – a paper that not only recorded Governor's testimony largely verbatim but captured the physicality of his retelling. In his court testimony, Jimmy Governor declared that on the night of the murders:

> I says to my wife, 'We'll go up and see Mrs Mawbey about these words she's been talking about us.' I says to my wife, 'I'll make

her mind what she's talking about.' I says to my wife, 'I'll put her through the court if she doesn't watch herself.' So I went up to the house. So I says, 'Did you tell my wife that a white woman who married a-----blackfellow ought to be shot?' I said, 'Did you ask her what kind of nature did I have; black or white, or what colour was it?' [Presumably his penis.] And with that Mrs Mawbey and Miss Kerz wheeled around and laughed at me like that, with a sneering laugh. (Prisoner imitated the posture he was describing.) And before I had the words out of my mouth, as I put it to the court, I struck Mrs Mawbey on the head with this nullah-nullah. (Prisoner dramatically went through the movement of striking.) And Miss Kerz says, 'Pooh, you black rubbish, you want shooting for marrying a white woman.' And with that I hit her with my hand. It was on the jaw and I knocked her down. Then I got angry and lost my temper, and everything, and I did not know anything after that.[45]

Governor's lawyers argued that this was a case of provocation. Jimmy had been pushed to his limits and lost control – meaning that he was not fully responsible for his actions. The aim was not to throw out the charges but reduce them from murder to manslaughter. For Governor's words to be accepted as a mitigation to murder, colonial Australians had to be convinced that he held similar values to those of respectable white men. Governor could only have been provoked by Miss Kerz and Mrs Mawbey if he believed that the things they said were offensive in the extreme. Having aspersions cast upon your character, your intimate relations ridiculed, your wife insulted, and your honour challenged would have been considered more than enough to incite a white man to violence. If anything, it was his duty to react to such a gross insult and disregard for propriety.[46] Although murder would have still been condemned, the reason for the crime would have been recognisable. But as we have already seen time and time again, Governor was not deemed equal to a white man. Colonists judged Indigenous Australians 'to live a debased and degraded existence, without claim to honour'.[47] And the brutal nature of Jimmy Governor's crimes prevented him being viewed as anything but 'savage'.

Although white colonists refused to recognise Governor's claims to be defending his honour, it is clear from other instances in his life that he set great store by his public reputation. Jimmy Governor proudly remarked to police that he was not a 'loafer'.[48] He did not live on public funds as other Aboriginal people were denigrated for doing, and before the murders, he was well liked and hard-working.[49] In his account of the Breelong murders, Governor initially wanted to use the court to stop Mrs Mawbey's slanderous remarks, and there is evidence that he had used similar, non-violent means to address a grievance like this in the past.[50] After receiving offensive comments from a woman at the Gulgong Show in 1899, Governor demanded an apology. On her refusal, he went to the police and the woman was made to publish a public apology in the Gulgong newspaper.[51] It appears the Mawbey women could not be similarly persuaded. By refusing to retract their statements or show contrition for their actions, they made a mockery of Jimmy Governor's claim to respect. It was only after Governor's negotiations with the Mawbey women had failed that he resorted to violence.

\*

Understanding Governor's grievances does not excuse his actions. He massacred women, children and old people. He killed them brutally, violently, and apparently without remorse.[52] Unpacking Governor's words is important because they show us something of his sense of self as well as the injustices that he and others like him faced. By pushing beyond the shorthand of 'savage' we can see that Governor challenged colonial culture by adopting it, appropriating it, and using it to defend his criminal actions. This is where things get messy, as Governor appealed to notions of honour and manhood epitomised by white bushranging legends. In defending his wife's honour, Governor tapped into the elite bushranger's respect for and protection of women.[53] That he murdered other white women to mount this defence certainly complicated matters but did not negate that original impulse. In another letter that Governor left for the police, he apparently stated that 'had it not been for her [Ethel] the murders would not have been committed'. The papers automatically assumed that Governor made 'this accusation out of a spirit of revenge' against Ethel to punish her for providing evidence at the Breelong inquest.[54] However, this too can be interpreted differently. Had Ethel not come to Jimmy, upset and aggrieved by the Mawbey women's taunts, then he may not have confronted them. If Jimmy Governor had not needed to come to his wife's aid, then the murders may never have taken place.

It was not only the Mawbey family who encouraged Jimmy Governor's turn to crime, but his own. In an extensive interview given to reporters upon his capture, Governor stated that most nights after work, he, Ethel, Jacky Underwood and his brother Joe would talk about bushranging:

> I told them if I was a bushranger I suppose I would take some catching ... My missus, Jacky Underwood and Joe laughed at the idea of bushranging. They said to me 'you are not game to go'. I said, 'That is forcing me to go'.[55]

From this statement, it seems that Jimmy Governor's family did not believe he had what it took to be a bushranger, and Governor draws a clear connection between this doubt and his decision to go on the run. These aspersions were 'forcing' him to go, to prove his family wrong and raise his position to one of esteem in their eyes.

Governor was well aware that he needed to perform daring feats to become a celebrated bushranger, even if he did not follow through with them in action. On 25 August, for example, the *Singleton Argus* reported that a third letter had been discovered from Jimmy Governor:

... who states that before long he will ride through the streets of Coonabarabran in broad daylight. He adds that the police will have a rare picnic before they catch him.[56]

These lines are wildly unsubstantiated. Most evidence suggests that the Governors travelled on foot rather than riding horses. Horses made a great deal of noise in the bush and left tracks that were easily followed. The Governors evaded capture for so long because they went to great measures to avoid being traced. The *Dubbo Dispatch* reported that the pair must have doubled back and 'walked along a fence for some distance' to avoid leaving tracks and escape the dogs and men pursuing them.[57] But the iconic bushranger was a man riding his horse, and it is this image that Governor draws on in his letter.[58] His threat was reminiscent of elite bushrangers who brazenly entered towns and held their inhabitants as (well-treated) hostages. In these instances the police were humiliated as they were unable to stop such a direct encroachment on their turf.[59] Although Jimmy Governor never rode into Coonabarabran in broad daylight, he drew inspiration from the white bushranging tradition. It just appears that he valued his safety more than carrying out his boast.

## CULTURE

White colonists never had a monopoly on bushranging, as Governor felt a deep affinity with celebrated bushranging heroes. Oral histories, ballads and folklore about bushrangers circulated around the colonies and these tales were commonly passed around campfires and shared among itinerant bushmen. Governor moved about the same country frequented by these legendary figures and it is unlikely that their tales would have escaped his notice.[60] Governor had also been reading about bushrangers before the murders.[61] It might not have been a coincidence that he demanded his first letter be published in the *Sydney Mail*, the

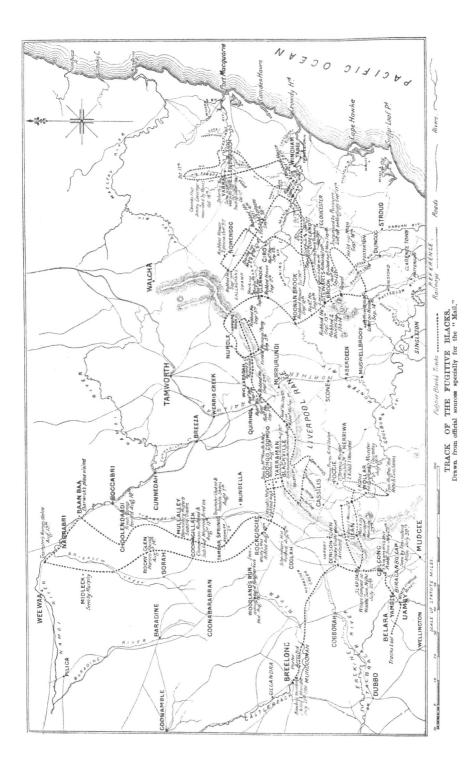

FIGURE 7. Unknown illustrator, *Tracks of the Governors*, 1900.

'*Tracks of the Governors,*' Sydney Mail (3 November 1900), p. 1056.

newspaper that published the famous bushranging serial, 'Robbery Under Arms' by Rolf Boldrewood in 1882–1883.[62] Governor was likely aware of the Kellys too. Although he was only five years old when the bushrangers were caught and killed, the *Mudgee Guardian* published a series of articles on the gang's exploits in 1899, one year before the Breelong attacks.[63] We know from Jimmy Governor's taunts to the police that he was reading the *Guardian* in 1900. He probably did so recreationally before he used the paper to ascertain the authorities' plans.[64]

Upon his capture in October 1900, Governor stated to reporters that he had never read 'any of Deadwood Dick's novels or any other books about bushranging until we came out that night [the night of the murders]'.[65] What is interesting here is that Governor referred to an American influence in his conception of bushranging, as *Deadwood Dick* 'dime-novels' were about American cowboys (see Plate 20).[66] Although he denied reading these books for long, Governor was not alone in conflating bushranging with the life of an American cowboy. An *Evening News* reporter declared that '[t]he little native camp at Breelong seems to have owed, at least, in part, some of its demoralisation to reading "Deadwood Dick" tales of highwaymen and bushrangers', and there were certainly connections between the two.[67] Bushrangers and cowboys operated on sprawling frontiers, often beyond the reach of established (colonial) society. And they walked a precarious line between being symbols of crime and disorder, and representing an alternative form of justice.[68] When they were fictional and confined to the printed page, bushrangers and cowboys could tread that line even more deliberately and so appeal to a wider audience. For instance literary scholar Daryl E Jones goes as far as to describe the character Deadwood Dick as a 'delightful rogue', as his bravery and survival in harsh country endeared him to his audience.[69]

Although Governor may have wanted to identify with Deadwood Dick, the cowboy and protagonist of these novels, the Native Americans in these stories may have struck a greater chord with him. English academic Michelle Abate notes that:

[f]rontier figures like ... Deadwood Dick ... spend most of their
time fighting indigenous tribal peoples. Frequently in these
novels, the current villain or longstanding enemy of the white
Western hero is either a solitary American Indian or an entire
tribe.[70]

Pitting cowboys against 'Indians' stood in stark contrast to Australian
bushranging yarns, where Aboriginal people were on the periphery
and white bushrangers were mostly fighting wealthy squatters or
corrupt authorities.[71] It is hard to believe that this divide between
white heroes and Indigenous villains would have been lost on Jimmy
Governor, and it is telling that Governor was reading these tales the
night before he committed the murders. For a man who already felt
persecuted, ridiculed and disrespected by colonial society, this fictive
representation may have compounded his feelings of frustration and
isolation.

*

After one hundred days at large, Jimmy Governor was captured by
civilians on 27 October 1900. By his own admission, his last days on
the run had been hard ones. Far from the glamorous life of a legendary
bushranger, Governor had spent the fourteen days before his capture
living on nothing but wild honey and water, and was emaciated when
the roving party caught up with him. At his trial the following month,
Jimmy Governor made a startling about-face, and disavowed his
interest in bushranging. To the court he declared that:

All this bushranging business that we was talking about – that's
a lie ... We made all that up ... [we said that] so that they'd know
that I was the main man. But all that was not true, it was only to
be said.[72]

It is very unlikely that Jimmy Governor fabricated his interest in bushranging. Not only is there a solid base of evidence contradicting this lone statement, but its timing is incredibly suspicious. Governor made this denial just before his lawyer argued that the Mawbey women's taunts had incited him to violence.[73] In law, provocation relied on a lack of premeditation. For Governor's charge to be reduced from murder to manslaughter, he could not have planned, let alone revelled in, his turn to crime.[74]

Before Governor had access to a lawyer, he spoke willingly to the press about his bushranging exploits. According to the *Singleton Argus*, Governor:

> ... did not seem at all anxious to hide a single detail of his doings during the period in which his name was a terror to thousands, but rather gloried in many of his performances, principally those which brought his bush craft into prominence, or exhibited his powers of cunning in outwitting the police and the others who were engaged in his pursuit.[75]

*

Jimmy Governor identified with bushrangers. Bushranging allowed him to articulate his own grievances through a mode that colonial Australians knew well. He appealed to notions of honour and frontier masculinity that these figures relied upon. He showcased skills typical of bushranging heroes. He made clear connections between his desire to be a bushranger and his turn to crime. And he embraced the forms of language and performance displayed by (real and fictional) bushranging legends. The fact that settler Australians refused to accept him as a bushranger should not blind us to the evidence that Governor sought to make bushranging his own. This material not only helps us to understand Jimmy Governor's actions, but the unstable, disruptive potential of national symbols. The popular, bushranging elite was composed of white men, but these figures had an appeal that transcended race. Colonial Australians might have killed Jimmy Governor – on 18 January 1901 at the hangman's noose in Darlinghurst Gaol – but they could not control how the bushranging legend was used, or by whom. It was turned against the society that created it. Jimmy Governor used the bushranging mythos to justify his crimes, and threaten the colonial state of which his victims were a part.

# AFTERWORD

When you next see the blunt rectangular shape of a 'Ned Kelly' helmet – on an artwork, a film trailer, a placard, a t-shirt, a stubby holder, or a bicep – perhaps you will imagine a different face beneath the mask. Although Kelly and his gang were the only ones to use this incredibly heavy and grossly impractical armour, they were not the only bushrangers. Aboriginal, African American and Chinese men and an Aboriginal woman were associated with bushranging in their own times, and many explicitly claimed the bushranging tradition for themselves. Some even committed the same crimes at the same time as famous white bushranging men, yet they have never entered the national bushranging mythos. Despite what we have been taught by history books and films, songs and podcasts, and despite what we have seen on merchandise and in our museums, bushrangers were not all white men. It would be wrong to assume that a white male face is the only one capable of being behind bushranging's symbolic armour.

Our national heroes are not natural figures who step into our hearts and minds fully formed. They are actively created and inherently political. Heroes are formed through a peculiar mix of distance and proximity. Distance because they are, by definition, exceptional. As the playful quip goes, if everyone was a hero, then no one would be. Heroes are rare, remarkable individuals, high above us mortals. But they cannot be too high. Heroes also require proximity. We must feel close to them. Their actions and values must resonate with our own. We aspire to be like them, emulate them and capture something of

170

their brilliance. Historian Eric Hobsbawm famously declared 'social bandits' to be criminals who are not seen as such by their supporters. As they represent the interests and champion the causes of their supporters, they are celebrated by that community.[1] Our national bushranging heroes tell us something about who we are and what we believe in. But the other bushrangers, the ones we have excluded, perhaps tell us even more.

The fact that the bushrangers we remember, commemorate and celebrate as a nation are exclusively white men is no accident. It was colonists' intent. We can see this in the way other bushrangers were maligned, demonised and dehumanised at the time they operated – and the way this has leached into records kept about them since. The nation's archives were created by settlers and enshrined their ideas, and so the 'public opinion' we see most clearly is that of the white, colonial public. Local or familial groups who supported other bushrangers are a lot harder to see than white colonists, and we often do not have enough material to bring these people squarely into view. Studies of bushranging in Australia currently privilege white colonists' perspectives. Other bushrangers were deliberately set apart from colonial society and the nascent Australian nation. Our country has changed a great deal since the 1800s and early 1900s. Yet our bushranging heroes remain largely the same.

It is important to remember that crime was never the reason that other bushrangers were placed beyond the pale. There were scores of colonists who supported criminals, protected bushrangers, and championed their cause. They hid white bushranging men in their homes, packed them provisions, provided them with information and misled the authorities to assist them. Some settlers might have helped these bushrangers due to fear or threats or violence, but there were enough genuine supporters to turn many of these white bushranging men into living legends. Ordinary people passed tales around campfires and sang songs of bravery and righting wrongs for years before these bushrangers reached the mainstream or permeated popular culture.

Crime was never the issue that prevented other bushrangers from being celebrated. Their race (and gender) were.

William Douglas, Sam Poo, Mary Ann Bugg and Jimmy Governor's lives did not resonate with white settlers. Unlike white bushranging men, their stories could not be used to legitimise colonial society, fashion white male colonisers into righteous champions or naturalise colonists' theft of Aboriginal Country. They did quite the opposite. Douglas, Poo, Bugg and Governor not only imperilled colonists' lives and livelihoods, but shook foundational narratives upon which the colonies were built. What if white colonists did not have a natural, preordained right to the wealth of the colonies? What if white men were not at the top of the food chain, let alone the social or evolutionary ladder? And critically, what of First Nations people? How were colonists to reconcile Aboriginal people's endurance, resilience and survival with their own desire to create a 'white man's country'? These are just some of the myriad challenging questions that other bushrangers raised. If white, settler masculinity was not an essential ingredient for bushrangers' appeal, our bushranging heroes would look different.

\*

This is not to say that other bushrangers were a blip in colonists' minds, fearsome and anxiety-inducing at the time they operated but instantly forgotten once the danger they posed had passed. Memory does not work that way. A switch could not be flicked, and their trace immediately erased. In historian Tom Griffiths' evocative phrase, there are 'seasons of memory' – cycles of movement and change, remembrance and forgetting.[2] The case of Jimmy Governor provides a striking example of this. After his execution in 1901 (an execution that was pushed back so as not to taint Federation celebrations), Jimmy Governor was still a sensation.[3] Far from forgetting his deeds, colonists showcased them. Waxwork figures were made of the 'protagonists' in the Breelong crimes and became part of a larger travelling show around the colonies.[4] Missionary Retta Dixon presented a lecture titled 'Jimmy Governor, Chief of Sinners' where she used Governor as a cautionary tale to promote early religious intervention in Aboriginal people's lives, lest they pursue similar murderous ends. She presented this in church and town halls almost the length of New South Wales.[5] Bush ballads were created, spread and sung – with Governor as villain, and white bushmen as noble heroes.[6] Jimmy Governor's enduring impact was not just felt by white colonists either. Aboriginal man Fred Locke committed a series of crimes, including the abduction of a white girl, in 1901, claiming that he wanted to be the next Jimmy Governor.[7] Family memory of Jimmy as a loving father and provider has been passed down through generations and now resides with Aunty Loretta Parsley, Governor's descendant and custodian of her family's story.[8] Other bushrangers were not erased completely. But they were scrubbed from national consciousness.

There are some signs of change. Another season of memory for other bushrangers appears to be beginning. Comedians Hannah and Eliza Reilly have used Mary Ann Bugg's story in their webseries *Sheilas: Badass women from Australian history*. Their show explicitly positions women like Mary Ann as alternative heroes to the 'bossy old white dudes' who dominate in Australian social memory.[9] On a more personal level, descendants of Jimmy Governor, and the O'Brien family (who were among Governor's murder victims) staged a play about their ancestors in 2015, while Lorraine Martyn – Mary Ann Bugg and Captain Thunderbolt's descendant – believes that there should be a public statue to Mary Ann and has traced the location of her grave.[10] Australian artists are also stirring this new wave of remembrance. In 2016 Kudjla/Gangalu artist Daniel Boyd transformed Jimmy Governor's colonial mugshots into striking dot portraits in black, yellow and red.[11] Since 2015, I have collaborated with Chinese-Australian artist Jason Phu to reimagine Sam Poo's story and return it to the public eye.[12] In the 1940s, it was modernist artist Sidney Nolan who captured something of Ned Kelly's legend and added a new edge to the symbol he is today, and so it is fitting that contemporary artists are now interrogating, deconstructing, and playing with the bushranging trope.[13] I would like to think that this book has a role in shaping this new season of memory too. I hope it also goes some way to reviving other bushrangers' stories and allowing us to face the colonial legacies that have kept them veiled from public view.

*

But in true historian fashion, I cannot end the story there. There needs to be some qualification about this book's relationship to the national bushranging legend. Because I have done a bit of 'market research' – I have chatted to people at conferences, over coffee and in supermarket checkout queues. I have had zooms and calls and in-person chats with friends and relatives and colleagues and collaborators and curious bystanders. When I tell people about this book, their response is usually shock:

'No way!? Really? There were *other* bushrangers?!'

– quickly followed by enthusiasm:

'That's so great! A Chinese Ned Kelly! An Aboriginal Ben Hall!'

Although I love the excitement, this type of conversation makes me uneasy. Other bushrangers *were* remarkable. They survived in treacherous conditions, traversed large swathes of country, assaulted and outwitted the police, pushed back against colonial constraints and fought hard to maintain their freedom. There is a strong push to include these 'hidden' figures in the national mythos, to place them as heroes alongside the likes of Ned Kelly and remark that the nation has always had a multicultural past. And while proffered in good faith, this approach is extremely problematic.

This framing adds other bushrangers directly into our national mythology without questioning it. No one asks why we did not know about these people. No one queries why other bushrangers were not already part of the Australian legend. Why weren't we told? The answer is the white masculinist tradition that has informed Australian nationalism for decades. The answer is that our colonial ancestors believed in racial and gendered hierarchies, and they placed white men at the top of the ladder. This not only affected other bushrangers' lives. This is our inheritance.

Other bushrangers were deliberately excluded from the burgeoning bushranging legend. Their posthumous inclusion in this tradition does not reflect the reality that they lived in. If we uncritically add William Douglas, Mary Ann Bugg, Sam Poo or Jimmy Governor to the bushranging legend, then we risk erasing their own worldviews and co-opting their stories for our own ends. This would be particularly egregious considering that each of these people was stripped of their personhood and used as some kind of vessel, myth or symbol to serve colonists' interests in their own times. We cannot let history repeat itself. We should not impose a settler framework onto other bushrangers' lives and flatten out the differences that defined their experience. In rushing to make them heroes, we can easily erase what made them human.

Other bushrangers were not mere derivatives of a white colonial character. They were not mimicking a tradition we know so well. We need to see other bushrangers on their own terms. And to do this, we cannot simply 'add a bit of colour' to the enduring bushranging legend. It is not enough to diversify. We need to challenge the frame of reference. We need to decolonise.

# ACKNOWLEDGMENTS

In some form or another, I have been writing (and rewriting) this book for much of my adult life. This means that the list of people I have to thank is far too long for my already blown-out word count. If you aren't mentioned here, I hope that I have made my gratitude palpable in other ways.

Although this book is a work of history, it is not solely about the past. Colonial prejudices about gender and race continue to impact everything, from the structures that oppress women and people of colour today to the national heroes we praise. Although I'm a woman, I benefit from these structures by being white. People of colour are chronically underrepresented in higher education, and the ongoing impact of colonisation means First Nations people are particularly affected. This presents a painful catch-22. Centuries of violence towards people of colour mean it is even more important that they have control over their own past and reclaim histories that were occluded, doctored or denied by white colonists. But because this power imbalance is ongoing, not enough people of colour have the time, space or resources to do so. Nor should they have to shoulder the burden of righting over 200 years of history alone.

I cannot express how grateful I am to have received cultural advice and undertaken collaborations with people who live this history. I am incredibly grateful to Lorraine Martyn for sharing the details of her family story. Lorraine has tirelessly supported this research and I can't thank her enough for our conversations over five years. I would also like to thank Aunty Loretta Parsley for her generosity in sharing Jimmy Governor's story. Although I was unable to contact Aunty Loretta personally, her public statements and creative works about her ancestor are an invaluable gift that have formed the foundations of chapters about him. To Jason Phu, for our collaborations and work together on memory, identity and hero-worship in this country as well as Jamie Preisz for our discussions about the potent legacy of criminal 'bad boys' in Australian mythology, I am incredibly grateful. I cannot thank enough everyone at Jumbunna, the Institute for Indigenous Education and Research at the University of Technology, Sydney; Nura Gili Centre for Indigenous Programs at the University of New South Wales, and Aboriginal Land Councils throughout New South Wales who have provided invaluable assistance and cultural advice over the years. I'd also like to recognise the work of Terri Janke and UNSW Press, whose Indigenous Cultural and Intellectual Property protocols provide a framework of ethical practice for non-Indigenous writers working with First Nations culture.

As I hope this book has shown, bushranging was never just an Australian story, and having experts on hand to discuss the international dimensions of this history has been invaluable. I would like to thank Newnham College, University of Cambridge, for supporting this project and providing me with the intellectual and financial resources to complete this book. This research has benefitted from the rich and diverse intellectual environment at the University of Cambridge, especially the World History Subject Group, World History Seminar and a reading group run by Professor Sujit Sivasundaram. I also have to thank members of the Australia-Pacific writing group based in Australia, for their advice, insights and support over many years. To everyone from these groups who has read, reviewed and discussed chapters, I am especially indebted.

An abridged version of Chapter 5 won the 2018 Aboriginal History Award from the History Council of New South Wales and appeared as 'Jimmy Governor and the Aboriginal People of Wollar' in *Australian Historical Studies* vol. 50, no. 3 in 2019. I would like to thank the History Council and judges for their continuing support of early career historians and promotion of Aboriginal history, as well as the editors and anonymous reviewers of *Australian Historical Studies* for their insightful comments on this piece.

I have received a number of formal and informal residencies throughout the course of this research. I am grateful to be a visiting fellow with the School of Humanities and Languages at my alma mater, the University of New South Wales, and to have gained invaluable support from both established and emerging academics there. I was welcomed as a visiting scholar at the University of Leicester in 2017, a Bicentennial scholar at King's College in London that same year and a visiting research student at the University of Cambridge from 2018–2019.

Thank you to Richard White and Cath Bishop, Paul Ashton and Pauline O'Loughlin as well as the Williams/Mazzella family for opening their homes to me and providing beautiful, restorative spaces for me to write. I am indebted to Marilyn Hoey, Paul van Reyk, Django and Sarge for agreeing to take in an impoverished stranger for a two and a half month stay and then due to the pandemic, border closures and illness, giving me a home for over two and a half years.

This project is the culmination of nearly ten years of research from all over the world. I am especially indebted to the archivists and librarians who have helped me wade through boxes of material, shared my euphoria when I discovered a game-changing source, and offered their expertise to make these discoveries possible. In particular, I would like to express my immense gratitude to the staff at the New South Wales State Archives and Records Office, the State Library of New South Wales and the Mitchell Library, the Public Record Office of Victoria, the British National Archives, the British Library, the East Sussex Records Office and the Museum of Rye. This research could also never have taken place without digital archives. I am greatly indebted to the Tasmanian Archives and Heritage Office, whose material on Tasmanian convicts is online, and Trove, whose digital newspaper collections form the backbone of this research.

Grace Karskens and Lisa Ford have been my stalwart supporters. Not only have they been invested in this project almost since its inception, they have been invested in me – in my development as an historian, and as a person. Words can't express how grateful I am for their mentorship and guidance.

To my friends and family who have been bombarded with bushranging stories, persevered through my excited rants about sources and whose eyes never glazed over when I regaled them with yet another tale, I am eternally indebted. Genevieve Dashwood, James Keating and Hollie Pich in particular listened eagerly to my book news, lifted me up when I was in an archival or writing gloom, and generally made my life so much better for having them in it.

To Richie Phillips and Archer Milton Phillips-Foster (my partner and chubby cat baby respectively), I owe so much. You support me in countless ways. From cooking dinners and delivering pep talks on demand (Richie), to tolerating my presence and being affectionate when you need food (Archie), you've built me up with love and tenderness. I cherish every moment with you. Even the annoying ones.

This book is dedicated to Dr Tracy Newlands, my high school history teacher, friend, and established historian in her own right. Tracy is one of the kindest, most generous, dedicated and intelligent people I know. She is also the first person to convince me that I could be an historian, and that time spent pursuing your passion is never wasted.

Doc, this book is for you.

# BIBLIOGRAPHY

## PRIMARY SOURCES

### ARCHIVAL SOURCES (AUSTRALIA)
#### New South Wales Registry of Births, Deaths and Marriages

NSW RBDM, *Edmund Baker and Mary A Bugg*, Marriage Certificate. Registration number 1848/518.
NSW RBDM, *Frederick Wordsworth Ward*, Birth Certificate. Registration number 1868/0016881.
NSW RBDM, *Maria Emily Ward*, Birth Certificate. Registration number 1861/7193.
NSW RBDM, *Mary Ann Bugg*, Baptism Certificate, vol. 23. Registration number 1839/1494.
NSW RBDM, *Mary Ann Burrows*, Death Certificate. Registration number 1905/5831.
NSW RBDM, *Sam Poo*, Death Certificate. Registration number 2742/1865.
NSW RBDM, *Thelma HR Governor*, Baptism Certificate. Registration number 18315/1901.

#### New South Wales State Archives

NSWSA: Board for the Protection of Aborigines; NRS 2, Minute Books [Aborigines Welfare Board], 1890–1901 [4/7108-15].
NSWSA: Board for the Protection of Aborigines; NRS 2, Minute Books [Aborigines Welfare Board], 1890–1901 [4/7113].
NSWSA: Circuit Court; NRS 7868, Justice Wise's Notebook, 1865 [2/7776].
NSWSA: Clerk of the Peace; NRS 847, Registers of Criminal Cases Tried at Sydney Quarter Sessions, 1839–1845 [5/2917], reel 2431.
NSWSA: Clerk of the Peace; NRS 880, Papers and Depositions of the Supreme Court on Circuit, 1865 [9/6474, 9/6475].
NSWSA: Darlinghurst Gaol; NRS 2137, Entrance and Description Books [Darlinghurst Gaol], 1900 [5/1947-53].
NSWSA: Darlinghurst Gaol; NRS 2163, Condemned Prisoners' Daily Record, 1900–1901 [5/1739].
NSWSA: Darlinghurst Gaol; NRS 2166, Diary of Officer Doing Duty Over Jimmy Governor, 1900–1901 [6/1029].
NSWSA: Department of Corrective Services; NRS 1993, Bathurst Gaol Entrance Book, 1865 [4/8492], reel 2321, entry for 'Sam Poo'.
NSWSA: Department of Corrective Services; NRS 2318, Maitland Gaol Entry Book 1860-65, 1871-76 [5/755-56, 5/790], reel 2370, entry for 'Mary Ann Ward'.
NSWSA: Department of Corrective Services; NRS 2318, Maitland Gaol Entry Book, 1866–1867, [5/747-50], reel 2368, entry for 'Mary Ann Ward'.
NSWSA: Department of Corrective Services; NRS 2329, Maitland Gaol Discharge Books [5/789], entry for 'Mary Ann Ward'.

NSWSA: Department of Corrective Services; NRS 2374, Entrance Books [Newcastle Gaol] 1832–1848 [2/2005], roll 136, entry for 'Harvey Henley'.

NSWSA: Department of Premier and Cabinet; NRS 905, Main Series of Letters Received [Colonial Secretary], Letters from Miscellaneous Persons, Names Starting M [4/2284.1].

NSWSA: Department of Premier and Cabinet; NRS 905, Main Series of Letters Received [Colonial Secretary], Letters from Miscellaneous Persons, Names Starting T [4/2285.1].

NSWSA: Department of Premier and Cabinet; NRS 905, Main Series of Letters Received [Colonial Secretary], 'Mary Ann Ward', 1867 [4/590, 67/1050].

NSWSA: Department of Premier and Cabinet; NRS 905, Main Series of Letters Received [Colonial Secretary], Police Port Stephens [4/2332.2].

NSWSA: Department of Premier and Cabinet; NRS 905, Main Series of Letters Received [Colonial Secretary], Re: Mary Ann Ward, 1866 [4/573, 66/1844].

NSWSA: [Police] Special Bundles; NRS 10923, Papers re-Joe and Jimmy Governor [4/8581] Doc 79.

NSWSA: Secretary to the Governor; NRS 1155, Musters and Papers Relating to Convict Ships, 1812–1840 [2/8269], reel 2425.

NSWSA: Superintendent of Convicts; NRS 12188, Convict Administration, Indents, 1830–42, [4/4019], reel 906.

NSWSA: Supreme Court of New South Wales; NRS 880, Papers and Depositions of the Supreme Court [9/7003] – papers relating to the trial of Jimmy Governor.

NSWSA: Supreme Court; NRS 6034, Justice Hargrave's Notebook, 1865 [2/4469].

NSWSA: Supreme Court; NRS 13705, Memoranda selected from Twenty-Four Years of Missionary Engagements in the South Sea Islands and Australia, by Lancelot Edward Threlkeld, Missionary to the Aborigines, New South Wales, 1838 [5/1123].

NSWSA: Sydney and Darlinghurst Gaol; NRS 2519, Entrance Books [Sydney Gaol and Darlinghurst Gaol], [4/6440–41], reel 854.

## Public Record Office of Victoria

PROV, VA 475 Chief Secretary's Department, VPRS 515/P0001 Central Register of Male Prisoners; Alexander Douglas, Unit 4, 1855.

PROV, VA 724 Victorian Police, VPRS 937/P0000 Inward Registered Correspondence; Avoca District, Unit 6, 1855.

PROV, VA 724 Victorian Police, VPRS 937/P0004 Inward Registered Correspondence; Miscellaneous Correspondence, 1855.

PROV, VA 862 Office of the Registrar-General and the Office of Titles, VPRS 24/P0000 Inquest Deposition Files, Unit 411, 1880/938, Inquest of Edward Kelly.

PROV, VA 1464 Penal and Gaols Branch, Chief Secretary's Department, VPRS 515/P0001 Central Register of Male Prisoners; Charles Douglas, Unit 38, 1886 and 1888.

PROV, VA 1464 Penal and Gaols Branch, Chief Secretary's Department, VPRS 515/P0001 Central Register of Male Prisoners; Charles Russell, Unit 44, 1892.

PROV, VA 2825 Attorney General's Department (previously known as the Law Department), VPRS 4966/P0 Kelly Historical Collection: Part 2: Crown Law Department, Unit 1, Item 3, Edward Kelly: Gives statement of his murders of Srgt. Kennedy and others; and makes other threats (Euroa Letter) 80/T12640, 1880.

PROV, VA 2889 Registrar-General's Department, VPRS 24/P0001 Inquests into Deaths (deposition files, 1840–1985), Unit 596, 1892.

**State Library of New South Wales**

Pratt, Ambrose and AS Joseph, *Thunderbolt Play Script*, date unknown, State Library of New South Wales, William Anderson Collection, MLMSS 1412.

Rede, Rege, *The Kelly Gang Play Script*, c1898, State Library of New South Wales, MLMSS 1412/8, Item 100.

**State Library of Victoria**

Nawton, William, *Diaries, 1852–53*, unpublished manuscript, State Library of Victoria, MS 10251.

**Victorian Register of Births, Deaths and Marriages**

Death: Charles Russell, Victorian Register of Births, Deaths and Marriages 1892/5199.

**Tasmanian Archives and Heritage Office**

TAHO: Convict Department (TA60); Conduct Registers of Male Convicts, CON35/1/1.

TAHO: George Town Police (TA1862); Returns of Crew and Passengers on Ships Departing from Launceston, POL220/1/1.


## ARCHIVAL SOURCES (ONLINE)
### Ancestry.com

Ancestry.com. *England, Select Births and Christenings, 1538–1975* [database online]. Provo, UT, USA: Ancestry.com Operations, Inc., 2014. FHL film number: 1473701 (David Taylor) and 1473701 (Charles Taylor).

Ancestry.com, Pigot, *Pigot's Sussex Directory* (Place of Publication Unknown: Pigot & Co., 1832).


## ARCHIVAL SOURCES (UNITED KINGDOM)
### East Sussex Records Office

ESRO, Criminal Indictments, RYE 8/134.

ESRO, Diary for Thomas Chester Daws for 1834, HMU/1/4/3/11.

**The National Archives of the United Kingdom**

TNA, ADM101/50/10.

TNA, HO8/43.

TNA, HO10/33.

TNA, HO10/41.

TNA, HO13/66.

TNA, HO27/50.

TNA, HO107/1109.

## AUSTRALIAN COURT RECORDS

*R. v. Charley* (1835). Published by Macquarie University. <www.law.mq.edu.au/scnsw/Correspondence/36.htm>. Taken from NSWSA: Supreme Court of New South Wales; NRS 13686, Miscellaneous correspondence relating to Aborigines, [5/1161], *R. v. Charley* (1835) No. 36.

## GOVERNMENT REPORTS

British House of Commons, *Parliamentary Papers*, vol. 42 (London: HM Stationery Office, 1938).

British House of Commons, 'Report of the Commissioner of Enquiry into the State of the Colony in New South Wales', *Parliamentary Papers* 1822 (156) (Bigge Report).

Great Britain, Commission for Inquiring into the State of the Several Municipal Corporations in England and Wales, *Introductory Report on the Cinque Ports* (England, 1834).

New South Wales Legislative Assembly [NSWLA], *New South Wales Legislative Assembly Minutes* (11 October 1900). (Sydney: Government Printer, 1900), p. 3891.

New South Wales Legislative Council, *Minutes of Evidence Taken Before the Committee on Police* (Sydney: Government Printer, 1835).

New South Wales Legislative Council, *Report from the Committee on the Aborigines Question, with the Minutes of Evidence* (Sydney: J Spilsbury, 1838).

Victorian Legislative Council, *Report from the Select Committee on Police* (Melbourne: John Ferres, 1852).

Victorian Legislative Council, *Report of the Select Committee of the Legislative Council on the Aborigines* (Melbourne: John Ferres, 1859).

Victorian Legislative Council, *Report of the Select Committee of the Legislative Council on the Gold Fields* (Melbourne: John Ferres, 1853).

Victorian Legislative Council, *Return Respecting the Goldfields* (Melbourne: John Ferres, 1851).

## LEGISLATION

*Aborigines Protection Act* 1909 (NSW).

*Aborigines Protection Amendment Act* 1915 (NSW).

*An Act for the Gradual Abolition of Slavery* 1780 (Pennsylvania). <avalon.law.yale.edu/18th_century/pennst01.asp>

*Bushranging Act* 1830 (NSW), 11 Geo. IV No. 10.

*Chinese Immigration Restriction Act* 1861 (NSW), 25 Vict. No. 3.

*Criminal Law and Evidence Amendment Act* 1891 (NSW), 55 Vict. No. 5.

*Dog and Goat Act* 1898 (NSW), No. 44.

*Felons Apprehension Act* 1865 (NSW), 28 Vict. No. 2.

*Felons Apprehension Act*, 1899 (NSW), 63 Vict. No. 26.

*Fugitive Slave Act* 1850 (USA).

*Marriages Act* 1855 (NSW), 19 Vict. No. 30.

*Married Women's Property Act* 1893 (NSW), 56 Vict. No. 11.

*Masters and Servants Act* 1828 (NSW) 9 Geo. IV No. 9.

*Minors Marriages Act* 1838 (NSW), 2 Vict. No. 13.
*Vagrancy Act* 1835 (NSW), 6 Will. IV No. 6.
*Vagrancy Act* 1851 (NSW), 15 Vict. No. 9.


## NEWSPAPERS AND GOVERNMENT CIRCULARS

*Age* (Melbourne, VIC)
*Albury Banner* (NSW)
*Argus* (Melbourne, VIC)
*Armidale Express* (NSW)
*Australian* (Sydney)
*Australian News for Home Readers* (Melbourne, VIC)
*Australian Star* (Sydney, NSW)
*Bathurst Free Press* (NSW)
*Bell's Life in Sydney and Sporting Reviewer* (NSW)
*Bendigo Advertiser* (VIC)
*Bendigo Independent* (VIC)
*Brisbane Courier* (QLD)
*Clarence River Examiner* (Grafton, NSW)
*Colonist* (Sydney, NSW)
*Cootamundra Herald* (NSW)
*Courier* (Hobart, TAS)
*Daily Telegraph* (Sydney, NSW)
*Dubbo Dispatch* (NSW)
*Dubbo Liberal* (NSW)
*Eastern Districts Chronicle* (York, WA)
*Empire* (Sydney, NSW)
*Evening News* (Sydney, NSW)
*Evening Star* (Boulder, WA)
*Fitzroy City Press* (VIC)
*Geelong Advertiser* (VIC)
*Goulburn Evening Penny Post* (NSW)
*Goulburn Herald and Chronicle* (NSW)
*Goulburn Penny Post* (NSW)
*Illawarra Mercury* (Wollongong, NSW)
*Independent* (Footscray, VIC)
*Kiama Independent* (NSW)
*Launceston Examiner* (TAS)
*Maitland Mercury* (NSW)
*Manaro Mercury* (NSW)
*Melbourne Punch* (VIC)
*Mercury* (Hobart, TAS)
*Mount Alexander Mail* (VIC)
*Mudgee Guardian* (NSW)
*National Advocate* (Bathurst, NSW)
*Nepean Times* (Penrith, NSW)

*New South Wales Police Gazette* (NSW)
*Newcastle Chronicle* (NSW)
*Northern Star* (Lismore, NSW)
*Richmond River Herald* (NSW)
*Riverine Herald* (Echuca, VIC)
*Rye's Own Magazine* (UK)
*Scone Advocate* (NSW)
*Singleton Argus* (NSW)
*Sydney Gazette* (NSW)
*Sydney Herald* (NSW)
*Sydney Mail* (NSW)
*Sydney Monitor* (NSW)
*Sydney Morning Herald* (NSW)
*Tasmanian Colonist* (Hobart Town, TAS)
*Truth* (Sydney, NSW)
*Tumut and Adelong Times* (NSW)
*Victorian Government Gazette* (Melbourne, VIC)
*Walcha Witness* (NSW)
*Western Post* (Newcastle, NSW)
*Wingham Chronicle* (NSW)


## ORAL HISTORIES

Martyn, Lorraine, interviewed by Meg Foster. iPhone recording, Newcastle, NSW 15 June 2017.


## PUBLISHED SOURCES

Bailliere, FF and Robert P Whitworth, *Bailliere's NSW Gazetteer, LO-Z* (Sydney: FF Bailliere, 1866).

Barnard, James, 'Observations on the statistics of Van Diemen's Land for 1849: compiled from official records in the Colonial Secretary's Office', *Papers and Proceedings of the Royal Society of Tasmania* vol. 2, no. 1 (1852), pp. 1–33.

Blackstone, William, *Commentaries on the Laws of England in Four Books* (Philadelphia: JB Lippincott Co., 1893).

Clacy, Mrs Charles, *A Lady's Visit to the Gold Diggings of Australia in 1852–53* (Melbourne: Lansdowne Press, 1963, c.1853).

Coghlan, TA, *The Decline of the Birth-Rate of New South Wales and Other Phenomena of Child-birth* (Sydney: William Applegate Gullick, 1903).

———, *The Wealth and Progress of New South Wales, 1898–1899* (Sydney: William Applegate Gullick, 1900).

Craig, William, *My Adventures on the Australian Goldfields* (Melbourne: Cassell and Company, 1903).

Ellery, RLJ et al, *Victoria and Its Metropolis, Past and Present. Volume 11A: The Colony and Its People in 1888* (Melbourne: McCarron, Bird & Co. Publishers, 1888).

————, *Victoria and Its Metropolis, Past and Present. Volume 11B: The Colony and Its People in 1888* (Melbourne: McCarron, Bird & Co. Publishers, 1888).

Giles, Herbert, *Glossary of Reference on Subjects Connected with the Far East* (Shanghai: Kelly & Walsh, 1900).

Hassall, James S, *In Old Australia: Records and reminiscences from 1794* (Brisbane: RS Hews & Co., 1902).

*Historical Records of Australia* [HRA] (Canberra: Library Committee of the Commonwealth Parliament, 1923).

*Historical Records of New South Wales* [HRNSW] (Sydney: Government Publisher, 1890–1901).

Horsfield, Thomas, *The History, Antiquities and Topography of the County of Sussex* (Lewes, UK: Sussex Press, 1835).

Jenkins, Joseph with William Evans (ed.), *Diary of a Welsh Swagman, 1869–1898* (Melbourne: Macmillan, 1975).

Lewis, Samuel, *A Topographical Dictionary of England* (London: S Lewis and Co., 1831).

Lush, Montague, *The Law of Husband and Wife* (London: Stevens and Sons Limited, 1896).

Melville, Henry, *The History of the Island of Van Diemen's Land, from the year 1824 to 1835 inclusive* (Cambridge: Cambridge University Press, c.1835, 2012).

Parry, JD, *An Historical and Descriptive Account of the Coast of Sussex* (London: E & W Books Ltd, 1970, c.1833).

Plunkett, John Hubert, *The Australian Magistrate* (Sydney: JJ Moore, 1866).

*Records of the Castlemaine Pioneers* (Melbourne: Rigby Limited, 1972).

Ryan, James Tobias, *Reminiscences of Australia: Containing 70 years of his knowledge and 35 years of his ancestors* (Sydney: George Robinson, 1894).

St Michel-Podmore, *Rambles and Adventures* (London: L Upcott Gill, 1909).

Therry, Roger, *Reminiscences of Thirty Years' Residence in New South Wales and Victoria* (London: Sampson Low Son & Co., 1863).

United Kingdom Poll Books, *East Sussex Election: List of the registered electors, with the votes of those who actually polled* (Lewes: RW Lower, 1837).

West, John, *The History of Tasmania* (Cambridge: Cambridge University Press, 2011, c.1852).

White, Charles, *Australian Bushranging: John Vane, bushranger* (NSW Bookstall Co. Ltd: Sydney, 1921).

## TREATIES

*Treaty of Nanking* 1842 (Nanjing). Taken from UCLA International Institute: Asia Pacific Centre, 2016. <www.international.ucla.edu/asia/article/18421>

# SECONDARY SOURCES

## FILMS

Schepisi, Fred, *The Chant of Jimmie Blacksmith* (film) (Melbourne: The Film House, 1978).

## GOVERNMENT REPORTS AND PARLIAMENTARY SUBMISSIONS

Grandmothers Against Removals, *Submission to the House of Representatives Standing Committee on Social Policy and Legal Affairs: Inquiry into Adoption* (May 2018), p. 2. <www.aph.gov.au/DocumentStore.ashx?id=12d80b1a-daf1-45eb-b064-b9b2e92309ac&subId=566046>

Human Rights and Equal Opportunity Commission [HREOC], *Bringing Them Home: Report of the National Inquiry into the Separation of Aboriginal and Torres Strait Islander Children from their Families* [Commissioner: Ronald Wilson] (Sydney: Human Rights and Equal Opportunity Commission, 1997). <www.austlii.edu.au/au/special/rsjproject/rsjlibrary/hreoc/stolen/>

## JOURNAL ARTICLES

Abate, Michelle Ann, '"Bury My Heart on Recent History": Mark Twain's "Hellfire Hotchkiss", the massacre at Wounded Knee, and the dime novel Western', *American Literary Realism* vol. 42, no. 2 (2010), pp. 114–128.

Antony, Robert J, 'Peasants, Heroes and Brigands: The problems of social banditry in early nineteenth-century South China', *Modern China* vol. 15, no. 2 (1989), pp. 123–148.

Attwood, Bain, 'Portrait of an Aboriginal as an Artist: Sally Morgan and the construction of Aboriginality', *Aboriginal History* vol. 25, no. 99 (1992), pp. 302–318.

Bacon, Jacqueline and Glen McClish, 'Reinventing the Master's Tools: Nineteenth-century African-American literary societies of Philadelphia and rhetorical education', *Rhetoric Society Quarterly* vol. 30, no. 4 (2000), pp. 19–47.

Bagnall, Kate, 'Rewriting the History of Chinese Families in Nineteenth-century Australia', *Australian Historical Studies* vol. 42, no. 1 (2011), pp. 62–77.

Bairstow, Damaris, '"With the Best Will in the World": Some records of early white contact with the Gampignal on the Australian Agricultural Company's estate at Port Stephens', *Aboriginal History* vol. 17 (1993), pp. 4–16.

Baxter, Carol and David Andrew Roberts, '"Mrs Thunderbolt": setting the record straight on the life and times of Mary Ann Bugg', *Journal of Australian Studies* vol. 99, no. 1 (2013), pp. 55–76.

Behrendt, Larissa, 'Consent in a (Neo) Colonial Society: Aboriginal women as sexual and legal "other"', *Australian Feminist Studies* vol. 15, no. 33 (2000), pp. 353–367.

Bellanta, Melissa, 'Leary Kin: Australian larrikins and the blackface minstrel dandy', *Journal of Social History* vol. 42, no. 3 (2009), pp. 677–695.

Bennett, James, 'Māori as Honorary Members of the White Tribe', *Journal of Imperial and Commonwealth History* vol. 29, no. 3 (2001), pp. 33–54.

Bennett, JM, 'The Day of Retribution: Bigge's inquiries in colonial New South Wales', *The American Journal of Legal History* vol. 15, no. 2 (1971), pp. 85–106.

Biber, Katherine, 'Besieged at Home: Jimmy Governor's Rampage', *Public Space: The journal of law and social justice* vol. 2 (2008), pp. 1–41.

——, 'In Jimmy Governor's Archive', *Archives and Manuscripts* vol. 42, no. 3 (2014), pp. 270–281.

Blackburn, Kevin, 'Mapping Aboriginal Nations: The "nation" concept of late nineteenth century anthropologists in Australia', *Aboriginal History* vol. 26 (2002), pp. 131–158.

Blyton, Greg and John Ramsland, 'Mixed Race Unions and Indigenous Demography in the Hunter Valley of New South Wales, 1788–1850', *Journal of the Royal Australian Historical Society* vol. 98, no. 1 (2012), pp. 125–148.

Britton, Clare, 'Posts in a Paddock: Revisiting the Jimmy Governor tragedy, approaching reconciliation and connecting families through the medium of theatre', *Journal of the European Association for Studies of Australia* vol. 4, no. 1 (2013), pp. 143–157.

Cahir, Fred and Ian Clark, '"why should they pay money to the Queen?": Aboriginal miners and land claims', *Journal of Australian Colonial History* vol. 10, no. 1 (2008), pp. 115–128.

Carey, Hilary and David Roberts, 'Smallpox and the Biaime Waganna of Wellington Valley, New South Wales, 1829–1840: the earliest nativist movement in Aboriginal Australia', *Ethnohistory* vol. 49, no. 4 (2002), pp. 821–869.

Colligan, Mimi, 'Waxworks Shows and Some of Their Proprietors in Australia, 1850–1910', *Australasian Drama Studies* vol. 34 (1999), pp. 86–107.

Davies, Peter, Susan Lawrence and Jodi Turnbull, 'Harvesting Water on a Victorian Goldfield', *Australasian Historical Archaeology* vol. 29 (2011), pp. 24–32.

Davison, Graeme, 'Sydney and the Bush: An urban context for the Australian legend', *Australian Historical Studies* vol. 18 (1978), pp. 191–209.

Denholm, Decie, 'Port Arthur: The men and the myth', *Australian Historical Studies* vol. 14, no. 55 (1970), pp. 406–423.

Dingle, AE, '"A Truly Magnificent Thirst": An historical survey of Australian drinking habits', *Australian Historical Studies* vol. 19, no. 75 (1980), pp. 229–249.

Duffield, Ian, 'From Slave Colonies to Penal Colonies: The West Indian convict transportees to Australia', *Slavery and Abolition* vol. 7, no. 1 (1986), pp. 25–45.

——, 'Skilled Workers or Marginalised Poor? The African population of the United Kingdom, 1812–52', *Immigrants and Minorities* vol. 12, no. 3 (1993), pp. 49–87.

Eburn, Michael, 'Outlawry in Colonial Australia: Felons Apprehension Acts, 1865–1899', *Australia and New Zealand Law and History* E-Journal (2005). Accessed 12 June 2019 via: < www.anzlhsejournal.auckland.ac.nz/pdfs_2005/Eburn.pdf >

Elbourne, Elizabeth, 'The Sin of the Settler: The 1835–36 Select Committee on Aborigines and debates over virtue and conquest in the early nineteenth-century British white settler Empire', *Journal of Colonialism and Colonial History* vol. 4, no. 3 (2003).

Ellinghaus, Katherine, 'Margins of Acceptability: Class, education and interracial marriage in Australia and North America', *Frontiers* vol. 23, no. 3 (2002), pp. 55–75.

Evans, Raymond and Bill Thorpe, 'Commanding Men: Masculinities and the convict system', *Journal of Australian Studies* vol. 22, no. 56 (1998), pp. 17–34.

—— and William Thorpe, 'Power, Punishment and Penal Labour: *Convict Workers* and Moreton Bay', *Australian Historical Studies* vol. 25, no. 98 (1992), pp. 90–111.

Evans, Tanya, 'Secrets and Lies: The radical potential of family history', *History Workshop Journal* no. 71 (2011), pp. 49–73.

Foxhall, Katherine, 'From Convicts to Colonists: The health of prisoners and the voyage to Australia, 1823–1853', *Journal of Imperial and Commonwealth History* vol. 39, no. 1 (2011), pp. 1–19.

Freeman, Ashley Thomas, 'Bushrangers, Itinerant Teachers and Constructing Educational Policy in 1860s NSW', *History of Education Review* vol. 48, no. 1 (2019), pp. 15–30.

Garton, Stephen, 'The Convict Origins Debate: Historians and the problem of the "criminal class"', *Australia and New Zealand Journal of Criminology* vol. 24 (1991), pp. 66–82.

Gilchrist, Catie, '"A Victim of His Own Temerity"? Silence, scandal and the recall of Sir John Eardley-Wilmot', *Journal of Australian Studies* vol. 28, no. 84 (2005), pp. 151–161.

Grimshaw, Patricia, 'Interracial Marriages and Colonial Regimes in Victoria and Aotearoa/New Zealand', *Frontiers* vol. 23, no. 3 (2003), pp. 12–28.

Hannah, Mark, 'Aboriginal Workers in the Australian Agricultural Company, 1824–1857', *Labour History* vol. 82 (2002), pp. 17–33.

Harris, Wendy, 'Spousal Competence and Compellability in Criminal Trials in the Twenty First Century', *Queensland University of Technology Law and Justice Journal* vol. 3, no. 2 (2003), pp. 274–296.

Haskins, Victoria and John Maynard, 'Sex, Race and Power: Aboriginal men and white women in Australian history', *Australian Historical Studies* vol. 36, no. 126 (2005), pp. 191–216.

Henriques, URQ, 'The Rise and Fall of the Separate System of Prison Discipline', *Past & Present* vol. 54 (1972), pp. 61–93.

Hirsch, Alison Duncan, 'Uncovering the "Hidden History of Mestizo America" in Elizabeth Drinker's Diary: Interracial relationships in late eighteenth-century Philadelphia', *Pennsylvania History: A journal of mid-Atlantic studies* vol. 68, no. 4 (2001), pp. 483–506.

Hirst, John, 'The Pioneer Legend', *Australian Historical Studies* vol. 18, no. 71 (1978), pp. 316–337.

Hobsbawm, Eric, 'Social Bandits: Reply', *Comparative Studies in Society and History* vol. 14, no. 4 (1972), pp. 503–505.

Hunter, Kathryn M, 'Silence in the Noisy Archives: Reflections of Judith Allen's "Evidence and Silence – feminism and the limits of history" (1986) in the era of mass digitisation', *Australian Feminist Studies* vol. 32, no. 91–92 (2017), pp. 202–212.

Jennings, Thelma, '"Us Colored Women Had to Go Through a Plenty": Sexual exploitation of African-American Slave Women', *Journal of Women's History* vol. 1, no. 3 (1990), pp. 45–74.

Jones, Daryl E, 'Blood'n Thunder: Virgins, villains and violence in the dime novel Western', *Journal of Popular Culture* vol. 4, no. 2 (1970), pp. 507–517.

Karskens, Grace, '"This Spirit of Emigration": The nature and meanings of escape in early New South Wales', *Journal of Australian Colonial History* vol. 7 (2005), pp. 1–34.

Kellerman, MH, 'Interesting Account of the Travels of Abraham Abrahamsohn', *Australian Jewish Historical Society* vol. 7 (1974), pp. 478–494.

Kent, David, 'Decorative Bodies: The significance of convicts' tattoos', *Journal of Australian Studies* vol. 21, no. 53 (1997), pp. 78–88.

——and Norma Townsend, 'Some Aspects of Colonial Marriage: A case study of the swing protesters', *Labour History* no. 74 (1998), pp. 40–53.

Kimber, Julie, 'Poor Laws: A historiography of vagrancy in Australia', *History Compass* vol. 11, no. 8 (2013), pp. 537–550.

Kociumbas, Jan, '"Mary Ann", Joseph Fleming and "Gentleman Dick": Aboriginal–convict relationships in colonial history', *Journal of Australian Colonial History* vol. 3, no. 1 (2001), pp. 28–54.

Lake, Marilyn, 'The Politics of Respectability: Identifying the masculinist context', *Australian Historical Studies* vol. 22, no. 86 (1986), pp. 116–131.

——, 'White Man's Country: The transnational history of a national project', *Australian Historical Studies* vol. 34, no. 112 (2003), pp. 346–363.

Lamley, Harry J, 'Hsieh-Tau: The pathology of violence in south-eastern China', *Ch'ing-shih wen-t'i* vol. 3, no. 7 (November 1977), pp. 1–39.

Lester, Alan, 'Settler Colonialism, George Grey and the Politics of Ethnography', *Environment and Planning D: Society and space* vol. 34, no. 3 (2016), pp. 492–507.

Lydon, Jane, 'Bullets, Teeth and Photographs: Recognising Indigenous Australians between the wars', *History of Photography* vol. 36, no. 3 (2012), pp. 275–287.

Mann, Susan, 'The Male Bond in Chinese History and Culture', *American Historical Review* vol. 105, no. 5 (2000), pp. 1600–1614.

Maxwell-Stewart, Hamish, 'The Rise and Fall of John Longworth: Work and punishment in early Port Arthur', *Tasmanian Historical Studies* vol. 6, no. 2 (1999), pp. 96–114.

McGowan, Barry, 'Reconsidering Race: The Chinese experience on the goldfields of southern NSW', *Australian Historical Studies* vol. 36, no. 124 (2004), pp. 312–331.

McGrath, Ann, 'Playing Colonials: Cowgirls, cowboys, and Indians in Australia and North America', *Journal of Colonialism and Colonial History* vol. 2, no. 1 (2001).

——, 'The White Man's Looking Glass: Aboriginal-colonial gender relations at Port Jackson', *Australian Historical Studies* vol. 24, no. 95 (1990), pp. 189–206.

Meredith, David and Deborah Oxley, 'Contracting Convicts: The convict labour market in Van Diemen's Land', *Australian Economic History Review* vol. 45, no. 1 (2005), pp. 45–72.

Morrissey, Doug, 'Ned Kelly and Horse and Cattle Stealing', *Victorian Historical Journal* vol. 66, no. 1 (1995), pp. 29–48.

Nettelbeck, Amanda, 'Creating the Aboriginal Vagrant: Protective governance and Indigenous mobility in colonial Australia', *Pacific Historical Review* vol. 87, no. 1 (2018), pp. 79–100.

Newman, Richard S, '"Lucky to be born in Pennsylvania": Free soil, fugitive slaves, and the making of Pennsylvania's anti-slavery borderland', *Slavery and Abolition* vol. 32, no. 3 (2011), pp. 413–430.

Noonan, Rodney, 'Chinese Bushrangers in Australian History and Literature', *Journal of Australian Studies* vol. 24, no. 65 (2000), pp. 127–135.

Okur, Nilgun Anadolu, 'Underground Railroad in Philadelphia, 1830–1860', *Journal of Black Studies* vol. 25, no. 5 (1995), pp. 537–557.

Oppenheimer, Jillian, 'Thunderbolt's Mary Ann – an Aboriginal bushranger', *Journal of the Royal Australian Historical Society* vol. 78, no. 3–4 (1992), pp. 92–107.

Pennington, Kenneth, 'Innocent Until Proven Guilty: The origins of a legal maxim', *The Jurist* vol. 63 (2003), pp. 106–124.

Petrow, Stefan, 'Policing in a Penal Colony: Governor Arthur's police system in Van Diemen's Land', *Law and History Review* vol. 18, no. 2 (2000), pp. 351–395.

Porter, Roy, 'The Drinking Man's Disease: The "pre-history" of alcoholism in Georgian Britain', *British Journal of Addiction* vol. 80 (1985), pp. 385–396.

Reeves, Keir, 'Goldfields Settler or Frontier Rogue?: The trial of James Acoy and the Chinese on the Mount Alexander Diggings', *Provenance: The journal of the public record office of Victoria* vol. 5 (2006).

Reynolds, Henry, 'Jimmy Governor and Jimmie Blacksmith', *Australian Literary Studies* vol. 9, no. 1 (1979), pp. 14–25.

Roberts, David Andrew, 'Bells Falls Massacre and Bathurst's History of Violence: Local tradition and Australian Historiography', *Australian Historical Studies* vol. 26, no. 105 (1995), pp. 615–633.

—— 'Masters, Magistrates and the Management of Complaint: The 1833 convict revolt at Castle Forbes and the failure of local governance', *Journal of Australian Colonial History* vol. 19 (2017), pp. 57–94.

—— and Carol Baxter, 'Exposing an Exposé: Fact versus fiction in the resurrection of Captain Thunderbolt', *Journal of Australian Studies* vol. 36, no. 1 (2012), pp. 1–15.

Rose, Deborah Bird, 'Ned Kelly Died for Our Sins', *Oceania* vol. 65, no. 2 (1994), pp. 175–186.

Salmond, Anne, 'Tuki's Universe', *New Zealand Journal of History* vol. 38, no. 2 (2004), pp. 215–232.

Shaw, AGL, 'The Origins of the Probation System in Van Diemen's Land', *Australian Historical Studies* vol. 6, no. 21 (1953), pp. 16–28.

——, 'Violent Protest in Australian History', *Australian Historical Studies* vol. 15, no. 60 (1973), pp. 545–561.

Smith, Bradley P and Carla A Litchfield, 'A Review of the Relationship Between Indigenous Australians, Dingoes (*Canis Dingo*) and Domestic Dogs (*Canis Familiaris*)', *Anthrozoos* vol. 22, no. 2 (2009), pp. 111–128.

Smith, Eric L, 'The End of Black Voting Rights in Pennsylvania: African Americans and the Pennsylvania constitution', *Pennsylvania History* vol. 65 (1998), pp. 279–299.

Spencer, Tracy, '"Woman Lives as a Lubra in Native Camp": Representations of shared space', *Journal of Australian Studies* vol. 28, no. 82 (2004), pp. 61–74.

Stafford, Robert, 'Preventing the "Curse of California": Advice for English emigrants to the Australian goldfields', *Historical Records of Australian Science* vol. 7, no. 3 (1987), pp. 215–230.

Standfield, Rachel, 'The Parramatta Māori Seminary and the Education of Indigenous Peoples in Early Colonial New South Wales', *History of Education Review* vol. 41, no. 2 (2012), pp. 119–128.

Taylor, Rebe, '"All I Know Is History": Memory and land ownership in the Dudley District, Kangaroo Island', *The UTS Review* vol. 5, no. 1 (1999), pp. 6–35.

——, *Unearthed: The Aboriginal Tasmanians of Kangaroo Island* (Kent Town, SA: Wakefield Press, 2002).

Twomey, Christina, 'Gender, Welfare and the Colonial State: Victoria's 1864 *Neglected and Criminal Children's Act*', *Labour History* vol. 73 (1997), pp. 169–186.

——, 'Without Natural Protectors: Responses to wife desertion in Gold Rush Victoria', *Australian Historical Studies* vol. 27, no. 108 (1997), pp. 22–46.

Urban, Andrew, 'Legends of Deadwood', *Journal of American History* vol. 94, no. 1 (2007), pp. 224–231.

Vines, Prue, 'Annie Ludford, Postmistress: The *Married Women's Property Acts* and public service employment in 1890s NSW', *Law and History* vol. 2 (2015), pp. 146–176.

Walker, RB, 'Bushranging in Fact and Legend', *Australian Historical Studies* vol. 11, no. 42 (1964), pp. 206–221.

———, 'Captain Thunderbolt, Bushranger', *Journal of the Royal Australian Historical Society* vol. 43, no. 5 (1957), pp. 223–251.

Walker, Robin, 'The New South Wales Police Force, 1862–1900', *Journal of Australian Studies* vol. 8, no. 15 (1984), pp. 25–38.

Waterhouse, Richard, 'Australian Legends: Representations of the bush, 1813–1913', *Australian Historical Studies* vol. 31, no. 115 (2000), pp. 201–221.

———, 'Bare Knuckle Prize Fighting, Masculinity and Nineteenth Century Australian Culture', *Journal of Australian Studies* vol. 26, no. 73 (2002), pp. 101–110.

West, Susan, '"Spiders in the Centre of their Webs": The NSW police and bushranging in the 1860s', *Journal of Australian Colonial History* vol. 8 (2006), pp. 1–22.

———, 'The Role of the "Bush" in 1860s bushranging', *Journal of the Royal Australian Historical Society* vol. 91, no. 2 (2005), pp. 133–147.

———, '"The Thiefdom": Bushrangers, supporters and social banditry in 1860s New South Wales', *Journal of the Royal Australian Historical Society* vol. 101, no. 2 (2015), pp. 134–155.

Wolf, Gabrielle, 'Innocent Convicts and Respectable Bushrangers: History and the nation in Melbourne melodrama, 1890–1914', *Journal of Australian Studies* vol. 28, no. 81 (2004), pp. 73–81.

Woollacott, Angela, 'Frontier Violence and Settler Manhood', *History Australia* vol. 6, no. 1 (2009), p. 11.1–11.15.

## MONOGRAPHS AND EDITED COLLECTIONS

Alexander, Alison and David Young, 'Boxing' in Alison Alexander (ed.), *The Companion to Tasmanian History* (Hobart: Centre for Tasmanian Historical Studies, 2005), p. 52.

Allen, Matthew, 'Australia and New Zealand' in Scott C Martin (ed.), *The Sage Encyclopaedia of Alcohol: Social, cultural and historical perspectives*, vol. 1 (Los Angeles: Sage Reference, 2015), pp. 195–197.

Anderson, Margaret, 'Mrs Charles Clacy, Lola Montez and Poll the Grog Seller: Glimpses of women on the early Victorian goldfields' in Iain McCalman, Alexander Cook and Andrew Rees (eds), *Gold: Forgotten histories and lost objects of Australia* (Cambridge: Cambridge University Press, 2001), pp. 225–249.

Annear, Robyn, *Nothing But Gold: The diggers of 1852* (Melbourne: Text Publishing, 1999).

Arneil, Barbara, *John Locke and America: The defence of English colonialism* (Oxford: Oxford University Press, 1996).

Bairstow, Damaris, *A Million Pounds, A Million Acres: The pioneer settlement of the Australian Agricultural Company* (Sydney: D. Bairstow, 2003).

Bate, Weston, *Victorian Gold Rushes* (Ballarat: Sovereign Hill Museums Association, 1999).

Bateson, Charles, *The Convict Ships, 1787–1868* (Glasgow: Brown, Son & Ferguson Ltd, 1959).

Baxter, Carol, *Captain Thunderbolt and His Lady: The true story of bushrangers Frederick Ward and Mary Ann Bugg* (Sydney: Allen & Unwin, 2011).

Bean, Charles EW, *Official History of Australia in the Great War* (Sydney: Angus and Robertson, 1935).

Beatty, Bill, *A Treasury of Australian Folk Tales and Traditions* (London: Edmund Ward Publishers, 1960).

Benton, Lauren and Lisa Ford, *Rage for Order: The British Empire and the origins of international law, 1800–1850* (Harvard: Harvard University Press, 2016).

Berlin, Ira, 'Slavery, Freedom, and Philadelphia's Struggle for Brotherly Love, 1685 to 1861' in Richard Newman and James Mueller (eds), *Antislavery and Abolition in Philadelphia: Emancipation and the long struggle for racial justice in the city of brotherly love* (Baton Rouge: Louisiana State University Press, 2011), pp. 19–44.

Birch, Tony, 'The Trouble with History' in Anna Clark and Paul Ashton (eds) *Australian History Now* (Sydney: NewSouth, 2013), pp. 232–250.

Blainey, Geoffrey, *A History of Victoria* (Cambridge: Cambridge University Press, 2006).

Boladeras, Jean, 'The Desolate Loneliness of Racial Passing' in Maureen Perkins (ed.), *Visibly Different: Face, place and race in Australia* (Bern: Peter Lang, 2007), pp. 49–63.

Bolster, W Jeffrey, *Black Jacks: African American seamen in the age of sail* (London: Harvard University Press, 1997).

Bongiorno, Frank, *The Sex Lives of Australians* (Melbourne: Black Inc., 2012).

Boxall, George E, *The Story of the Australian Bushrangers* (London: Swann Sonnenschien, 1899).

Bradshaw, Jack, *The True Story of the Australian Bushrangers* (Sydney: WJ Anderson & Co., 1924).

Brand, Ian, *The Convict Probation System: Van Diemen's Land, 1839–1854* (Hobart: Blubber Head Press, 1990).

Broome, Richard, *Aboriginal Australians* (Sydney: Allen & Unwin, 2019).

Brown, Christopher L, *Moral Capital: Foundations of British Abolitionism* (Chapel Hill: University of North Carolina Press, 2006).

Burchall, Michael J, *Sussex Convicts Transported to Australia 1789–1867* (Hampshire, Parish Register Transcription Society, 2011).

Byrne, Paula, *Criminal Law and Colonial Subject: New South Wales, 1810–1830* (Cambridge: Cambridge University Press, 1993).

Cahir, Fred, *Black Gold: Aboriginal people on the goldfields of Victoria, 1850–1870* (Canberra: ANU Press, 2012).

Caldwell, JC, 'Population' in Wray Vamplew (ed.), *Australians: Historical statistics* (Sydney: Fairfax, Syme & Weldon Associates, 1987), pp. 23–41.

Cameron, Roy, 'Breelong Tragedy' in Kathielyn Job (ed.), *Around the Black Stump* (Coolah: Council Shire of Coolah, 1993), pp. 87–102.

Carpenter, Lloyd, 'Finding "Te Wherro in Otakou": Otago Māori and the gold rush', in Lloyd Carpenter and Lyndon Fraser (eds), *Rushing for Gold: Life and commerce on the goldfields of New Zealand and Australia* (Dunedin: Otago University Press, 2016), pp. 87–100.

Carrodus, Geraldine, *Gold, Gamblers and Sly Grog: Life on the goldfields, 1851–1900* (Oxford: Oxford University Press, 1981).

Chadban, John, *Stroud and the AA Co.* (Stroud, NSW: Stroud Shire Council, 1970).

Chan, Henry, 'Becoming Australasian but Remaining Chinese: the future of the down under Chinese past' in Henry Chan, Ann Curthoys and Nora Chiang (eds), *The Overseas Chinese in Australasia: History, settlement and interactions* (Taipei: Interdisciplinary Group for Australasian Studies and the Centre for the Study of the Chinese Diaspora, 2001), pp. 1–15.

Chan, Henry, Ann Curthoys and Nora Chiang (eds), *The Overseas Chinese in Australasia: History, settlement and interactions* (Taipei: Interdisciplinary Group for Australasian Studies and the Centre for the Study of the Chinese Diaspora, 2001).

Chee-Beng, Tan, 'Introduction' in Tan Chee-Beng (ed.), *The Routledge Handbook of the Chinese Diaspora* (Oxford: Routledge, 2012), pp. 1–12.

Ching-Hwang, Yen, *Coolies and Mandarins: China's protection of overseas Chinese during the late Ch'ing period (1851–1911)* (Singapore: Singapore University Press, 1985).

Clune, Frank, *Jimmy Governor* (Sydney: Horwitz, 1959).

Connors, Libby, 'Uncovering the Shameful: Sexual violence on an Australian colonial frontier' in Robert Mason (ed.), *Legacies of Violence: Rendering the unspeakable past in modern Australia* (New York: Berghahn Books, 2017), pp. 33–52.

Conor, Liz, *Skin Deep: Settler impressions of Aboriginal women* (Crawley: UWA Press, 2016).

Couzens, Andrew James, *A Cultural History of the Bushranger Legend in Theatres and Cinemas, 1828–2017* (London: Anthem Press, 2019).

Currey, CH, *Sir Francis Forbes: The first chief justice of the Supreme Court of New South Wales* (Sydney: Angus and Robertson, 1968).

Curthoys, Ann, 'Good Christians and Useful Workers: Aborigines, church and state in New South Wales, 1870–1883' in Sydney Labour History Group (eds), *What Rough Beast? The State and social order in Australian History* (Sydney: Allen & Unwin, 1982), pp. 31–56.

—, '"Men of All Nations, Except Chinamen": Europeans and Chinese on the goldfields of New South Wales' in Iain McCalman, Alexander Cook and Andrew Reeves (eds), *Gold: Forgotten histories and lost objects of Australia* (Cambridge: Cambridge University Press, 2001), pp. 103–123.

Darnell, Maxine, 'Master and Servant, Squatter and Shepherd: The regulation of indentured Chinese labourers to NSW, 1847–1853' in Henry Chan, Ann Curthoys and Nora Chiang (eds.), *The Overseas Chinese in Australasia: History, settlement and interactions* (Taipei and Canberra: Interdisciplinary Group for Australasian Studies and the Centre for the Study of the Chinese Southern Diaspora, 2001), pp. 44–53.

Davey, Gwenda and Graham Seal, 'Bushrangers' in Gwenda Davey and Graham Seal (eds), *Oxford Companion to Australian Folklore* (Oxford: Oxford University Press, 1993), pp. 58–61.

Davis, Richard, 'Exile' in Alison Alexander (ed.), *The Companion to Tasmanian History* (Hobart: Centre for Tasmanian Historical Studies, 2005), pp. 432–437.

Dening, Greg, *Mr Bligh's Bad Language: Passion, power and theatre on the Bounty* (Cambridge: Cambridge University Press, 1992).

Dickey, Brian, *No Charity There: A short history of social welfare in Australia* (Sydney: Allen & Unwin, 1980).

Douglas, Heather and Mark Finnane, *Indigenous Crime and Settler Law: White sovereignty after empire* (Basingstoke: Palgrave Macmillan, 2012).

Duffield, Ian, '"I asked how the vessel could go": The contradictory experiences of African and African diaspora mariners and port workers in Britain, 1750–1850' in Anne J Kershen (ed.), *Language, Labour and Migration* (London: Routledge, 2000), pp. 121–154.

Edmonds, Penelope, 'The Intimate, Urbanising Frontier' in Tracey Banivanua Mar and Penelope Edmonds (eds.), *Making Settler Colonial Space* (London: Palgrave Macmillan, 2010), pp. 129–154.

Egan, Richard, *Neither Amity Nor Kindness: Government policy towards Aboriginal people of New South Wales 1788–1969* (Sydney: R Egan, 2012).

Ellinghaus, Katherine, *Taking Assimilation to Heart: Marriages of white women and Indigenous men in the United States and Australia, 1887–1937* (Lincoln: University of Nebraska Press, 2006).

Evans, Tanya, *Fractured Families: Life on the margins in colonial New South Wales* (Sydney: New South, 2015).

Fels, Marie, *Good Men and True: Aboriginal police of the Port Phillip District, 1837–1853* (Melbourne: Melbourne University Press, 1988).

Finnane, Mark, *Police and Government: Histories of policing in Australia* (Melbourne: Oxford University Press, 1994).

Fitchett, WH, *In the Days of Thunderbolt and Moonlite: The dramatic story of the second generation of bushrangers* (Melbourne: Fitchett Brothers Pty Ltd, 1938).

Fitzgerald, Ross and Trevor L Jordan, *Under the Influence: A history of alcohol in Australia* (Sydney: Harper Collins, 2009).

Fletcher, JJ, *Clean, Clad and Courteous: A history of Aboriginal education in New South Wales* (Sydney: Southwood Press, 1989).

Foster, Meg, 'Murder for White Consumption: Jimmy Governor and the Bush Ballad' in Yu-ting Huang and Rebecca Weaver-Hightower (eds), *Archiving Settler Colonialism: Culture, race and space* (London: Routledge, 2018), pp. 173–189.

Garland, Maurie, *Jimmy Governor: Blood on the tracks* (Melbourne: Brolga Press, 2009).

Garton, Stephen, *Out of Luck: Poor Australians and social welfare, 1788–1988* (Sydney: Allen & Unwin, 1990).

Geertz, Clifford, *The Interpretation of Cultures* (New York: Basic Books, 1973).

Gerzina, Gretchen, *Black London: Life before emancipation* (New Brunswick: Rutgers University Press, 1995).

Gigantino, James, 'Slavery and the Slave Trade' in *The Encyclopedia of Greater Philadelphia* (New Brunswick: Rutgers University, 2012). <philadelphiaencyclopedia.org/archive/slavery-and-the-slave-trade/>

Gillen, Mollie, *The Founders of Australia: A biographical dictionary of the First Fleet* (Sydney: Library of Australian History, 1989).

Goodall, Heather, *Invasion to Embassy: Land in Aboriginal politics in New South Wales, 1770–1972* (Sydney: Sydney University Press, 1996, 2008).

Goodman, David, 'Gold and the Public in the Nineteenth Century Gold Rushes', in Benjamin Mountford and Stephen Tuffnell (eds), *A Global History of Gold Rushes* (Oakland: University of California Press, 2018), pp. 65–87.

—— *Gold Seeking: Victoria and California in the 1850s* (Sydney: Allen & Unwin, 1994).

—— 'The Gold Rushes of the 1850s' in Alison Bashford and Stuart Macintyre (eds), *The Cambridge History of Australia*, vol. 1 (Cambridge: Cambridge University Press, 2013), pp. 170–188.

Gunson, Niel (ed.), *Australian Reminiscences and Papers of LE Threlkeld: Missionary to the Aborigines, 1824–1859* (Canberra: Australian Institute of Aboriginal Studies, 1974).

Guotu, Zhuang, 'China's Policies on Chinese Overseas' in Tan Chee-Beng (ed.), *The Routledge Handbook of the Chinese Diaspora* (Oxford: Routledge, 2012), pp. 31–41.

Grant, Stan, *On Thomas Keneally* (Melbourne: Black Inc., 2021).

Griffiths, Billy, *Deep Time Dreaming: Uncovering ancient Australia* (Melbourne: Black Inc. Books, 2018).

Griffiths, Tom, *Hunters and Collectors: The antiquarian imagination in Australia* (Cambridge: Cambridge University Press, 1996).

Grimshaw, Patricia, et al., *Creating a Nation, 1788–1990* (Ringwood, Victoria: Penguin Books, 1996).

—— and Graham Willett, 'Women's History and Family History: An exploration of colonial family structure' in Norma Grieve and Patricia Grimshaw (eds), *Australian Women: Feminist perspectives* (Oxford: Oxford University Press, 1981), pp. 134–155.

Haebich, Anna, *Broken Circles: Fragmenting families, 1800–2000* (Fremantle, WA: Fremantle Arts Centre Press, 2000).

Haldane, Robert, *The People's Force: A history of the Victorian police* (Melbourne: Melbourne University Press, 1986).

Harman, Kristyn, *Aboriginal Convicts: Australian, Khoisan and Māori exiles* (Sydney: NewSouth Books, 2012).

Hay, Douglas, et al. (eds), *Albion's Fatal Tree: Crime and society in eighteenth century England* (New York: Pantheon, 1975).

Hiatt, LR, *Arguments About Aborigines: Australia and the evolution of social anthropology* (Cambridge: Cambridge University Press, 1996).

Hirst, John, *Convict Society and Its Enemies: A history of early Sydney* (Sydney: Allen & Unwin, 1983).

——, *Freedom on the Fatal Shore: Australia's first colony* (Melbourne: Black Inc., 2008).

——, *The Strange Birth of Colonial Democracy: New South Wales, 1848–1884* (Sydney: Allen & Unwin, 1998).

Hobsbawm, Eric, *Bandits* (Harmondsworth: Penguin Books, 1969).

——, *Primitive Rebels: Studies in archaic forms of social movement in the nineteenth and twentieth centuries* (Manchester: Manchester University Press, 1959).

——, 'Social Banditry' in Henry A Landsberger (ed.), *Rural Protest: Peasant movements and social change* (London: Palgrave Macmillan, 1974), pp. 142–157.

Houghton, Walter, *The Victorian Frame of Mind, 1830–1870* (New Haven: Yale University Press, 1957).

Huggins, Jackie and Thom Blake, 'Protection or Persecution? Gender relations in the era of racial segregation' in Kay Saunders and Raymond Evans (eds), *Gender Relations in Australia: Domination and negotiation* (Sydney: Harcourt Brace, 1994), pp. 42–58.

Irish, Paul, *Hidden in Plain View: The Aboriginal people of coastal Sydney* (Sydney: NewSouth Books, 2017).

Karskens, Grace, *The Colony: A history of early Sydney* (Sydney: Allen & Unwin, 2010).

——, *People of the River* (Sydney: Allen & Unwin, 2020).

——, *The Rocks* (Melbourne: Melbourne University Press, 1997).

Keneally, Thomas, *The Chant of Jimmie Blacksmith* (Melbourne: Penguin Books, 1972).

Kennedy, Leo and Mic Looby, *Black Snake: The real story of Ned Kelly* (Melbourne: Affirm Press, 2018).

Khan, Jeff (ed.), *Posts in the Paddock: Performance space, point 4, exchange* (Sydney: Performance Space Limited, 2011).

Kingston, Beverley, *The Oxford History of Australia*, vol. 3 (Melbourne: Oxford University Press, 1988).

Lake, Marilyn and Henry Reynolds, *Drawing the Global Colour Line: White men's country and the question of racial equality* (Cambridge: Cambridge University Press, 2012).

Lawrence, Susan, 'After the Gold Rush: material culture and settlement on Victoria's central goldfields' in Iain McCalman, Alexander Cook and Andrew Rees (eds), *Gold: Forgotten histories and lost objects of Australia* (Cambridge: Cambridge University Press, 2001), pp. 250–266.

Lecaudey, Helene, 'Behind the Mask: Ex-slave women and interracial sexual relations' in Patricia Morton (ed.), *Discovering the Women in Slavery: Emancipating perspectives on the American Past* (Athens: University of Georgia Press, 1996), pp. 260–277.

Linebaugh, Peter and Marcus Rediker, *The Many Headed Hydra: Sailors, commoners and the hidden history of the Revolutionary Atlantic* (Boston: Beacon Press, 2000).

Livingstone, David, *Adam's Ancestors: Race, religion and the politics of human origin* (Baltimore: John Hopkins University Press, 2008).

Longley, RA, *Rye Street Directory 1822/3* (St Leonards-On-Sea: RA and KJ Longley, 2006).

Lydon, Jane, *The Flash of Recognition: Photography and the emergence of Indigenous rights* (Sydney: NewSouth Books, 2012).

Macintyre, Stuart and Anna Clark, *The History Wars* (Melbourne: Melbourne University Press, 2003).

Macleod, AR, *The Transformation of Manellae: A history of Manilla* (Sydney: Halstead Press, 1949).

Manne, Robert, 'Aboriginal Child Removal and the Question of Genocide, 1900–1940' in A Dirk Moses (ed.), *Genocide and Settler Society: Frontier violence and stolen Indigenous children in Australian history* (New York: Berghahn Books, 2004), pp. 217–243.

Maxwell-Stewart, Hamish and James Bradley, 'Embodied Explorations: Investigating convict tattoos and the transportation system' in Ian Duffield and James Bradley (eds), *Representing Convicts: New perspectives on convict forced labour migration* (London: Leicester University Press, 1997), pp. 183–203.

McDonald, Peter and Patricia Quiggin, 'Lifecourse Transitions in Victoria in the 1880s' in Patricia Grimshaw, Chris McConville and Ellen McEwen (eds), *Families in Colonial Australia* (Sydney: Allen & Unwin, 1985), pp. 64–82.

McGowan, Barry, 'Mullock Heaps and Tailing Mounds: Environmental effects of alluvial goldmining' in Iain McCalman, Alexander Cook and Andrew Rees (eds), *Gold: Forgotten histories and lost objects of Australia* (Cambridge: Cambridge University Press, 2001), pp. 85–100.

McGowen, Randall, 'The Well-Ordered Prison: England, 1780–1865' in Norval Morris and David J Rothman (eds), *The Oxford History of the Prison: The practice of punishment in western society* (Oxford: Oxford University Press, 1995), pp. 79–110.

McGrath, Ann, *Illicit Love: Interracial sex and marriage in the United States and Australia* (Lincoln, Nebraska: University of Nebraska Press, 2015).

McGregor, Russell, *Imagined Destinies: Aboriginal Australians and the Doomed Race Theory 1880–1939* (Melbourne: Melbourne University Press, 1997).

McKenzie, Kirsten, 'Defining and Defending Honour in Law' in Penny Russell and Nigel Worden (eds), *Honourable Intentions? Violence and virtue in Australian and Cape colonies, c.1750 to 1850* (London: Routledge, 2016), pp. 17–30.

——, *Imperial Underworld: An escaped convict and the transformation of the British colonial order* (Cambridge: Cambridge University Press, 2016).

Molony, John, *Eureka* (Melbourne: Melbourne University Press, 2001).

Monaghan, E Jennifer, *Reading for the Enslaved, Writing for the Free? Reflections on liberty and literacy* (Worcester: American Antiquarian Society, 2000).

Monaghan, Jay, *Australians and the Gold Rush: California and Down-Under, 1849–1854* (Berkeley: University of California Press, 1966).

Moore, Laurie and Stephan Williams, *The True Story of Jimmy Governor* (Sydney: Allen & Unwin, 2001).

Morgan, Sally, *My Place* (Fremantle: Fremantle Press, 1987).

Morrissey, Doug, *Ned Kelly: A lawless life* (Brisbane: Connor Court Publishing, 2015).

——*Ned Kelly: selectors, squatters and stock thieves* (Brisbane: Connor Court Publishing, 2018).

Nai'an, Shi and Luo Guanzhong, *Outlaws of the Marsh* (Hong Kong: The Commercial Press, 1991).

Nash, Gary, *Forging Freedom: The formation of Philadelphia's black community, 1720–1840* (Cambridge, Mass.: Harvard University Press, 1991).

—— and Jean Soderlund, *Freedom by Degrees: Emancipation in Pennsylvania and its aftermath* (Oxford: Oxford University Press, 1991).

Neal, David, *The Rule of Law in a Penal Colony: Law and power in early NSW* (Cambridge: Cambridge University Press, 1991).

Nettelbeck, Amanda, 'Intimate Violence in the Pastoral Economy: Aboriginal women's labour and protective governance' in Penelope Edmonds and Amanda Nettelbeck (eds), *Intimacies of Violence in the Settler Colony: Economies of dispossession around the Pacific Rim* (London: Palgrave Macmillan, 2018), pp. 67–87.

Newman, Richard and James Mueller, 'Introduction' in Richard Newman and James Mueller (eds), *Antislavery and Abolition in Philadelphia* (Louisiana: Louisiana University Press, 2011), pp. 1–18.

Ngai, Mae M, 'The Chinese Question: The gold rushes and global politics, 1849–1910' in Benjamin Mountford and Stephen Tuffnell (eds), *A Global History of Gold Rushes* (Oakland, California: University of California Press, 2018), pp. 109–136.

Nicholas, Stephen, 'The Care and Feeding of Convicts' in Stephen Nicholas (ed.), *Convict Workers: Reinterpreting Australia's past* (Cambridge: Cambridge University Press, 1998), pp. 180–198.

Nixon, Allan, *100 Australian Bushrangers, 1789–1901* (Adelaide: Rigby, 1982).

No Attributed Author, *Wollar, 1885–1985: The sleeping village* (Wollar: Wollar Centenary Publishing Committee, 1985).

O'Brien, Anne, *Philanthropy and Settler Colonialism* (Basingstoke: Palgrave Macmillan, 2015).

Ogborn, Miles, *Global Lives: Britain and the World, 1550–1800* (Cambridge: Cambridge University Press, 2008).

Osborn, Betty and Trenear DuBourg, *Maryborough: A social history, 1854–1904* (Maryborough: Maryborough City Council, 1985).

*Oxford English Dictionary* (Oxford: Oxford University Press, 2008).

Oxley, Deborah, *Convict Maids: The forced migration of women to Australia* (Cambridge: Cambridge University Press, 1996).

Parsley, Aunty Loretta, 'Blood on his hands, cleansed in salt water' in Jeff Khan (ed.), *Posts in the Paddock: Performance space, point 4, exchange* (Sydney: Performance Space Limited, 2011), pp. 15–18.

Penzig, Edgar, *Troopers, Villains, Vipers and Vixens: An illustrated history of police and colonial crime 1850–1915* (Katoomba: Tranter Enterprises, 1995).

Poskett, James, *Materials of the Mind: Phrenology, race, and the global history of science, 1815–1920* (Chicago: University of Chicago Press, 2019).

Pybus, Cassandra, *Black Founders: The unknown story of Australia's first black settlers* (Sydney: UNSW Press, 2006).

Read, Peter, *The Stolen Generations: The removal of Aboriginal children in New South Wales, 1883–1969* (Sydney: NSW Department of Aboriginal Affairs, 1998).

Reece, RHW, *Aborigines and Colonists: Aborigines and colonial society in New South Wales in the 1830s and 40s* (Sydney: Sydney University Press, 1974).

Reynolds, Henry, *Frontier: Aborigines, settlers, land* (Sydney: Allen & Unwin, 1987).

——, *The Other Side of the Frontier: Aboriginal resistance to the European invasion of Australia* (Sydney: UNSW Press, 2006).

——, *With the White People: The crucial role of Aborigines in the exploration and development of Australia* (Sydney: Penguin Books, 1990).

Rixon, A, *Captain Thunderbolt* (Sydney: Annie Rixon, 1951).

Rodger, NAM, *The Wooden World: An anatomy of the Georgian navy* (London: Collins, 1986).

Rose, Deborah Bird, *Dingo Makes Us Human: Life and land in an Australian Aboriginal culture* (Cambridge: Cambridge University Press, 2000).

Russell, Penny and Nigel Worden, 'Introduction' in Penny Russell and Nigel Worden (eds), *Honourable Intentions? Violence and virtue in Australian and Cape colonies, c.1750 to 1850* (London: Routledge, 2016), pp. 13–28.

——, 'Honour, Morality and Sexuality in Nineteenth-century Sydney' in Penny Russell and Nigel Worden (eds), *Honourable Intentions? Violence and virtue in Australian and Cape colonies, c.1750 to 1850* (London: Routledge, 2016), pp. 202–217.

Salmond, Anne, *Between Worlds: Early exchanges between Māori and Europeans, 1773–1815* (Honolulu: University of Hawaii Press, 1998).

——, 'Kidnapped: Tuki and Huru's involuntary visit to Norfolk Island in 1793' in Robin Fisher and Hugh Johnston (eds), *From Maps to Metaphors: The Pacific World of George Vancouver* (Vancouver: University of British Columbia Press, 1993), pp. 191–226.

Sayers, Andrew, *Sidney Nolan: The Ned Kelly story* (New York: Metropolitan Museum of Art, 1994).

Seal, Graham, *Hidden Culture: Folklore in Australian society* (Melbourne & Oxford: Oxford University Press, 1989).

——, *Outlaw Heroes in Myth and History* (London: Anthem Press, 2011).

——, 'Tell 'Em I Died Game': The legend of Ned Kelly* (Melbourne: Hyland House Publishing, 2002).

——, *The Outlaw Legend: A cultural tradition in Britain, America and Australia* (Cambridge: Cambridge University Press, 1996).

Serle, Geoffrey, *The Golden Age: A history of the colony of Victoria, 1851–1861* (Melbourne: Melbourne University Press, 1963).

Slocomb, Margaret, *Among Australia's Pioneers: Chinese indentured pastoral workers on the Northern Frontier 1848–c.1880* (Bloomington, IN: Balboa Press, 2014).

Smith, Babette, *Australia's Birthstain: The startling legacy of the convict era* (Sydney: Allen & Unwin, 2008).

Soderlund, Jean R, *Quakers and Slavery: A divided spirit* (Princeton: Princeton University Press, 1985).

Sproud, Michael, 'The Probation System' in Alison Alexander (ed.), *The Companion to Tasmanian History* (Hobart: Centre for Tasmanian Historical Studies, 2005).

Standfield, Rachel, *Race and Identity in the Tasman World, 1769–1840* (London: Pickering and Chatto, 2012).

Sutton, Peter, *Native Title in Australia: An ethnographic perspective* (Cambridge: Cambridge University Press, 2003).

Swain, Tony, *A Place for Strangers: Towards a history of Australian Aboriginal being* (Cambridge: Cambridge University Press, 1993).

Threadgold, Terry, 'Black Man, White Woman, Irresistible Impulse: media, law and literature making the black murderer' in Pheng Cheah, David Fraser and Judith Grbich (eds), *Thinking Through the Body of the Law* (New York: New York University Press, 1996), pp. 163–187.

Travers, Robert, *Rogues' March: A chronicle of colonial crime in Australia* (Melbourne: Hutchinson Group, 1973).

Turner, Edward, *The Negro in Pennsylvania: Slavery, servitude, freedom* (Washington: American Historical Association, 1911).

Vidler, Leopold Amon, *A New History of Rye* (Hove, Sussex: Combridges, 1934).

Waldrep, Christopher, *The Many Faces of Judge Lynch: Extralegal violence and punishment in America* (New York: Palgrave Macmillan, 2002).

Wang, Sing-wu, *The Organisation of Chinese Emigration, 1848–1888: With special reference to Chinese emigration to Australia* (San Francisco: Chinese Materials Centre Inc., 1978).

Wannan, Bill, *The Australian: Yarns, ballads, legends, traditions of the Australian people* (London & Sydney: Angus & Robertson, 1964).

Ward, Russel, *The Australian Legend* (Melbourne: Oxford University Press, 1958).

Waterhouse, Richard, *Private Pleasures, Public Leisure: A history of Australian popular culture since 1788* (Sydney: Longman, 1995).

——, *The Vision Splendid: A social and cultural history of rural Australia* (Fremantle: Curtin University Press, 2005).

West, Susan, *Bushranging and the Policing of Rural Banditry in NSW, 1860–1880* (Melbourne: Australian Scholarly Publishing, 2009).

White, Charles, *The History of Australian Bushranging* (Sydney: Angus and Robertson, 1900).

White, Richard, *Inventing Australia: Images and identity, 1688–1980* (Sydney: Allen & Unwin, 1981).

Wickham, Dorothy, *Women of the Diggings, Ballarat 1854* (Ballarat: Ballarat Heritage Publishing, 2009).

Wilcox, Craig, *Australia's Boer War: The war in South Africa, 1899–1902* (Melbourne: Oxford University Press, 2002).

Williams, Stephan, *A Ghost Called Thunderbolt: The career and legend of Frederick Ward, bushranger throughout northern NSW* (Canberra: Popinjay Publications, 1987).

——, *Sam Poo: The Chinese bushranger* (Canberra: Popinjay Publications, 1987).

Wood, Marilyn, 'The "Breelong Blacks"' in Gillian Cowlishaw and Barry Morris (eds), *Race Matters: Indigenous Australians and "our" society* (Canberra: Aboriginal Studies Press, 1997), pp. 97–120.

Woods, Gregory D, *A History of Criminal Law in New South Wales: The colonial period, 1788–1900* (Sydney: The Federation Press, 2002).

Wright, Clare, *The Forgotten Rebels of Eureka* (Melbourne: Text Publishing, 2013).

## PRIVATE CORRESPONDENCE

Finch, Ely, *Private Correspondence with the Author* (5 January 2017).

## PUBLIC LECTURES

Kaladelfos, Andy, 'Citizens of Mercy: Bushrangers, punishment and public opinion in colonial NSW', David Scott Mitchell Memorial Lecture (Sydney: State Library of NSW, 2010).

## TELEVISION

Davie, Michael and Steve Westh, 'Ned Kelly', *Lawless: The real bushrangers*, season 1, episode 1.

Reilly, Hannah and Eliza Reilly, *Sheilas: Badass women from Australian history*, Sheilas TV. <www.youtube.com/channel/UCTiKCOvMDU46Q3BSOOww9WA>

## THESES

Allen, Matthew, 'The Temperance Shift: Drunkenness, responsibility and the regulation of New South Wales', PhD Thesis (University of Sydney, 2013).

Bierens, Kali, 'The Captain's Lady: Mary Ann Bugg', Honours Thesis (University of Tasmania, 2008).

Curthoys, Ann, 'Race and Ethnicity: A study of the response of British colonists to Aborigines, Chinese and non-British Europeans in New South Wales', PhD Thesis (Macquarie University, 1973).

Darnell, Maxine, 'The Chinese Labour Trade to NSW 1783–1853', PhD Thesis (University of New England, 1997).

Egan, Richard, 'Power and Dysfunction: The New South Wales Board for the Protection of Aborigines', PhD Thesis (UNSW, 2019).

Foster, Meg, '"Black Bushrangers": A Colonial Paradox: Representations of Aboriginal bushrangers in Australian popular culture, 1864–1903', Honours Thesis (University of Sydney, 2013).

Howitt, Rohan, 'Poihākena: Māori travellers and workers in New South Wales, 1793–1840', Honours Thesis (University of Sydney, 2014).

Maxwell-Stewart, Hamish, 'The Bushrangers and the Convict System of Van Diemen's Land', PhD Thesis (University of Edinburgh, 1990).

McKinnon, Jennifer, 'Convict Bushrangers in New South Wales, 1824–1834', Master's Thesis (LaTrobe University, 1979).

Parry, Naomi, '"Such a longing": Black and white children in welfare in Tasmania and New South Wales, 1880–1940', PhD Thesis (UNSW, 2007).

Roginski, Alexandra, 'A Touch of Power: Popular phrenology in the Tasman world', PhD Thesis (ANU, 2018).

Wang, Sing-wu, 'The Organisation of Chinese Emigration, 1848–1888: With special reference to Chinese emigration to Australia', Master's Thesis (ANU, 1969).

Wickham, Dorothy, 'Women in Ballarat 1851–1871: A case study in agency', PhD Thesis (University of Ballarat, 2008).

Zhang, Ye, 'The Marsh and the Bush: Outlaw hero traditions in China and the West', PhD Thesis (Curtin University of Technology, 1998).

## WEBSITES

Barker, Theo, 'White, Charles (1845–1922)', Australian Dictionary of National Biography Online. <www.adb.anu.edu.au/biography/white-charles-4834>

Baxter, Carol, 'Ada Gertrude Burrows: Baptism entry 1887', Thunderbolt Bushranger. <www.thunderboltbushranger.com.au/ada-gertrude-burrows-baptism-1887.html>

————, 'Mary Ann Bugg and her husband Edmund Baker', Thunderbolt Bushranger.
　　<www.thunderboltbushranger.com.au/mary-ann-bugg-and-edmund-baker.html>
————, 'Timeline: James and Charlotte Bugg and Family', Thunderbolt Bushranger.
　　<www.thunderboltbushranger.com.au/timeline-bugg-family.html >
Bergman, GFP, 'Davis, Edward, 1816–1841', Australian Dictionary of National Biography.
　　<adb.anu.edu.au/biography/davis-edward-1964>
Bureau of Meteorology [BOM], *Climate Statistics for Australian Locations: Dubbo*.
　　<www.bom.gov.au/climate/averages/tables/cw_065012.shtml>
'Bushranger (n.)', Australian National Dictionary Online. <www.australiannationaldictionary.
　　com.au/oupnewindex1.php>
'Convict Facts', Convict Records (in association with ancestry.com). <convictrecords.com.au/
　　facts>
'Dubbo', Dubbo Regional Council.
'Dubbo Railway Station and Yard Group', NSW Office for Environment and Heritage
　　[NSW OEH]. <www.environment.nsw.gov.au/heritageapp/ViewHeritageItemDetails.
　　aspx?ID=5011998>
'Early Australian Bushrangers', Australian Government. <www/australia.gov.au/about-
　　australia/australian-story/early-austn-bushrangers>
Evershed, Nick and Lorena Allam, 'Indigenous Children's Removal on the Rise 21 Years After
　　*Bringing Them Home*', *Guardian* (25 May 2018). <www.theguardian.com/australia-
　　news/2018/may/25/australia-fails-to-curb-childrens-removal-from-indigenous-
　　families-figures-show>
Foster, Meg, 'Bugg, Mary Ann (1834–1905)', People Australia. <peopleaustralia.anu.edu.au/
　　biography/bugg-mary-ann-29654>
————and Jason Phu, 'The Artist, the Historian and the Case of the Chinese Bushranger',
　　Museum of Contemporary Art (8 November 2018). <www.mca.com.au/stories-and-
　　ideas/artist-historian-and-case-chinese-bushranger/>
'Gulgong', Anglican Diocese of Bathurst. <www.bathurstanglican.org.au/Parishes/Gulgong.
　　html>
'Historical Currency Converter', The National Archives (UK).'Honour Role', NSW Police Force. <www.police.nsw.gov.au/about_us/proud_traditions>
'Jolly Sailor', Hasting's Pub History. <www.hastingspubhistory.com/page20.html>
National Museum of Australia [NMA], 'Jerilderie Letter'. <www.nma.gov.au/collections/
　　collection_interactives/jerilderie_letter>
Oxley, Deborah, 'Convict Indents', Digital Panopticon. <www.digitalpanopticon.org/
　　Convict_Indents_(Ship_and_Arrival_Registers)_1788-1868>
'Phrenology', Cambridge English Dictionary. <dictionary.cambridge.org/dictionary/english/
　　phrenology>
'Robbery Under Arms', AUSTLIT Database. <www.austlit.edu.au/austlit/page/C252884>
Roscoe, Katherine, 'Tasmania: Van Diemen's Land, 1804-1853', Convict Voyages: a global
　　history of convicts and penal colonies, University of Leicester. <https://web.archive.
　　org/web/20190209022944/convictvoyages.org/expert-essays/tasmania>
Rydon, Joan, 'Chanter, John Moore*, Australian Dictionary of Biography Online. <adb.anu.
　　edu.au/biography/chanter-john-moore-5553>
Smit, Lauren, 'Australia's Most Notorious Bushrangers', Australian Geographic
　　Online (23 October 2014). <www.australiangeographic.com.au/topics/history-
　　culture/2014/10/australias-most-notorious-bushrangers/>

'Stroud House', NSW Government Office of Environment and Heritage [GOEH]. <www.
environment.nsw.gov.au/heritageapp/ViewHeritageItemDetails.aspx?ID=5060873>

Tapsell, Miranda, 'Mary Ann Bugg: Bushranger and Spy', ABC Radio National (4 March
2016). <www.abc.net.au/radionational/programs/archived/pocketdocs/mary-ann-
bugg-bushranger-and-spy/7160138>

'*The Chant of Jimmie Blacksmith*, novel, historical fiction', AUSTLIT Database. <www.austlit.
edu.au/austlit/page/C268065>

'The Last Outlaws' (podcast). October–September 2021. <thelastoutlaws.com.au/episodes/>

'The Last Stand of Ned Kelly, Sites in Glenrowan: the railway line', Culture Victoria.
Ward, Richard, 'Transportation Under the Microscope', The Digital Panopticon.
Ward, Russel, 'Donohoe, John (Jack) (1806-1830)', Australian Dictionary of National
Biography Online. <adb.anu.edu.au/biography/donohoe-john-jack-1985>

Wilson, Jane, 'Bushrangers in the Australian Dictionary of Biography', Australian Dictionary
of National Biography Online. <adb.anu.edu.au/essay/12>

# NOTES

**Introduction**

1 'Bushranger (n.)', Australian National Dictionary Online; Wilson, 'Bushrangers'; Davey and Seal, 'Bushrangers', pp. 58–61.
2 Keneally, *The Chant*; Schepisi, *The Chant*.
3 Melville, *The History*; West, *The History of Tasmania*; Therry, *Reminiscences*, p. 126; Ryan, *Reminiscences*, pp. 124–128; Hassall, *In Old Australia*, pp. 28, 107–108.
4 Seal, *The Outlaw Legend*, pp. 119–164; Wannan, *The Australian*, pp. 13–22; Beatty, *A Treasury*, pp. 122–145, 265–272; Davey and Seal, 'Bushrangers', pp. 58–61; Waterhouse, *The Vision Splendid*, pp. 172–173, 185–186; Seal, *Hidden Culture*, pp. 25–31; Couzens, *A Cultural History*.
5 Boxall, *The Story*; White, *The History*.
6 Barker, 'White, Charles'.
7 Lake, 'White Man's Country', pp. 346–363; Lake and Reynolds, *Drawing the Global Colour Line*, pp. 137–165.
8 For Donohoe: Wilson, 'Bushrangers'; Davey and Seal, 'Bushrangers', p. 59; Wannan, *The Australian*, pp. 13–14. For Caesar: Pybus, *Black Founders*, pp. 1–136.
9 Ward, 'Donohoe, John'.
10 Gillen, *The Founders of Australia*, p. 63; Pybus, *Black Founders*.
11 For example: Reynolds, 'Jimmy Governor'; Reynolds, *Frontier*, pp. 78–80; Wood, 'The "Breelong Blacks"', pp. 97–120; Noonan, 'Chinese Bushrangers', pp. 127–135; Baxter and Roberts, 'Mrs Thunderbolt', pp. 55–76.
12 This includes popular histories. Garland, *Jimmy Governor*; Moore and Williams, *The True Story*; Baxter, *Captain Thunderbolt and His Lady*.
13 Macintyre and Clark, *The History Wars*.
14 Kaladelfos, 'Citizens of Mercy'; Freeman, 'Bushrangers, Itinerant Teachers', pp. 15–30.

**1 The legendary Black Douglas**

1 *Age* (14 May 1855), p. 3.
2 ibid.; *Age* (14 May 1855), p. 6; *Geelong Advertiser* (18 May 1855), p. 2; *Sydney Morning Herald* (25 May 1855), p. 5; *Courier* (23 May 1855), p. 3; *Maitland Mercury* (26 May 1855), p. 1; *Mount Alexander Mail* (11 May 1855), p. 2.
3 *Geelong Advertiser* (18 May 1855), p. 2.
4 *Age* (14 May 1855), p. 3; *Mount Alexander Mail* (11 May 1855), p. 2.
5 *Tasmanian Colonist* (19 April 1852), p. 3.
6 *Geelong Advertiser* (18 May 1855), p. 2.
7 Ellery et al., *Victoria and Its Metropolis* vol. 11A, pp. 180, 234; Ellery et al., *Victoria and Its Metropolis*, vol 11B, pp. 224, 304.
8 Clacy, *A Lady's Visit*, p. 37; JF Hughes in *Records of the Castlemaine Pioneers*, p. 2.
9 'Early Australian Bushrangers', Australian Government; Smit, 'Australia's Most Notorious Bushrangers'.

10  *Geelong Advertiser* (18 May 1855), p. 2 (the *Geelong Advertiser* took its story from the *Mount Alexander Mail*); *Maitland Mercury* (26 May 1855), p. 1; *Courier* (23 May 1855), p. 3.

11  *Geelong Advertiser* (18 May 1855), p. 2.

12  *Independent* (30 July 1887), p. 3; Nixon, *100 Australian Bushrangers*, p. 49.

13  *Age* (14 May 1855), p. 6; *Geelong Advertiser* (18 May 1855), p. 2; *Argus* (15 May 1855), p. 5; *Bendigo Advertiser* (20 February 1857), p. 2; *Mount Alexander Mail* (20 February 1857), p. 5; PROV, VA 475, VPRS 515/P0001 (William Douglas went by many aliases over the years).

14  *Geelong Advertiser* (18 May 1855), p. 2.

15  *Bendigo Advertiser* (20 February 1857), p. 2; *Mount Alexander Mail* (20 February 1857), p. 5; *Bendigo Advertiser* (4 April 1857), p. 2; *Bendigo Advertiser* (23 June 1857), p. 3.

16  PROV, VA 475, VPRS 515/P0001; PROV, VA 1464, VPRS 515/P0001 Unit 38; PROV, VA 1464, VPRS 515/P0001 Unit 44.

17  *Geelong Advertiser* (7 May 1855), p. 2; *Sydney Morning Herald* (12 May 1855), p. 4; *Age* (14 May 1855), p. 6.

18  *Geelong Advertiser* (12 May 1855), p. 2; *Argus* (9 May 1855), p. 5; *Victorian Government Gazette*, no. 41 (8 May 1855), p. 1141.

19  Blainey, *A History of Victoria*, p. 40; Bate, *Victorian Gold Rushes*, pp. 27–28; Serle, *The Golden Age*.

20  Bate, *Victorian Gold Rushes* pp. 27–28; Serle, *The Golden Age*, pp. 75–76.

21  Serle, *The Golden Age*, p. 82.

22  *Geelong Advertiser* (12 May 1855), p. 2; *Argus* (9 May 1855), p. 5; *Victorian Government Gazette*, no. 41 (8 May 1855), p. 1141; *Geelong Advertiser* (18 May 1855), p. 2.

23  Wright, *The Forgotten Rebels*, p. 131.

24  Anderson, 'Mrs Charles Clacy', pp. 225–249; Osborn and DuBourg, *Maryborough*, p. 48.

25  ibid.; Wickham, 'Women in Ballarat'; Wickham, *Women of the Diggings*.

26  Grimshaw et al., *Creating a Nation*, pp. 73–131.

27  Anderson, 'Mrs Charles Clacy', pp. 225–249; Grimshaw and Willett, 'Women's History', p. 139; Ottey in *Records of the Castlemaine Pioneers* (Melbourne: Rigby Limited, 1972), p. 58; PROV, VA 724, VPRS 937/P0000; Nawton, *Diaries*, 1852–53.

28  Wright, *The Forgotten Rebels*; Molony, *Eureka*.

29  *Geelong Advertiser* (12 May 1855), p. 2; *Argus* (9 May 1855), p. 5; *Victorian Government Gazette*, no. 41 (8 May 1855), p. 1141.

30  PROV, VA 724, VPRS 937/P0000.

31  PROV, VA 724, VPRS 937/P0004.

32  Goodman, 'Gold and the Public', p. 79.

33  *Argus* (14 June 1855), p. 4.

34  Osborn and DuBourg, *Maryborough*, p. 40.

35  Goodman, *Gold Seeking*, pp. 88–104; Waldrep, *The Many Faces*, 49–66.

36  Goodman, *Gold Seeking*, pp. 64–70; Stafford, 'Preventing the "Curse of California"', pp. 215–230; Monaghan, *Australians and the Gold Rush*, pp. 180–193.

37  Anderson, 'Mrs Charles Clacy', p. 233; Nawton, *Diaries*.

38  PROV, VA 724, VPRS 937/P0000.

39  Twomey, 'Without Natural Protectors', p. 29.

40  *Geelong Advertiser* (4 July 1855), p. 2.

41  Twomey, 'Without Natural Protectors', pp. 23–24; Twomey, 'Gender, Welfare', pp. 169–186.

42  Woollacott, 'Frontier Violence', p. 11.1–11.15.

43  Twomey, 'Without Natural Protectors', pp. 22–46.

44  Cahir, *Black Gold*, pp. 49–54; Fels, *Good Men and True*, pp. 212–220; Henry Dana in *Select Committee on Police*.

45  *Age* (11 April 1855), p. 7; *Sydney Morning Herald* (21 April 1855), p. 3.

46  *Geelong Advertiser* (18 May 1855), p. 2; *Courier* (23 May 1855), p. 3; *Maitland Mercury* (26 May 1855), p. 1; Smit, 'Australia's Most Notorious Bushrangers'.

47  *Argus* (14 June 1855), p. 4.

48  Carpenter, 'Finding "Te Wherro in Otakou"', pp. 90–91; Cahir, *Black Gold*.
49  *Argus* (4 March 1852), p. 2; *Launceston Examiner* (13 March 1852), p. 4.
50  Lester, 'Settler Colonialism', pp. 495–496; Livingstone, *Adam's Ancestors*; McGregor, *Imagined Destinies*, pp. 1–21.
51  Annear, *Nothing But Gold*, p. 289; Cahir and Clark, 'why should they pay?', pp. 115–128; Cahir, *Black Gold*, p. 86; Jenkins with Evans (ed.), *Diary*, p. 38
52  McGowan, 'Mullock Heaps', pp. 85–100; Davies, Lawrence and Turnbull, 'Harvesting Water', pp. 24–32.
53  Cahir and Clark, 'why should they pay?', p. 122; George Robins in *Records of the Castlemaine Pioneers*, pp. 176–177; Kellerman, 'Interesting Account', pp. 488–489.
54  *Select Committee on the Aborigines*, p. iv.
55  Elbourne, 'The Sin of the Settler'; Arneil, *John Locke*; Hiatt, *Arguments*, pp. 13–35.
56  Serle, *The Golden Age*, pp. 82, 126; Haldane, *The People's Force*, p. 19; Shaw, 'Violent Protest', p. 553.
57  TAHO: (TA60), CON35/1/1, p. 184.
58  TAHO: (TA1862), POL220/1/1, p. 425; *Return Respecting the Goldfields*, p. 7.
59  TAHO: (TA1862), POL220/1/1, pp. 425–426.
60  *Argus* (15 April 1852), p. 4.
61  Ward, *The Australian Legend*, pp. 17–19, 23.
62  *Argus* (15 April 1852), p. 4.
63  *Argus* (22 April 1852), p. 4.
64  Blackstone, *Commentaries on the Laws of England in Four Books*, p. 359; Pennington, 'Innocent', pp. 106–124.
65  Neal, *The Rule of Law*, pp. 1–60; Harman, *Aboriginal Convicts*.
66  *Melbourne Punch* (2 August 1855), p. 50.
67  *Courier* (4 December 1852), p. 3; *Argus* (19 April 1853), p. 9; *Argus* (28 June 1853), p. 5; *Argus* (8 July 1853), p. 5; *Age* (14 November 1854), p. 5; *Bendigo Advertiser* (20 February 1857), p. 2; *Mount Alexander Mail* (20 February 1857), p. 5; *Bendigo Advertiser* (4 April 1857), p. 2; *Bendigo Advertiser* (23 June 1857), p. 3.
68  Serle, *The Golden Age*, p. 82; Goodman, *Gold Seeking*, pp. 174–176.
69  Serle, *The Golden Age*, p. 82.
70  Samuel Lazarus in Goodman, *Gold Seeking*, p. 174.
71  *Select Committee on the Gold Fields*, p. 4.
72  Dingle, 'A Truly Magnificent Thirst', p. 238.
73  ibid., p. 235.
74  Serle, *The Golden Age*, p. 83.
75  O'Brien, *Philanthropy*, p. 48.
76  Samuel Lazarus in Goodman, *Gold Seeking*, p. 174.
77  Dingle, 'A Truly Magnificent Thirst', p. 238.
78  Allen, 'The Temperance Shift', p. 233.
79  Waterhouse, *Private Pleasures*, p. 39; Goodman, *Gold Seeking*, p. 74; Carrodus, *Gold, Gamblers*; Reeves, 'Goldfields Settler or Frontier Rogue?'.
80  McGowan, 'Mullock Heaps', pp. 85–100; Serle, *The Golden Age*, p. 80; Fitzgerald and Jordan, *Under the Influence*, pp. 65–66.
81  McGowan, 'Mullock Heaps', pp. 85–100; Davies, Lawrence and Turnbull, 'Harvesting Water', pp. 24–32.
82  Goodman, *Gold Seeking*, p. 174.
83  Allen, 'The Temperance Shift', p. 237.
84  Karskens, *People of the River*, pp. 399–405.
85  Porter, 'The Drinking Man's Disease', pp. 385–387.
86  James Robertson in *Records of the Castlemaine Pioneers*, p. 45; Craig, *My Adventures*, pp. 38–53.
87  Lawrence, 'After the Gold Rush', p. 258.
88  Serle, *The Golden Age*, p. 82.

89   *Select Committee on the Goldfields*, p. 4.
90   Allen, 'Australia and New Zealand', pp. 195–196.
91   Serle, *The Golden Age*, p. 82.
92   *Select Committee on the Goldfields*, pp. 43, 46.
93   ibid., p. 21.
94   *Argus* (8 July 1853), p. 5.

**2    The life and times of William Douglas**
1    Bateson, *The Convict Ships*, pp. 302–303; NSWSA: NRS 1155 [2/8269], p. 285.
2    ibid.; Bateson, *The Convict Ships,* p. 214.
3    Bateson, *The Convict Ships*, p. 302.
4    TNA, ADM 101/50/10.
5    Bateson, *The Convict Ships,* p. 334; NSWSA: NRS 12188 [4/4019].
6    Oxley, 'Convict Indents'.
7    William Gunn in Maxwell-Stewart and Bradley, 'Embodied Explorations', p. 191.
8    TNA, HO8/43, p. 81; TNA, HO27/50, p. 352; ESRO, Criminal Indictments, RYE 8/134.
9    NSWSA: NRS 12188 [4/4019].
10   Karskens, *The Colony*; Karskens, 'This Spirit of Emigration', pp. 1–34.
11   Oxley, *Convict Maids*, p. 21.
12   NSWSA: NRS 12188 [4/4019].
13   *Gradual Abolition Act* 1780 (Pennsylvania).
14   Newman, 'Lucky to be born in Pennsylvania', p. 414.
15   *Gradual Abolition Act* 1780 (Pennsylvania).
16   Gigantino, 'Slavery'; Berlin, 'Slavery, Freedom', p. 20; Soderlund, *Quakers and Slavery*, p. 80.
17   Nash and Soderlund, *Freedom By Degrees*, p. 183.
18   Jennings, 'Us Colored Women Had to Go Through a Plenty', pp. 45–74; Lecaudey, 'Behind the Mask', pp. 260–277; Hirsch, 'Uncovering the "Hidden History of Mestizo America"', pp. 483–506; Turner, *The Negro*, p. 31.
19   *Gradual Abolition Act* 1780 (Pennsylvania). Berlin, 'Slavery, Freedom', p. 1.
20   Brown, *Moral Capital*.
21   Newman and Mueller (eds), *Antislavery and Abolition*; Okur, 'Underground Railroad', pp. 537–557.
22   Nash, *Forging Freedom*, pp. 66, 247.
23   Newman and Mueller, 'Introduction', p. 6.
24   ibid., pp. 3–4.
25   ibid., p. 7.
26   Bacon and McClish, 'Reinventing the Master's Tools', pp. 21–22.
27   Monaghan, *Reading*, pp. 309–341.
28   Newman and Mueller, 'Introduction', p. 2.
29   Nash, *Forging Freedom*, pp. 1–2, 4.
30   Smith, 'The End', pp. 279–299.
31   This was the federal *Fugitive Slave Act* 1850 (USA).
32   Bolster, *Black Jacks*, pp. 3–4.
33   ibid., p. 236.
34   ibid., p. 239.
35   NSWSA: NRS 12188 [4/4019].
36   Kent, 'Decorative Bodies', p. 81.
37   Ogborn, *Global Lives*, pp. 150–151.
38   Linebaugh and Rediker, *The Many Headed Hydra*, p. 151.
39   Ogborn, *Global Lives*, p. 146.
40   Ibid., p. 151; Linebaugh and Rediker, *The Many Headed Hydra*, p. 157.
41   Ogborn, *Global Lives*, pp. 146–150.
42   Bolster, *Black Jacks*, p. 77.

43 Ogborn, *Global Lives*, p. 152.
44 NSWSA, NRS 12188 [4/4019].
45 Gigantino, 'Slavery'; Nash and Soderlund, *Freedom By Degrees*, p. 181.
46 Rodger, *The Wooden World*, p. 27.
47 'Dispatch from Sir John Franklin, to Lord Glenelg', p. 4. Taken from *Parliamentary Papers*, vol. 42.
48 Duffield, 'Skilled Workers', pp. 60–64; Gerzina, *Black London*, pp. 29–67; Duffield, 'I asked how the vessel could go', pp. 121–154.
49 ESRO, Criminal Indictments, RYE 8/134.
50 Bolster, *Black Jacks*, pp. 72–73.
51 Dening, *Mr Bligh's*, p. 118.
52 Bolster, *Black Jacks*, pp. 72–73.
53 NSWSA: NRS 12188 [4/4019].
54 Horsfield, *The History*, pp. 497–498; Lewis, *A Topographical*, p. 630.
55 ESRO, Criminal Indictments, RYE 8/134.
56 Garton, 'The Convict Origins', p. 77; ESRO, Criminal Indictments, RYE 8/134.
57 'Historical Currency Converter', TNA.
58 'Convict Facts', Convict Records.
59 Burchall, *Sussex Convicts*.
60 Parry, *An Historical*, p. 299.
61 ESRO, Summary Offences, RYE 11/1–72.
62 Commission of Inquiry, *Introductory Report*, p. 1035.
63 Horsfield, *The History*, pp. 487–488.
64 Parry, *An Historical*, p. 297.
65 Horsfield, *The History*, p. 488; Commission of Inquiry, *Introductory Report*, p. 1038.
66 Commission of Inquiry, *Introductory Report*, pp. 921–927, 1029–1039.
67 Vidler, *A New History*, pp. 161–163.
68 Commission of Inquiry, *Introductory Report*, p. 1032.
69 ibid., pp. 1031–1035.
70 Vidler, *A New History*, pp. 162–163.
71 Longley, *Rye*, pp. 3, 6, 8, 11; Vidler, *A New History*, pp. 120, 162.
72 *Births and Christenings* 1473701 (David) and 1473701 (Charles).
73 Vidler, *A New History*, p. 123.
74 TNA, HO107/1109, Book: 4; Folio: 14; GSU roll: 464159; ESRO, HMU/1/4/3/11.
75 Burchall, *Sussex Convicts*.
76 Commission of Inquiry, *Introductory Report*, p. 1035.
77 For Charles Taylor, see TNA, HO107/1109, Book: 4; Folio: 14; GSU roll: 464159; Pigot, *Pigot's Sussex Directory*. For James Newbery see TNA, HO107/1109; Book: 4; Folio: 16; GSU roll: 464159. For Thomas Hearsfield see United Kingdom Poll Books, *East Sussex Election*, p. 88. The fourth witness at the trial that we know about is George Allen who lived at Cottage Spring Cliff in Rye in 1841. For George Allen, see TNA HO107/1109; Book: 5; Folio: 10; GSU roll: 464159.
78 Pigot, *Pigot's Sussex Directory*; Longley, *Rye*, p. 9.
79 'Jolly Sailor', Hasting's Pub History. <www.hastingspubhistory.com/page20.html>; Russell, 'The Jolly Sailor', *Rye's Own Magazine*.
80 TNA, HO 13/66, p. 116.
81 TNA, HO 10/33, p. 14.
82 Hirst, *Convict Society*; Karskens, *The Colony*.
83 McKenzie, *Imperial Underworld*, pp. 52–55; Benton and Ford, *Rage for Order*, pp. 62–66; Bennett, 'The Day of Retribution', pp. 85–106; British House of Commons, *Bigge Report*.
84 Evans and Thorpe, 'Power', p. 101.
85 TAHO, CON35/1/1, p. 184.
86 Hirst, *Convict Society*, pp. 57–58.

87     TAHO, CON35/1/1, p. 184.
88     Hirst, *Convict Society*, pp. 76–77.
89     Nicholas, 'The Care', p. 181.
90     TAHO, CON35/1/1, p. 184.
91     Evans and Thorpe, 'Commanding Men', p. 26; Hirst, *Convict Society*, p. 60.
92     NSWSA: NRS 12188 [4/4019]; Maxwell-Stewart, 'The Rise', p. 98.
93     *Sydney Herald* (19 August 1841), p. 2. While the original article stated that the pair were sentenced to seven years penal servitude, they were actually sentenced to ten years. NSWSA: NRS 847 [5/2917]; TAHO, CON35/1/1, p. 184; TNA, HO10/41, p. 29.
94     *Sydney Monitor* (20 August 1841), p. 2.
95     NSWSA: NRS 2519 [4/6440–41].
96     Byrne, *Criminal Law*, pp. 130, 132.
97     Seal, *The Outlaw Legend*, pp. 121–124; Byrne, *Criminal Law*, pp. 132–136, 139; Bergman, 'Davis, Edward'.
98     Byrne, *Criminal Law*, pp. 129–151; McKinnon, 'Convict Bushrangers'.
99     New South Wales Legislative Council, *Committee on Police*, p. 26.
100    *Sydney Herald* (19 August 1841), p. 2.
101    Byrne, *Criminal Law*, p. 132; McKinnon, 'Convict Bushrangers', p. 69.
102    *Sydney Monitor* (20 August 1841), p. 2.
103    Byrne, *Criminal Law*, pp. 134–135.
104    ibid., pp. 139–141.
105    *Bushranging Act* 1830 (NSW).
106    Burton to Bourke (19 August 1834), *HRA*, s. I, vol. XVII, pp. 523–533.
107    *Bushranging Act* 1830 (NSW).
108    Currey, *Sir Francis Forbes*, pp. 417–418.
109    Goderich to Darling (23 March 1831), *HRA*, s. I, vol. XVI, p. 115.
110    TAHO, CON35/1/1, p. 184.
111    ibid.
112    Brand, *The Convict*; Sproud, 'The Probation System', p. 290; Meredith and Oxley, 'Contracting Convicts', pp. 45–70; Shaw, 'The Origins', pp. 16–28.
113    Hay, *Albion's Fatal Tree*; McGowen, 'The Well-Ordered Prison'.
114    Brand, *The Convict*; Sproud, 'The Probation System', p. 290; Meredith and Oxley, 'Contracting Convicts', pp. 45–70; Shaw, 'The Origins', pp. 16–28.
115    Sproud, 'The Probation System', p. 290.
116    TAHO, CON35/1/1, p. 184.
117    McGowen, 'The Well-Ordered Prison', pp. 79–110; Henriques, 'The Rise', pp. 61–93; Brand, *The Convict*, pp. 7–8.
118    Davis, 'Exile', pp. 432–437.
119    Foxhall, 'From Convicts', p. 11.
120    ibid., p. 12.
121    ibid., pp. 1–19.
122    Maxwell-Stewart, 'The Bushrangers', pp. 97–110; Sproud, 'The Probation System', p. 290.
123    Denholm, 'Port Arthur', p. 406.
124    Maxwell-Stewart, 'The Bushrangers', pp. 97–110.
125    TAHO, CON35/1/1, p. 184.
126    McGowen, 'The Well-Ordered Prison', p. 84; Petrow, 'Policing', p. 360; Shaw, 'The Origins', pp. 19–20.
127    Ward, 'Transportation'.
128    Roscoe, 'Tasmania'; Meredith and Oxley, 'Contracting Convicts', pp. 45–72.
129    Denholm, 'Port Arthur', p. 406.
130    Roscoe, 'Tasmania'.
131    Gilchrist, 'A Victim', pp. 151–161.
132    Barnard, 'Observations', pp. 1–2.

133 TAHO, CON35/1/1, p. 184.
134 *Bell's Life in Sydney* (26 October 1850), p. 2.
135 Waterhouse, 'Bare Knuckle', p. 107.
136 Maxwell-Stewart, 'The Bushrangers', pp. 151, 154–155; Shaw, 'The Origins', pp. 16–28.
137 Waterhouse, 'Bare Knuckle', p. 103; Alexander and Young, 'Boxing', p. 52
138 'Toddlers' was also a term for police. *Bell's Life in Sydney* (26 October 1850), p. 2.
139 Duffield, 'From Slave', p. 30.
140 RBDM 1892/5199; PROV, VA 2889, VPRS 24/P0001, Unit 596, 1892.
141 'Phrenology', Cambridge English Dictionary.
142 Poskett, *Materials*, p. 1.
143 *Bendigo Advertiser* (17 May 1892), p. 3; *Age* (17 May 1892), p. 6.
144 Roginski, 'A Touch of Power'.

**3    The many histories of Sam Poo**

1    *Sydney Morning Herald* (10 February 1865), p. 4.
2    *Sydney Mail* (14 October 1865), p. 12.
3    NSWSA: NRS 6034 [2/4469]; NSWSA: NRS 880 [9/6474, 9/6475]; Penzig, *Troopers*, p. 82.
4    West, *Bushranging*, pp. 18–19.
5    West, 'Spiders', p. 2; West, *Bushranging*, p. 23.
6    *Sydney Mail* (14 October 1865), p. 12; NSWSA: NRS 880 [9/6474, 9/6475].
7    *Sydney Morning Herald* (10 February 1865), p. 4.
8    *Maitland Mercury* (18 February 1865), p. 5.
9    *Sydney Morning Herald* (10 February 1865), p. 4; *Maitland Mercury* (11 February 1865), p. 1.
10   *Maitland Mercury* (18 February 1865), p. 5.
11   ibid.
12   Hirst, *The Strange*, p. 223.
13   West, 'Spiders', p. 2.
14   Walker, 'Bushranging', p. 211.
15   White, *Inventing Australia*, pp. 63–84.
16   West, *Bushranging*, p. 82.
17   Walker, 'Bushranging', p. 206.
18   ibid., p. 209.
19   West, *Bushranging*, p. 298.
20   West, 'The Thiefdom', p. 136.
21   ibid.; West, 'The Role', p. 135.
22   West, 'The Role', p. 133.
23   ibid; West, 'The Thiefdom', p. 137.
24   Hirst, *The Strange*, pp. 119–131; Ward, *The Australian Legend*; Davison, 'Sydney and the Bush',
     pp. 191–209; Waterhouse, 'Australian Legends', pp. 201–221.
25   *Sydney Morning Herald* (11 July 1864), p. 4.
26   *Maitland Mercury* (18 February 1865), p. 5.
27   *Sydney Mail* (25 February 1865), p. 4.
28   West, 'The Role', p. 134.
29   *Age* (4 March 1865), p. 7; *Australian News for Home Readers* (18 March 1865), p. 14.
30   West, 'The Thiefdom', pp. 135–155; West, *Bushranging*, pp. 121–158; West, 'The Role', p. 143.
31   *Sydney Morning Herald* (3 October 1867), p. 4; *Sydney Morning Herald* (7 February 1865), p. 4.
32   West, *Bushranging*, pp. 17–62; *Bathurst Free Press* (14 September 1861), p. 2; Kaladelfos,
     'Citizens of Mercy'; Ward, *The Australian Legend*, pp. 135–166; Seal, *The Outlaw Legend*.
33   *Sydney Mail* (25 February 1865), p. 4.
34   *Maitland Mercury* (18 February 1865), p. 5.
35   Foster, 'Black Bushrangers', pp. 61–67. A similar argument was put forward to explain the skills
     of Indigenous trackers. Reynolds, *Frontier*, p. 103; McGregor, *Imagined Destinies*, pp. 46–47.
36   *Maitland Mercury* (25 February 1865), p. 3.

37 *Sydney Mail* (25 February 1865), p. 4.
38 Hirst, *Freedom*, pp. 345–353; Curthoys, 'Men of All Nations', pp. 110–113.
39 Hirst, *The Strange*, p. 162.
40 Curthoys, 'Race and Ethnicity', pp. 250–347; Ngai, 'The Chinese Question', pp. 109–136.
41 *Bathurst Free Press* (15 September 1858), p. 3.
42 Curthoys, 'Men of All Nations', pp. 109; *Bathurst Free Press* (20 March 1858), p. 2.
43 Goodman, 'The Gold Rushes', p. 182.
44 Curthoys, 'Men of All Nations', p. 106.
45 Goodman, 'The Gold Rushes', pp. 182–184; Curthoys, 'Men of All Nations', pp. 106–107; Lake and Reynolds, *Drawing the Global Colour Line*, pp. 18–19; Woods, *A History*, pp. 185–186.
46 Curthoys, 'Men of All Nations', p. 108.
47 ibid., p. 115. There were also instances of cooperation and camaraderie between Chinese people and Europeans, but because racist voices were louder, and instances of violence towards Chinese miners more pressing, these peaceful encounters were constantly overlooked. McGowan, 'Reconsidering Race', pp. 312–331.
48 *Treaty of Nanking* 1842 (Nanjing).
49 Curthoys, 'Men of All Nations', p. 111.
50 Woods, *A History*, p. 186.
51 James Henley in Woods, *A History*, p. 187.
52 Hirst, *The Strange*, p. 221; Walker, 'The New South Wales', p. 26.
53 ibid.; Curthoys, 'Men of All Nations', p. 113.
54 Finnane, *Police and Government*, pp. 28–29; Hirst, *The Strange*, pp. 218–241.
55 West, 'Spiders', pp. 1–22.; Finnane, *Police and Government*, pp. 58–59.
56 *Empire* (17 February 1863), p. 4.
57 West, 'The Thiefdom', p. 143; West, 'Spiders', pp. 1–22.
58 ibid.; Hirst, *The Strange*, pp. 217–241; Seal, *The Outlaw Legend*, pp. 119–164.
59 *Maitland Mercury* (18 February 1865), p. 5.
60 'Honour Role', NSW Police Force.
61 *Western Post* as quoted in *Maitland Mercury* (11 February 1865), p. 1.
62 This is remarkably similar to the 'Outlaw Hero'. Seal, *The Outlaw Legend*.
63 *Sydney Morning Herald* (7 February 1865), p. 4.
64 *Sydney Mail* (25 February 1865), p. 4.
65 *Felons Apprehension Act* 1865 (NSW); Woods, *A History*, pp. 203–204; Eburn, 'Outlawry'.
66 *Sydney Morning Herald* (17 May 1865), p. 5; *Sydney Morning Herald* (10 October 1863), p. 4; *Sydney Morning Herald* (9 February 1865), p. 8; *Sydney Morning Herald* (10 February 1865), p. 4; Seal, *The Outlaw Legend*, pp. 134–135.
67 *Empire* (13 April 1865), p. 2; *Sydney Morning Herald* (13 April 1865), p. 8.
68 *Maitland Mercury* (2 March 1865), p. 4; *Illawarra Mercury* (24 February 1865), p. 2.
69 NSWSA: NRS 7868 [2/7776]; *Empire* (13 April 1865), p. 2; *Sydney Morning Herald* (13 April 1865), p. 8.
70 Douglas and Finnane, *Indigenous Crime*, pp. 57–59.
71 NSWSA: NRS 880 [9/6474].
72 *Maitland Mercury* (20 April 1865), p. 3.
73 *Empire* (13 October 1865), p. 5; *Sydney Morning Herald* (13 October 1865), p. 5; *Sydney Mail* (14 October 1865), p. 12.
74 Hirst, *The Strange*, p. 225.
75 *Sydney Mail* (14 October 1865), p. 12.
76 NSWSA: NRS 6034 [2/4469].
77 *Illawarra Mercury* (20 October 1865), p. 2.
78 Although the *Bathurst Free Press* article no longer exists, every article that references Sam Poo's execution states that it is copied from the *Free Press*. *Empire* (25 December 1865), p. 5; *Brisbane Courier* (30 December 1865), p. 5; *Sydney Mail* (30 December 1865), p. 2; *Clarence and Richmond Examiner* (2 January 1866), p. 3.

79  *Bathurst Free Press* quoted in *Empire* (25 December 1865), p. 5.
80  *Sydney Mail* (30 December 1865), p. 2.
81  *Queenslander* (20 February 1936), p. 10; *Daily Liberal* (7 February 2015).
82  The *Sydney Morning Herald* and the *Sydney Mail* were the only papers to broadcast the alternative view that was presented to the court on this matter. This was likely because they were published hundreds of kilometres from the scene of bushranging and murder, safely out of harm's way. *Sydney Morning Herald* (13 October 1865), p. 5; *Sydney Mail* (14 October 1865), p. 12.
83  NSWSA: NRS 6034 [2/4469].
84  White, *Australian Bushranging*, pp. 19–23.
85  West, *Bushranging*, p. 55.
86  Curthoys, 'Race and Ethnicity', pp. 374–435; *Chinese Immigration Restriction Act* 1861 (NSW).
87  Coghlan, *The Wealth*, pp. 558–559; Caldwell, 'Population', p. 26.
88  *Sydney Morning Herald* (13 October 1865), p. 5; NSWSA: NRS 880, [9/6474, 9/6475]; NSWSA: NRS 6034 [2/4469].
89  NSWSA: NRS 880 [9/6475].
90  Bailliere and Whitworth, *Bailliere's*, pp. 376–377; Curthoys, 'Race and Ethnicity', p. 375. There were also Chinese in the pastoral industry who travelled in search of work. Curthoys, 'Race and Ethnicity', p. 409.
91  Coghlan, *The Wealth*, p. 559.
92  NSWSA: NRS 880 [9/6474, 9/6475]; *Sydney Morning Herald* (13 October 1865), p. 5; *Sydney Mail* (14 October 1865), p. 12.
93  *Sydney Morning Herald* (13 October 1865), p. 5.
94  NSW RBDM, 2742/1865.
95  *Western Post* as quoted in *Maitland Mercury* (2 March 1865).
96  *Sydney Mail* (14 October 1865), p. 12.
97  ibid; *Sydney Morning Herald* (13 October 1865), p. 5; Plunkett, *The Australian Magistrate*, p. 222.
98  Kaladelfos, 'Citizens of Mercy'; Freeman, 'Bushrangers, Itinerant Teachers', pp. 15–30.
99  Penzig, *Troopers*, p. 82; Travers, *Rogues' March*, pp. 87–88; *Queenslander* (20 February 1936), p. 10; Williams, *Sam Poo*.
100 NSWSA: NRS 1993 [4/8492].
101 Curthoys, 'Men of All Nations', pp. 104–105.
102 Chee-Beng, 'Introduction', p. 4; Ching-Hwang, *Coolies*, pp. 72–76; Guotu, 'China's Policies', p. 34.
103 Wang, *The Organisation*, p. 120. Chinese labourers were also sent to Cuba, Honolulu, Peru and Demerara at this time. Wang, 'The Organisation', p. 105.
104 This stemmed from European miners' belief that the Chinese had no right to the riches of the goldfields. Curthoys, 'Men of All Nations', p. 108; Lake and Reynolds, *Drawing*, pp. 15–45.
105 Darnell, 'The Chinese', pp. 64–82; Lamley, 'Hsieh-Tau', pp. 1–39.
106 Darnell, 'The Chinese', p. 79.
107 NSW BDM 2742/ 1865. It is unclear how this information came to be registered on Poo's death certificate when he did not speak after he was caught by the police.
108 Chan, 'Becoming Australian', pp. 8–9; Bagnall, 'Rewriting', pp. 66, 73–76.
109 Darnell, 'The Chinese', pp. 78–80.
110 Wang, *The Organisation*, pp. 59–60.
111 ibid., p. 60.
112 ibid., pp. 62–64.
113 Curthoys, 'Men of All Nations', pp. 104–116.
114 Darnell, 'The Chinese', pp. 331–348; Slocomb, *Among Australia's Pioneers*.
115 Waterhouse, *The Vision Splendid*, p. 101.
116 ibid., pp. 101–102; Darnell, 'The Chinese', pp. 258–275.
117 Giles, *Glossary*, p. 70; Finch, *Private Correspondence*.
118 Slocomb, *Among Australia's Pioneers*, p. xiii; Darnell, 'The Chinese', p. 152. As Hokkien was a minority dialect of Chinese in New South Wales at this time, the translator at Sam Poo's trial was unlikely to have spoken to him in his own tongue.

119 Darnell, 'The Chinese', p. 158.
120 Darnell, 'Master and Servant', pp. 57–59.
121 Darnell, 'The Chinese', p. 158.
122 *Sydney Morning Herald* (12 April 1852), p. 2.
123 Darnell, 'The Chinese', pp. 278–284; Darnell, 'Master and Servant', pp. 54–65.
124 The average duration of a contract was five years. Wang, *The Organisation*, p. 43.
125 Darnell, 'The Chinese'; Slocomb, *Among Australia's Pioneers*.
126 As Chinese indentured labourers to New South Wales arrived between 1848 and 1852, Sam Poo would have lived in New South Wales for between thirteen and seventeen years by 1865. As the average duration of a labour contract was five years, this means that by 1865, he would have remained in the colony between seven and twelve years after his contract ended. Wang, *The Organisation*, pp. 43, 120.
127 Slocomb, *Among Australia's Pioneers*.
128 Seal, *The Outlaw Legend*.
129 Zhang, 'The Marsh', pp. 75–76.
130 Nai'an and Guanzhong, *Outlaws of the Marsh*; Seal, *Outlaw Heroes*, pp. 18–21; Antony, 'Peasants, Heroes and Brigands', p. 124.
131 Seal, *Outlaw Heroes*, pp. 18–21, 105–107; Zhang, 'The Marsh', pp. 74–111; Antony, 'Peasants', p. 126.
132 Zhang, 'The Marsh', p. 98; Antony, 'Peasants', pp. 138–141.
133 Hobsbawm, 'Social Banditry', p. 149; Darnell, 'The Chinese', pp. 64–82; Lamley, 'Hsieh-Tau', pp. 1–39.
134 Zhang, 'The Marsh', pp. 74–111; Antony, 'Peasants', pp. 128–135.
135 Xu Ke in Zhang, 'The Marsh', p. 94.
136 Zhang, 'The Marsh', pp. 78–89; Mann, 'The Male Bond', pp. 1603, 1607–1611.
137 Lamley, 'Hsieh-Tau', pp. 1–39; Antony, 'Peasants', pp. 134–136.
138 Zhang, 'The Marsh', p. 106.

**4    The making of Mary Ann Bugg**
1 *Empire* (2 May 1865), p. 5.
2 ibid.; Oppenheimer, 'Thunderbolt's Mary Ann', p. 102.
3 *Empire* (2 May 1865), p. 5.
4 *Maitland Mercury* (18 April 1865), p. 2.
5 *Empire* (2 May 1865), p. 5.
6 *Maitland Mercury* (18 April 1865), p. 2.
7 NSW RBDM 1839/1494.
8 Although the pair had a relationship before this time as their daughter, Marina Emily Ward, was born in October 1861. NSW RBDM 1861/7193.
9 Bradshaw, *The True Story*, pp. 53–54; Fitchett, *In the Days*, pp. 30–31; Williams, *A Ghost*; Macleod, *The Transformation*, pp. 21–27.
10 Baxter and Roberts, 'Mrs Thunderbolt', pp. 60–64; Williams, *A Ghost*, p. 25; Macleod, *The Transformation*, p. 23; Rixon, *Captain Thunderbolt*; Walker, 'Captain Thunderbolt', p. 227.
11 Baxter and Roberts, 'Mrs Thunderbolt', p. 62.
12 'Stroud House', NSW GOEH; Chadban, *Stroud*, p. 6; Bairstow, *A Million Pounds*.
13 Newspapers commonly referred to Mary Ann as a 'half-caste woman' and used the phrase as a pejorative reminder of her 'mixed race' heritage.
14 *NSW Police Gazette* (2 May 1866), p. 160.
15 NSWSA: NRS 2318 [5/747-50]; *Maitland Mercury* (3 April 1866), p. 2.
16 *Sydney Morning Herald* (3 April 1866), p. 5; *Clarence River Examiner* (10 April 1866), p. 3; *Tumut Times* (12 April 1866), p. 2.
17 NSWSA: NRS 905 [4/573, 66/1844]; *NSW Police Gazette* (4 April 1866), p. 122.
18 Kimber, 'Poor Laws', pp. 537–550; Nettelbeck, 'Creating the Aboriginal Vagrant', pp. 79–100.
19 NSWSA: NRS 2318 [5/747-50]; *Maitland Mercury* (3 April 1866), p. 2.

20    NSWSA: NRS 905 [4/573, 66/1844].
21    ibid.; Roberts and Baxter, 'Mrs Thunderbolt', p. 59.
22    *Empire* (2 May 1865), p. 5.
23    McGrath, *Illicit Love*, p. 7.
24    *Married Women's Property Act* 1893 (NSW); Vines, 'Annie Ludford', pp. 146–176.
25    Baxter, 'Timeline: James and Charlotte'. NSWSA: NRS 905 [4/573, 66/1844]; NSW RBDM 1848/518.
26    Baxter, 'Mary Ann Bugg and her husband Edmund Baker'.
27    *Minors Marriages Act* 1838 (NSW); *Marriages Act* 1855 (NSW).
28    Baxter and Roberts, 'Mrs Thunderbolt', pp. 57, 70.
29    Caldwell, 'Population', pp. 27–28.
30    'Phillip's Views (1787)', *HRNSW*, vol. I, pt. 2, pp. 52–53; 'Phillip's Instructions (25 April 1787)', *HRNSW* vol. I, pt. 2, p. 90; 'Governor Phillip to Lord Sydney (15 May 1788)', *HRNSW* vol. I, pt. 2, p. 127.
31    Reynolds, *The Other Side*, pp. 76–77; Grimshaw, *Creating a Nation*, pp. 139, 146; Kociumbas, 'Mary Ann', p. 40.
32    Bierens, 'The Captain's Lady', p. 2.
33    NSWSA: NRS 905, [4/2332.2], letter 35/7317.
34    Connors, 'Uncovering the Shameful', pp. 33–52; Behrendt, 'Consent', pp. 353–367; Nettelbeck, 'Intimate Violence', p. 68.
35    Edmonds, 'The Intimate', pp. 129–154.
36    Reece, *Aborigines and Colonists*, pp. 205–206.
37    *Maitland Mercury* (3 April 1866), p. 2; *Mercury* (10 April 1866), p. 3.
38    'Lady, n.', *Oxford English Dictionary*; Houghton, *The Victorian*, pp. 372–393.
39    West, *Bushranging*, pp. 17–62; *Bathurst Free Press* (14 September 1861), p. 2; Kaladelfos, 'Citizens of Mercy'.
40    *Maitland Mercury* (3 April 1866), p. 5.
41    NSWSA: NRS 905 [4/573, 66/1844].
42    *Maitland Mercury* (29 March 1866), p. 2; *Armidale Express* (7 April 1866), p. 4; *Mercury* (10 April 1866), p. 3.
43    NSWSA: NRS 2318, [5/755-56, 5/790]; *Maitland Mercury* (3 April 1866), p. 2; *Armidale Express* (7 April 1866), p. 3; *Mercury* (10 April 1866), p. 3; NSWSA: NRS 905 [4/573, 66/1844].
44    *Sydney Morning Herald* (6 April 1866), p. 3; *Maitland Mercury* (10 April 1866), p. 2.
45    *Vagrancy Act* 1835 (NSW).
46    *Sydney Morning Herald* (6 April 1866), p. 3; *Maitland Mercury* (10 April 1866), p. 2.
47    ibid.; *Empire* (6 April 1866), pp. 2–3.
48    *Sydney Mail* (7 April 1866), p. 4; *Goulburn Herald and Chronicle* (11 April 1866), p. 4; *Newcastle Chronicle* (11 April 1866), p. 3; *Tumut Times* (12 April 1866), p. 3; *Goulburn Herald and Chronicle* (11 April 1866), p. 4; *Empire* (6 April 1866), pp. 2–3.
49    *Sydney Morning Herald* (6 April 1866), p. 3; *Maitland Mercury* (10 April 1866), p. 2.
50    West, *Bushranging*, p. 88. A lack of education and religious instruction among the rural population were said to have caused the 1860s 'bushranging crisis'. *Sydney Morning Herald* (26 July 1864), p. 2; West, *Bushranging*, pp. 86–91.
51    NSWSA: NRS 905 [4/573, 66/1844]; Roberts and Baxter, 'Mrs Thunderbolt', pp. 56–57.
52    *Empire* (6 April 1866), pp. 2–3.
53    ibid.
54    NSWSA: NRS 905 [4/573, 66/1844]; *Sydney Morning Herald* (6 April 1866), p. 3; *Maitland Mercury* (10 April 1866), p. 2. See also below.
55    *Sydney Morning Herald* (6 April 1866), pp. 3, 4; *Maitland Mercury* (10 April 1866), p. 2; *Armidale Express* (14 April 1866), p. 4; *Brisbane Courier* (12 April 1866), p. 4; *Empire* (6 April 1866), pp. 2–3; *Sydney Mail* (7 April 1866), p. 4; *Goulburn Herald and Chronicle* (11 April 1866), p. 4; *Newcastle Chronicle* (11 April 1866), p. 3; *Tumut Times* (12 April 1866), p. 3;

*Sydney Morning Herald* (17 April 1866), p. 8; *Maitland Mercury* (15 May 1866), p. 3; *Maitland Mercury* (28 April 1866), p. 3.

56  *Sydney Morning Herald* (11 May 1866), p. 5. At this time, Cockatoo Island in Sydney Harbour was a place of confinement and punishment for secondary offenders.

57  NSWSA: NRS 2318 [5/755-56, 5/790].

58  NSWSA: NRS 905 [4/573, 66/1844].

59  *Empire* (30 August 1866), p. 6.

60  Geertz, *The Interpretation*.

61  NSW RBDM 1839/1494.

62  NSWSA: NRS 13686, [5/1161], *R. v. Charley* (1835).

63  NSWSA: NRS 905 [4/2332.2], letters 35/7317, 36/6621, 35/4014; *R. v. Charley* (1835); *Sydney Gazette* (30 May 1835), p. 4.

64  NSWSA: NRS 905 [4/2332.2], letter 35/ 4014.

65  The first newspaper to mention these deaths was the *Australian* (22 May 1835), p. 2. However, the authorities already knew of the murders. NSWSA: NRS 905 [4/2332.2].

66  *Committee on the Aborigines Question*, p. 58.

67  NSWSA: NRS 905 [4/2332.2], letter 35/ 4014.

68  Conor, *Skin Deep*.

69  Baxter and Roberts, 'Mrs Thunderbolt', pp. 55–76; Baxter, *Captain Thunderbolt and His Lady*; Oppenheimer, 'Thunderbolt's Mary Ann', pp. 92–107.

70  *Committee on the Aborigines Question*, p. 58; Baxter, *Captain Thunderbolt and His Lady*, p. 17.

71  Blyton and Ramsland, 'Mixed Race Unions', p. 127.

72  Irish, *Hidden*, pp. 17–19; Blackburn, 'Mapping Aboriginal Nations', pp. 131–158; Sutton, *Native Title*.

73  Irish, *Hidden*, p. 20.

74  Bairstow, *A Million Pounds*, p. 288.

75  Bairstow, 'With the Best Will in the World', pp. 5–8.

76  NSWSA: NRS 905 [4/2332.2], letter 35/ 4014.

77  Bierens, 'The Captain's Lady', p. 2; Karskens, *The Colony*, p. 419; McGrath, 'The White Man's Looking Glass', p. 193; McGrath, *Illicit Love*, p. 103.

78  Swain, *A Place for Strangers*.

79  Bairstow, 'With the Best Will in the World', p. 13; Bairstow, *A Million Pounds*, pp. 291–292.

80  Bairstow, *A Million Pounds*, p. 292; Hannah, 'Aboriginal Workers', pp. 17–33.

81  Bairstow, 'With the Best Will in the World', p. 12.

82  Haskins and Maynard, 'Sex, Race and Power', p. 206.

83  Karskens, *People of the River*, chapter 15; Carey and Roberts, 'Smallpox', pp. 821–869.

84  *R. v Charley* (1835); NSWSA: NRS 13705 [5/1123]; Gunson, *Australian Reminiscences*, pp. 50–51, 122; *Sydney Gazette* (27 June 1835), p. 2; *Sydney Monitor* (26 August 1835), p. 4; *Sydney Herald* (27 August 1835), p. 3; *Sydney Herald* (3 September 1835), p. 2.

85  *Australian* (12 June 1835), p. 2. For a lone voice of dissent see *Sydney Gazette* (27 June 1835), p. 2.

86  However, Governor Richard Bourke did pursue the issue when he examined depositions relating to the attacks. NSWSA: NRS 905 [4/2284.1], letter 35/ 4450.

87  *Sydney Herald* (1 June 1835), p. 3; *Sydney Monitor* (3 June 1835), p. 3; *Sydney Gazette* (4 June 1835), p. 2; *Colonist* (4 June 1835), p. 5; *Sydney Herald* (11 June 1835), p. 2; *Colonist* (11 June 1835), p. 4; *Australian* (12 June 1835), p. 2.

88  *Sydney Herald* (1 June 1835), p. 3.

89  NSWSA: NRS 905 [4/2332.2], letter 35/ 4014; Douglas and Finnane, *Indigenous Crime*, pp. 57–59.

90  NSWSA: NRS 905 [4/2284.1], letter 35/ 4270.

91  NSWSA: NRS 905 [4/2285.1], letter 25/ 4405; NSWSA: NRS 2374 [2/2005].

92  *R. v Charley* (1835).

93  In the 1830s, there were instances of Aboriginal people actively assisting bushrangers. However, these were usually individuals, rather than Aboriginal groups, and there is no connection between

these figures and the 1835 'outrages'. Kociumbas, 'Mary Ann', pp. 28–54.

94    Roberts, 'Masters', pp. 57–94.

95    NSWSA: NRS 905 [4/2332.2], letter 35/4014; *Sydney Gazette* (11 June 1835), p. 2; *Sydney Herald* (11 June 1835), p. 2; *Colonist* (11 June 1835), p. 4; *Sydney Monitor* (13 June 1835), p. 2; NSWSA: NRS 905 [4/2284.1], letter 35/4270.

96    NSWSA: NRS 905 [4/2332.2], letter 35/4014.

97    *R. v Charley* (1835).

98    *Sydney Herald* (3 August 1835), p. 3.

99    Reynolds, *The Other Side*, pp. 159–175.

100    Bairstow, 'With the Best Will in the World', p. 14; Bairstow, *A Million Pounds*, p. 288.

101    *Australian* (12 June 1835), p. 2.

102    In Aboriginal stories, Ned Kelly '... aligned himself with the moral position of those who were being dispossessed.' Bird Rose, 'Ned Kelly Died for Our Sins', pp. 175–186.

103    Goodall, *Invasion*, pp. 124–125; Waterhouse, 'Australian Legends', p. 209.

104    *Maitland Mercury* (28 August 1866), p. 2; *Newcastle Chronicle* (29 August 1866), p. 3; *Armidale Express* (1 September 1866), p. 3; *Kiama Independent* (6 September 1866), p. 2.

105    *Maitland Mercury* (3 April 1866), p. 2.

106    Grimshaw, *Creating a Nation*, pp. 159–162; Garton, *Out of Luck*, pp. 43–61; Evans, *Fractured Families*, pp. 82–107; Lake, 'The Politics of Respectability', pp. 123, 125–126.

107    *NSW Police Gazette* (23 January 1867), p. 33; NSWSA: NRS 2329 [5/789]; NSWSA: NRS 905 [4/590, 67/1050].

108    Baxter and Roberts, 'Mrs Thunderbolt', pp. 64–66.

109    Like many Aboriginal people, Lorraine only came to know about her family story by researching history. Attwood, 'Portrait', pp. 304–305; Taylor, 'All I Know Is History', pp. 6–35.

110    Martyn, interviewed by Foster.

111    Baxter and Roberts, 'Mrs Thunderbolt', pp. 64–70.

112    Seal, *The Outlaw Legend*.

113    We know from Mary Ann's previous, determined efforts to follow Ward that she could have stayed with him, if she desired. This, combined with the context of their parting, makes it appear that it was Mary Ann's choice to leave Frederick Ward.

114    NSW RBDM 1868/0016881; Baxter and Roberts, 'Mrs Thunderbolt', pp. 66–70.

115    Roberts and Baxter, 'Exposing an Exposé', pp. 1–15; Baxter, 'Ada Gertrude Burrows'.

116    Baxter and Roberts, 'Mrs Thunderbolt', pp. 66–70; NSW RBDM 1905/5831.

117    Baxter and Roberts, 'Mrs Thunderbolt', p. 69.

118    Evans, 'Secrets', p. 68; Kent and Townsend, 'Some Aspects', pp. 41–43. McGrath, *Illicit Love*, p. 10.

119    McDonald and Quiggin, 'Lifecourse Transitions', p. 75; Karskens, *People of the River*, Chapter 10; Karskens, *The Rocks*, pp. 80–102.

120    Baxter and Roberts, 'Mrs Thunderbolt', p. 69.

121    Martyn, interviewed by Foster.

122    Tapsell, 'Mary Ann Bugg'.

123    Foster, 'Bugg, Mary Ann'.

124    Hunter, 'Silence in the Noisy Archives:', pp. 209–210.

125    NSW RBDM 1905/5831.

126    *Empire* (3 July 1865), p. 5.

127    Martyn, interviewed by Foster.

128    Standfield, *Race;* Standfield, 'The Paramatta', pp. 119–128; Bennett, 'Māori', pp. 33–54.

129    There was an alternative discourse that painted Māori as fearsome cannibals utterly removed from civilisation, but overall, Māori garnered a degree of respect that was never given to Indigenous Australians. Salmond, *Between Worlds*; Standfield, *Race*; Howitt, 'Poihākena'.

130    While there are still debates as to whether Māori ceded sovereignty of the land or kāwanatanga (governorship) of the land to the British with the Treaty of Waitangi, the fact a treaty was entered into is significant, as the British recognised that Māori had pre–existing rights to the land that needed to be transferred to them. The same was not the case for Indigenous Australians.

131 Standfield, *Race;* Standfield, 'The Parramatta', pp. 119–128; Bennett, 'Māori', pp. 33–54; Grimshaw, 'Interracial Marriages', pp. 12–28. For early encounters, see Salmond, 'Kidnapped', pp. 191–226; Salmond, 'Tuki's Universe', pp. 215–232; Howitt, 'Poihākena', pp. 17–36; Salmond, *Between Worlds.*

132 Martyn, interviewed by Foster.

133 Curthoys, 'Good Christians', p. 33.

134 ibid., pp. 31–56; Egan, *Neither Amity*, pp. 85–102.

135 Egan, 'Power and Dysfunction', pp. 105–106; Parry, 'Such a longing', p. 169.

136 Egan, *Neither Amity*, pp. 95–98; Goodall, *Invasion*, pp. 104–114; McGregor, *Imagined Destinies.*

137 In reality, the Board's close connections with the New South Wales police meant that children were removed arbitrarily without legal sanction. See Chapter 5.

138 Egan, *Neither Amity*, pp. 85–109; Haebich, *Broken Circles*, pp. 181–186; Fletcher, *Clean*, pp. 39–107; Read, *The Stolen Generations.*

139 Haebich, *Broken Circles*, pp. 131–132.

140 *Aborigines Protection Act* 1909 (NSW); Egan, *Neither Amity*, pp. 110–117; Read, *The Stolen Generations*, p. 9; Goodall, *Invasion to Embassy*, pp. 143–148.

141 *Aborigines Protection Amendment Act* 1915 (NSW); Egan, *Neither Amity*, pp. 117–121; Read, *The Stolen Generations*, p. 10.

142 This date reflects when state policy was officially changed. In many ways Stolen Generations are ongoing as Indigenous children are significantly more likely than non-Indigenous children to be removed from their families by social services. Evershed and Allam, 'Indigenous Children's Removal'; Grandmothers Against Removals, *Submission.*

143 HREOC, *Bringing Them Home*; Haebich, *Broken Circles*; Read, *The Stolen Generations*; Manne, 'Aboriginal Child Removal', pp. 217–243.

144 Taylor, *Unearthed*, pp. 220–248; Attwood, 'Portrait', p. 313; Morgan, *My Place*; Boladeras, 'The Desolate', pp. 49–63.

145 Seal, *The Outlaw Legend*, pp. 9–10.

146 ibid., pp. 10–12.

147 Roberts and Baxter, 'Exposing an Exposé', pp. 1–15.

**5    The Governor family**

1   *Nepean Times* (28 July 1900), p. 3; Garland, *Jimmy Governor*, pp. 3–17; *Sydney Morning Herald* (24 July 1900), p. 5; *Evening News* (23 November 1900), p. 3; *Mudgee Guardian* (29 November 1900), p. 9.

2   Garland, *Jimmy Governor*; Moore and Williams, *The True Story*, quote from page vii.

3   *Nepean Times* (28 July 1900), p. 3; Moore and Williams, *The True Story*, p. 36.

4   Keneally, *The Chant*; Schepisi, *The Chant.*

5   'The Chant', AUSTLIT Database.

6   Clune, *Jimmy Governor*; Foster, 'Murder', pp. 173–189.

7   Wiradjuri journalist and author Stan Grant sees in Keneally's book an opportunity to examine the dehumanisation of First Nations people in colonial society as well as their resistance to it. Grant, *On Thomas Keneally.*

8   Reynolds, 'Jimmy Governor', pp. 14–25. As well as the works cited above, see Ellinghaus, *Taking Assimilation*, pp. 158–160; Wood, 'The "Breelong Blacks"', pp. 97–120; Biber, 'In Jimmy Governor's Archive', pp. 270–281; Biber, 'Besieged', pp. 1–41.

9   Foster, 'Murder', p. 173.

10  Parsley, 'Blood on his hands, cleansed in salt water', p. 15. See also 'The Last Outlaws'.

11  NSWSA: NRS 880 [9/7003].

12  Reynolds, *With the White People*, p. 114; Ellinghaus, 'Margins of Acceptability', p. 67; Ellinghaus, *Taking Assimilation*, pp. 157–158; Spencer, 'Woman Lives', p. 63.

13  Coghlan, *The Decline.*

14  Ellinghaus, *Taking Assimilation*, p. 155.

15  Garland, *Jimmy Governor*, p. 118; Ellinghaus, *Taking Assimilation,* p. 153; Moore and Williams, *The True Story*, p. 18; 'Gulgong', Anglican Diocese of Bathurst.

16 *Singleton Argus* (26 July 1900), p. 2.
17 *Mudgee Guardian* (9 August 1900), p. 3.
18 Bongiorno, *The Sex*, p. 100.
19 Coghlan, *The Decline*.
20 *Singleton Argus* (26 July 1900), pp. 2–3.
21 *Evening News* (23 November 1900), p. 3.
22 NSWSA: NRS 2166 [6/1029]; NSWSA: NRS 2163 [5/1739].
23 *Singleton Argus* (26 July 1900), pp. 2–3; *Truth* (28 October 1900), p. 3.
24 *Singleton Argus* (26 July 1900), pp. 2–3.
25 As quoted in Cameron, 'Breelong Tragedy', p. 88.
26 NSW RBDM 18315/1901.
27 Maurie Garland is the only historian to do so. Garland, *Jimmy Governor*, p. 273.
28 *Dubbo Liberal* (3 October 1900), p. 3; Moore and Williams, *The True Story*, p. 47.
29 *Mudgee Guardian* (25 October 1900), p. 13.
30 *Sydney Morning Herald* (23 November 1900), p. 7; *Felons Apprehension Act* 1899 (NSW).
31 Dickey, *No Charity*, pp. 72–108; Garton, *Out of Luck*, pp. 74–83.
32 *Evening News* (1 November 1900), p. 6.
33 Moore and Williams, *The True Story*, p. 55; *Sydney Morning Herald* (23 July 1900), p. 8; *Northern Star* (28 July 1900), p. 5; *Bathurst Free Press* (25 July 1900), p. 2.
34 *Mudgee Guardian* (16 August 1900), p. 20.
35 Ellinghaus, *Taking Assimilation*; Ellinghaus, 'Margins of Acceptability', pp. 56–75; Haskins and Maynard, 'Sex, Race and Power', p. 206.
36 Huggins and Blake, 'Protection or Persecution?', p. 49; Wood, 'The "Breelong Blacks"', p. 113.
37 Douglas and Finnane, *Indigenous Crime*.
38 Lush, *The Law of Husband and Wife*, pp. 473.
39 Harris, 'Spousal Competence', pp. 2–3.
40 *Criminal Law and Evidence Amendment Act* 1891 (NSW); Woods, *A History*, pp. 367–368.
41 *Mudgee Guardian* (23 July 1900), p. 5; *Sydney Morning Herald* (24 July 1900), p. 5; *Dubbo Liberal* (3 October 1900), p. 3; *Evening News* (23 November 1900), p. 3.
42 *Sydney Morning Herald* (23 November 1900), p. 7; *Evening News* (23 November 1900), p. 3. The issue of whether Ethel's evidence was admissible was also raised in Jacky Underwood's trial. *Dubbo Liberal* (3 October 1900), p. 3.
43 *Evening News* (23 November 1900), p. 3.
44 ibid.; *Sydney Morning Herald* (23 November 1900), p. 7. See also Threadgold, 'Black Man, White Woman', p. 183.
45 *Sydney Morning Herald* (27 July 1900), p. 8.
46 Britton, 'Posts in a Paddock', p. 156.
47 Although there was debate in Australia during the 2000s about the number of Aboriginal casualties, it is widely accepted by historians that their deaths ranged in the tens of thousands. Reynolds, *The Other Side*, pp. 9–11, 125–131.
48 Goodall, *Invasion*, pp. 124–125; Waterhouse, 'Australian Legends', p. 209. It is important to note that in the north and west of the country colonisation was later and uneven, and frontier violence continued into the twentieth century.
49 *Singleton Argus* (31 July 1900), p. 2; *Daily Telegraph* (30 July 1900), p. 7.
50 *Singleton Argus* (31 July 1900), p. 2.
51 *Maitland Mercury* (1 August 1896), p. 13.
52 *Evening News* (31 July 1900), p. 8; *Daily Telegraph* (30 July 1900), p. 7.
53 No attributed author, *Wollar*; *Age* (31 July 1900), taken from NSWSA: NRS 10923 [4/8581].
54 *Dubbo Dispatch* (1 August 1900), p. 2.
55 *Sydney Morning Herald* (1 August 1900), p. 11; *Dubbo Dispatch* (1 August 1900), p. 2.
56 *Cootamundra Herald* (1 August 1900), p. 2.
57 *Sydney Morning Herald* (1 August 1900), p. 11.
58 *Daily Telegraph* (30 July 1900), p. 7.

59  NSWSA: NRS 10923 [4/8581].
60  ibid. *Sydney Morning Herald* (28 July 1900), p. 2; *Maitland Mercury* (4 August 1900), p. 7; *Daily Telegraph* (23 August 1900), p. 6.
61  St Michel-Podmore, *Rambles and Adventures*, p. 49; Waterhouse, 'Australian Legends', p. 209; Waterhouse, *The Vision Splendid*, p. 170.
62  McGregor, *Imagined Destinies*, pp. 29–59.
63  Irish, *Hidden*, p. 103.
64  ibid., p. 91.
65  Egan, *Neither Amity*, pp. 85–102; Fletcher, *Clean*, pp. 31–96.
66  Moore and Williams, *The True Story*, pp. 8–20.
67  Reynolds, 'Jimmy Governor', pp. 14–25; Moore and Williams, *The True Story*, p. 20.
68  *Evening News* (31 August 1900), p. 8.
69  *Mudgee Guardian* (16 August 1900), p. 3; NSWSA: NRS 10923 [4/8581].
70  *Scone Advocate* (3 August 1900), p. 4.
71  NSWSA: NRS 10923 [4/8581].
72  *Evening News* (7 August 1900), p. 5; *Mudgee Guardian* (16 August 1900), p. 3.
73  NSWSA: NRS 10923 [4/8581].
74  *Bathurst Free Press* (24 August 1900), p. 2.
75  *Bathurst Free Press* (21 August 1900), p. 2. Only one letter to the editor of the *Daily Telegraph* outright condemned these actions as shameful and illegal. *Daily Telegraph* (23 August 1900), p. 6.
76  *Bathurst Free Press* (24 August 1900), p. 2.
77  Nettelbeck, 'Creating the Aboriginal "Vagrant"', pp. 79–100.
78  *Vagrancy Act* 1851 (NSW).
79  *Evening News* (31 August 1900), p. 2.
80  Rydon, 'Chanter, John Moore'.
81  McGrath, 'Playing Colonials'; Goodall, *Invasion*, pp. 124–125; Waterhouse, 'Australian Legends', p. 209.
82  McGrath, 'Playing Colonials'.
83  Lydon, 'Bullets, Teeth and Photographs', pp. 275–287; Lydon, *The Flash*.
84  Griffiths, *Hunters and Collectors*, pp. 115–118; Smith, *Australia's Birthstain*.
85  NSWSA: NRS 10923 [4/8581]; Moore and Williams, *The True Story*.
86  These people were: Alexander McKay (23 July), Elizabeth O'Brien and her young son James (24 July) as well as Kieran Fitzpatrick (27 July).
87  NSWSA: NRS 10923 [4/8581].
88  *Evening News* (27 July 1900), p. 3; NSWSA: NRS 2 [4/7108-15]. Board Minutes for 26 July 1900.
89  *Singleton Argus* (4 September 1900), p. 1; *Northern Star* (5 September 1900), p. 6.
90  Roberts, 'Bells Falls Massacre', pp. 615–633.
91  Waterhouse, 'Australian Legends', pp. 208–209.
92  NSWSA: NRS 10923 [4/8581].
93  ibid.
94  *Evening News* (1 September 1900), p. 6; *Mudgee Guardian* (3 September 1900), p. 2; *Mudgee Guardian* (16 August 1900), p. 3.
95  *Mudgee Guardian* (16 August 1900), p. 3.
96  Waterhouse, 'Australian Legends', pp. 201–221; Waterhouse, *The Vision Splendid*, pp. 163–193; Hirst, 'The Pioneer Legend', pp. 316–337; Lake, 'The Politics of Respectability', pp. 116–131.
97  NSWSA: NRS 10923 [4/8581]. Hunting was also a popular masculine pastime in this period. Kingston, *The Oxford History of Australia*, pp. 190–193, 304.
98  Waterhouse, 'Australian Legends', pp. 201–221.
99  NSWSA: NRS 10923 [4/8581].
100 ibid.
101 Griffiths, *Hunters and Collectors*, pp. 117–118; Bean, *Official History*; Australia's involvement in the Sudanese War preceded the Boer War.

102  Wilcox, *Australia's Boer War*.
103  NSWSA: NRS 10923 [4/8581].
104  *Evening News* (27 October 1900), p. 5; *Sydney Morning Herald* (29 October 1900), p. 7; *Mudgee Guardian* (29 October 1900), p. 2; Moore and Williams, *The True Story*, pp. 119–120.
105  *Maitland Mercury* (1 November 1900), p. 3; *Evening News* (1 November 1900), p. 5; *Daily Telegraph* (1 November 1900), p. 5; Moore and Williams, *The True Story*, p. 126.
106  Foster, 'Murder for White Consumption?', pp. 173–189.
107  *Mudgee Guardian* (17 September 1900), p. 2.
108  Irish, *Hidden*, p. 137; Egan, *Neither Amity*, pp. 100–125; Fletcher, *Clean*, pp. 57–58.
109  *Mudgee Guardian* (24 September 1900), p. 2; *Armidale Express* (25 September 1900), p. 5; *Manaro Mercury* (24 September 1900), p. 2; *Riverine Herald* (25 September 1900), p. 2; *Evening News* (8 March 1901), p. 7; *Albury Banner* (15 March 1901), p. 28; NSWSA: NRS 2 [4/7108-15].
110  *Evening News* (12 October 1900), p. 8; *Evening News* (12 October 1900), p. 4; NSWSA: NRS 2 [4/7108-15].
111  *Evening News* (1 December 1900), p. 7; *Mudgee Guardian* (13 December 1900), p. 18.
112  *Mudgee Guardian* (22 October 1900), p. 2.
113  Jimmy and Jacky Underwood's defence lawyers tried to make Ethel admit that she was at the scene of the crime under cross-examination, and in her dying declaration, Mrs Mawbey had stated that she heard a woman's voice outside the house on that bloody night in July. *Dubbo Liberal* (3 October 1900), p. 3; *Dubbo Liberal* (6 October 1900), p. 4.
114  *Sydney Morning Herald* (24 November 1900), p. 11; Reynolds, 'Jimmy Governor', pp. 14–25; Ellinghaus, 'Margins of Acceptability', p. 67.

**6  Jimmy Governor the bushranger**

1  *Maitland Mercury* (11 August 1900), p. 3; *Wingham Chronicle* (15 August 1900), p. 3.
2  Although there is evidence the Governors demanded, and received, some assistance from several Aboriginal people. Michael Bennett, *Pathfinders: a history of Aboriginal trackers in NSW* (Sydney: NewSouth, 2020), pp. 92–117.
3  *Mudgee Guardian* (9 August 1900), p. 10; *Wingham Chronicle* (15 August 1900), p. 3.
4  *Maitland Mercury* (18 August 1900), p. 7; *Sydney Mail* (25 August 1900), p. 423; *Maitland Mercury* (11 August 1900), p. 3; *Walcha Witness* (18 August 1900), p. 4; *Manaro Mercury* (10 August 1900), p. 2; *Wingham Chronicle* (15 August 1900), p. 3; *Scone Advocate* (14 August 1900), p. 4; *Mudgee Guardian* (9 August 1900), p. 10.
5  A brief mention of Governor and bushranging comes from Reynolds, 'Jimmy Governor', pp. 19–21.
6  *Sydney Morning Herald* (24 July 1900), p. 6; *Evening News* (24 July 1900), p. 4; *Daily Telegraph* (24 July 1900), p. 7.
7  *Sydney Morning Herald* (25 July 1900), p. 8; *Clarence and Richmond Examiner* (28 July 1900), p. 5; *Mudgee Guardian* (23 July 1900), p. 5; *Evening News* (1 September 1900), p. 5; Moore and Williams, *The True Story*, pp. 14–16.
8  *Australian Star* (24 July 1900), p. 5; *Evening News* (24 July 1900), p. 4; *Daily Telegraph* (24 July 1900), p. 7.
9  Exceptions include, *Richmond River Herald* (2 November 1900), p. 4; *Evening News* (29 October 1900), p. 4; *Daily Telegraph* (6 August 1900), p. 7. In the latter article, the reporter has Jimmy reading and rereading *The Life of Ned Kelly* 'until he knew it by heart'.
10  *Clarence and Richmond Examiner* (27 November 1900), p. 4.
11  ibid., pp. 8–10; Wannan, *The Australian*, pp. 9–10, 13–29.
12  Seal, *The Outlaw Legend*.
13  Doug Morrissey argues that the Kelly gang often coerced their 'supporters' into assisting them. Morrissey, 'Ned Kelly and Horse and Cattle Stealing', pp. 29–48.
14  Seal, 'Tell 'Em I Died Game', p. 94.
15  ibid.; 'The Last Stand of Ned Kelly', Culture Victoria.

16  PROV, VA 2825, VPRS 4966/P0 Part 2, Unit 1, Item 3, 80/T12640, 1880, pp. 9–12; Davie and Westh, 'Ned Kelly'; Kennedy and Looby, *Black Snake*; Morrissey, *Ned Kelly: a lawless life*; Morrissey, *Ned Kelly: selectors*.

17  West, *Bushranging*, pp. 121–158.

18  West, *Bushranging*; Waterhouse, *The Vision Splendid*, p. 69.

19  PROV, VA 862, VPRS 24/P0000 Unit 411, 1880/938.

20  Ward, *The Australian Legend*, pp. 152–153.

21  Waterhouse, *The Vision Splendid*, p. 186.

22  Wolf, 'Innocent Convicts', pp. 73–81; Rede, *The Kelly Gang*; Pratt and Joseph, *Thunderbolt Play Script*; Bellanta, 'Leary Kin', pp. 677–795.

23  Ward, *The Australian Legend*, pp. 135–166.

24  Lake and Reynolds, *Drawing the Global Colour Line*, pp. 137–165.

25  Griffiths, *Deep Time Dreaming*.

26  Broome, *Aboriginal Australians*.

27  NMA, 'Jerilderie Letter'.

28  *Maitland Mercury* (4 September 1900), p. 3; *Singleton Argus* (6 September 1900), p. 3.

29  *Maitland Mercury* (18 August 1900), p. 7.

30  *Mudgee Guardian* (16 August 1900), p. 3.

31  *Dog and Goat Act* 1898 (NSW).

32  Smith and Litchfield, 'A Review', pp. 111–128.

33  Bird Rose, *Dingo Makes Us Human*; Smith and Litchfield, 'A Review', pp. 111–128.

34  Smith and Litchfield, 'A Review', p. 123.

35  ibid., pp. 119–121.

36  Irish, *Hidden*. It is believed that Governor's family were Wiradjuri, from the central west of New South Wales. Garland, *Jimmy Governor*, p. 107.

37  NSWLA, *NSWLA Minutes* (11 October 1900). (Sydney: Government Printer, 1900), p. 3891.

38  ibid., pp. 3891–3892; NSWSA: NRS 2 [4/7113], minutes for 25/9/1890, 2/6/1882, 18/8/1892, 29/9/1892, 26/4/1894, 3/5/1894, 31/5/1894, 25/10/1894. Many thanks to Paul Irish for bringing these sources to my attention. Δ164

39  *Maitland Mercury* (18 August 1900), p. 7.

40  BOM, *Climate Statistics: Dubbo*; 'Dubbo', Dubbo Regional Council.

41  'Dubbo Railway Station and Yard Group', NSW OEH; *Evening News* (24 July 1900), p. 3.

42  Moore and Williams, *The True Story*, pp. 25, 27.

43  Garland, *Jimmy Governor*, p. 121.

44  *Maitland Mercury* (18 August 1900), p. 7.
    The people of Dubbo were particularly affected by Governor's crimes as one of the murder victims, the Mawbeys' live-in schoolteacher, Miss Kerz, was originally from Dubbo and was well known to its inhabitants. *Dubbo Dispatch* (25 July 1900), p. 2.

45  *Australian Star* (23 November 1900), p. 5.

46  McKenzie, 'Defining and Defending', pp. 17–30; Russell, 'Honour, Morality and Sexuality', pp. 202–217.

47  Russell and Worden, 'Introduction', p. 9.

48  *Sydney Morning Herald* (23 November 1900), p. 7.

49  Moore and Williams, *The True Story*, p. 20.

50  *Australian Star* (23 November 1900), p. 5.

51  Moore and Williams, *The True Story*, pp. 19–20.

52  However, female missionary Retta Dixon claimed that Governor repented for his sins on death row. *Goulburn Penny Post*, (29 September 1904), p. 2.

53  Beatty, *A Treasury*, pp. 123–127; Seal, *The Outlaw Legend*, pp. 7–8.

54  *National Advocate* (24 August 1900), p. 2; *Evening News* (24 August 1900), p. 6.

55  *Goulburn Evening Penny Post* (30 October 1900), p. 4.

56  *Singleton Argus* (25 August 1900), p. 2.

57  *Dubbo Dispatch* (12 September 1900), p. 2.

58      Ward, *The Australian Legend*, p. 141. Compare to West, *Bushranging*, pp. 47, 85.
59      Hirst, *The Strange*, pp. 218–240.
60      Laurie Moore and Stephan Williams note that on the run, Governor travelled some of the same route that the Aboriginal murderers known as the 'Dora Dora Blacks' had travelled before him, and that he might have also looked to them for inspiration for his crimes. Moore and Williams, *The True Story*, pp. 97, 157–159.
61      ibid., pp. 9, 11, 177; *Sydney Morning Herald* (25 July 1900), p. 8; *Clarence and Richmond Examiner* (28 July 1900), p. 5; *Mudgee Guardian* (23 July 1900), p. 5; *Goulburn Evening Penny Post* (30 October 1900), p. 4.
62      'Robbery Under Arms', AUSTLIT; *Sydney Mail* (1 July 1882 – 11 August 1883).
63      'In the Bad Old Days: Knights of the Road', *Mudgee Guardian* (January–March 1899). Jimmy Governor was 25 at the time of his capture in 1900. NSWSA: NRS 2137 [5/1947-53].
64      *Mudgee Guardian* (9 August 1900), p. 10; *Mudgee Guardian* (16 August 1900), p. 3.
65      *Goulburn Evening Penny Post* (30 October 1900), p. 4.
66      Urban, 'Legends of Deadwood', p. 225.
67      *Evening News* (29 October 1900), p. 4.
68      McGrath, 'Playing Colonials'.
69      Jones, 'Blood'n Thunder', p. 7.
70      Abate, 'Bury My Heart on Recent History', p. 122.
71      McGrath, 'Playing Colonials'.
72      *Evening News* (23 November 1900), p. 4; *Bathurst Free Press*, (26 July 1900), p. 3.
73      *Evening News* (23 November 1900), p. 4.
74      *Sydney Morning Herald* (24 November 1900), p. 11.
75      *Singleton Argus* (8 November 1900), p. 4.

**Afterword**
1       Hobsbawm, *Primitive Rebels*; Hobsbawm, *Bandits*.
2       Griffiths, *Hunters and Collectors*, pp. 195–218.
3       Biber, 'Besieged', p. 1.
4       *Fitzroy City Press* (11 January 1901), p. 3; *Evening Star* (26 April 1901), p. 3; *Eastern Districts Chronicle* (23 February 1901), p. 2; Colligan, 'Waxworks Shows', p. 103.
5       *Singleton Argus* (18 April 1903), p. 4; *Mudgee Guardian* (6 October 1904), p. 7; *Goulburn Penny Post* (29 September 1904), p. 2.
6       Foster, 'Murder', pp. 173–189.
7       *Daily Telegraph* (26 March 1901), p. 5; *Bendigo Independent* (27 March 1901), p. 3.
8       Parsley, 'Blood on his hands, cleansed in salt water', p. 15; 'The Last Outlaws' (podcast).
9       Reilly and Reilly, 'Sheilas'.
10      Britton, 'Posts in a Paddock', pp. 143–157; Khan (ed.), *Posts in the Paddock*; Martyn, interviewed by Foster.
11      Boyd, *Untitled* (JG 26.I), 2016; Boyd, *Untitled* (JG 26.II), 2016.
12      Foster and Phu, 'The Artist, the Historian'.
13      Sayers, *Sidney Nolan*.

# INDEX

Lightning Source UK Ltd.
Milton Keynes UK
UKHW050635240123
415866UK00004B/24